D0085299

JUL 2 4 2007

ANNE RICE

Recent Titles in
Critical Companions to Popular Contemporary Writers
Kathleen Gregory Klein, Series Editor

V. C. Andrews: A Critical Companion
E. D. Huntley

Anne McCaffrey: A Critical Companion
Robin Roberts

Pat Conroy: A Critical Companion
Landon C. Burns

John Saul: A Critical Companion
Paul Bail

James Clavell: A Critical Companion
Gina Macdonald

Stephen King: A Critical Companion
Sharon A. Russell

Colleen McCullough: A Critical Companion
Mary Jean DeMarr

Tony Hillerman: A Critical Companion
John M. Reilly

James A. Michener: A Critical Companion
Marilyn S. Severson

Howard Fast: A Critical Companion
Andrew Macdonald

Dean Koontz: A Critical Companion
Joan G. Kotker

Tom Clancy: A Critical Companion
Helen S. Garson

ANNE RICE

A Critical Companion

Jennifer Smith

CRITICAL COMPANIONS TO POPULAR CONTEMPORARY WRITERS
Kathleen Gregory Klein, Series Editor

Greenwood Press
Westport, Connecticut • London

Library of Congress Cataloging-in-Publication Data

Smith, Jennifer.
    Anne Rice : a critical companion / Jennifer Smith.
      p. cm.—Critical companions to popular contemporary
writers, ISSN 1082–4979)
    Includes bibliographical references and index.
    ISBN 0–313–29612–X (alk. paper)
    1. Rice, Anne, 1941– —Criticism and interpretation. 2. Women
and literature—United States—History—20th century. 3. Fantastic
fiction, American—History and criticism. 4. Horror tales,
American—History and criticism. 5. Gothic revival (Literature)—
United States. 6. Witchcraft in literature. 7. Vampires in
literature. 8. Mummies in literature. I. Title. II. Series.
PS3568.I265Z88   1996
813'.54—dc20   96–5459

British Library Cataloguing in Publication Data is available.

Library of Congress Catalog Card Number: 96–5459
ISBN: 0–313–29612–X
ISSN: 1082–4979

First published in 1996

Greenwood Press, 88 Post Road West, Westport, CT 06881
An imprint of Greenwood Publishing Group, Inc.

Printed in the United States of America

The paper used in this book complies with the
Permanent Paper Standard issued by the National
Information Standards Organization (Z39.48–1984).

P

This book is for
the people who taught me
the things that are in this book:
Lee K. Abbott, Dan Barnes, Elinor Bault,
David Frantz, John Gabel, James Hughes, Lisa Kiser,
Mary Beth Pringle, Barbara Rigney,
and Les Tannenbaum.

Contents

Series Foreword *by Kathleen Gregory Klein*   ix

1. The Life of Anne Rice   1

2. Supernatural Genres: Horror, Gothic, and Fantasy   9

THE VAMPIRES

3. *Interview with the Vampire* (1976)   21

4. *The Vampire Lestat* (1985)   43

5. *The Queen of the Damned* (1988)   63

6. *The Tale of the Body Thief* (1992)   83

7. *Memnoch the Devil* (1995)   99

THE MUMMY

8. *The Mummy or Ramses the Damned* (1989)   115

THE WITCHES

9. *The Witching Hour* (1990)   133

10. *Lasher* (1993)   151

Contents

11. *Taltos* (1994)   159

Bibliography   171

Index   187

Series Foreword

The authors who appear in the series Critical Companions to Popular Contemporary Writers are all best-selling writers. They do not have only one successful novel, but a string of them. Fans, critics, and specialist readers eagerly anticipate their next book. For some, high cash advances and breakthrough sales figures are automatic; movie deals often follow. Some writers become household names, recognized by almost everyone.

But novels are read one by one. Each reader chooses to start and, more importantly, to finish a book because of what she or he finds there. The real test of a novel is in the satisfaction its readers experience. This series acknowledges the extraordinary involvement of readers and writers in creating a best-seller.

The authors included in this series were chosen by an Advisory Board composed of high school English teachers and high school and public librarians. They ranked a list of best-selling writers according to their popularity among different groups of readers. Writers in the top-ranked group who had not received book-length, academic literary analysis (or none in at least the past ten years) were chosen for the series. Because of this selection method, Critical Companions to Popular Contemporary Writers meets a need that is not addressed elsewhere.

The volumes in the series are written by scholars with particular expertise in analyzing popular fiction. These specialists add an academic focus to the popular success that the best-selling writers already enjoy.

The series is designed to appeal to a wide range of readers. The general reading public will find explanations for the appeal of these well-known writers. Fans will find biographical and fictional questions answered. Students will find literary analysis, discussions of fictional genres, carefully organized introductions to new ways of reading the novels, and bibliographies for additional research. Students will also be able to apply what they have learned from this book to their readings of future novels by these best-selling writers.

Each volume begins with a biographical chapter drawing on published information, autobiographies or memoirs, prior interviews, and, in some cases, interviews given especially for this series. A chapter on literary history and genres describes how the author's work fits into a larger literary context. The following chapters analyze the writer's most important, most popular, and most recent novels in detail. Each chapter focuses on a single novel. This approach, suggested by the Advisory Board as the most useful to student research, allows for an in-depth analysis of the writer's fiction. Close and careful readings with numerous examples show readers exactly how the novels work. These chapters are organized around three central elements: plot development (how the story line moves forward), character development (what the reader knows about the important figures), and theme (the significant ideas of the novel). Chapters may also include sections on generic conventions (how the novel is similar to or different from others in its same category of science fiction, fantasy, thriller, etc.), narrative point of view (who tells the story and how), symbols and literary language, and historical or social context. Each chapter ends with an "alternative reading" of the novel. The volume concludes with a primary and secondary bibliography, including reviews.

The Alternative Readings are a unique feature of this series. By demonstrating a particular way of reading each novel, they provide a clear example of how a specific perspective can reveal important aspects of the book. In each alternative reading section, one contemporary literary theory—such as feminist criticism, Marxism, new historicism, deconstruction, or Jungian psychological critique—is defined in brief, easily comprehensible language. That definition is then applied to the novel to highlight specific features that might go unnoticed or be understood differently in a more general reading of the novel. Each volume defines two or three specific theories, making them part of the reader's understanding of how diverse meanings may be constructed from a single novel.

Taken collectively, the volumes in the Critical Companions to Popular

Contemporary Writers series provide a wide-ranging investigation of the complexities of current best-selling fiction. By treating these novels seriously as both literary works and publishing successes, the series demonstrates the potential of popular literature in contemporary culture.

Kathleen Gregory Klein
Southern Connecticut State University

1

The Life of Anne Rice

Anne Rice was born on October 4, 1941, in New Orleans, but her name wasn't Anne then. Instead, her parents named her Howard Allen O'Brien because they thought it was a powerful name that would give her a head start in life. She was baptized at St. Alphonsus Church, the same church in which she would later have all the Mayfair witches baptized, and she grew up in the neighborhoods in which the witches grew up, hearing ghost stories that were accepted as truth and dreaming of the great houses and their mysteries. New Orleans gave her both Catholicism and voodoo, a potent inspiration for any beginning writer. By the time she started school, she was already writing stories.

She was also showing signs that she was going to surprise people. On her first day of school in 1947, when her teaching nun Sister Hyacinth asked what her name was, she said "Anne" before her mother could say "Howard." "All right," her mother said. "If she wants to be Anne, let her be Anne." And Anne she was from that day on. Her mother's agreement was not that much of a surprise. A deeply religious woman who was also the finest storyteller Anne had ever heard, Anne's mother had always encouraged the creativity of all her children, telling them that she expected them to be geniuses and giving them plenty of freedom. Thus Anne not only read a lot but she also went to the movies, especially the horror films she loved. When she was nine, she learned about vampires for the first time when she saw the film *Dracula's Daughter*, later saying of it, "I loved the tragic figure of the daughter as a regretful creature who didn't want to kill but was driven to it" (Ramsland, "Interview," 34). At school, she also heard the story "The White Silk Dress" about a child vampire, and both stories made a profound impression on her.

She was also extremely religious, wanting to be a saint, but a little confused about some of the details. In her video biography, *Anne Rice: Birth of the Vampire*, she remembers being told about the dead rising on Judgment Day, but she also remembers thinking that she'd be conscious all that time and how boring it would be to wait in her coffin until then, a detail that would surface later in her vampire stories. She craved the security of the church because there was little security at home; her mother had become an alcoholic, spending most of her nights drinking and most of her days in an alcoholic stupor. Her mother told her that drinking was like a craving in the blood and that the craving was inherited, passed down from previous generations. Anne would remember that later and incorporate it, too, into her vampire mythology.

Anne continued to write over the next ten years, writing a novella about two aliens from Mars when she was ten, and several plays by the time she was twelve. But then things changed. In 1956, when Anne was fourteen, her mother died from alcoholism, and Anne's life was never the same. One important change was her loss of religion. She has said of that time that her faith "just went. . . . It struck me as really evil—the idea that you could go to hell for French-kissing someone" (Ferraro, 67). Another important change came the next year when Anne's father moved the family to Texas, away from the New Orleans that Anne loved. However, Texas brought her a new love, a boy who worked on the school paper named Stan Rice.

Stan remembers her as being bright and vivacious; Anne remembers that he sat down beside her and she fell in love instantly. But Stan was dating someone else, and Anne needed to find a city big enough so that she could both go to school and work to support herself. In 1959, she graduated and went to Texas Women's University; but Texas wasn't enough, and the next year, Anne moved to San Francisco. The move woke Stan up to his mistake of taking her for granted, and he wrote his first love letter to her. They wrote for two years until Stan proposed by a special delivery letter in 1961.

They were married in Texas, and Stan returned to San Francisco with Anne so that they could take night courses at the University of San Francisco until they could enroll in San Francisco University. They lived in

Haight-Ashbury and watched the beginnings of the hippie revolution outside their front door, and this also had tremendous impact on Anne's work. During this time, Anne wrote her first unpublished novels, *The Sufferings of Charlotte* and *Nicholas and Jean*, and they both graduated in 1964, Anne in political science and Stan in creative writing. At that point, a family friend remembers that most people thought of Stan as the star and Anne as the little wife typing in the kitchen. Anne published a short story in 1965, but the great event in both Stan and Anne's life was the birth of their first child, Michele, in 1966.

By this time, Anne was in graduate school, and Stan was teaching creative writing at San Francisco State University, doing so well with his writing that he won a poetry grant. They moved to Berkeley, and Anne wrote another short story, "Interview with the Vampire," along with the novella *Katherine and Jean* that would later serve as her master's thesis. Their lives were perfect, and the center of that perfection was always Michelle, an incredibly bright and generous child who gave their lives meaning. But in 1970, the same year that Anne began a master's degree program and Stan won another award, Michelle was diagnosed with leukemia.

For two years, the Rices struggled to save their child, and in the midst of the horror, Anne even managed to finish her degree. But the struggle ended in 1972, when Michelle died after suffering terribly. For the next two years, both Rices descended into alcoholism, spending their days and nights in a drunken haze. Both finally pulled through this period because of their writing, Stan with a collection of poems about Michelle's death called *Some Lamb*, published in 1975, and Anne with a groundbreaking book about addiction, loss, and despair called *Interview with the Vampire*, published in 1976.

Interview with the Vampire features a narrator as lost in misery as Anne was—Louis the vampire who loathes his vampire nature and tries to deny it. In both Louis and his opponent the vampire Lestat, Anne created fully developed figures with human needs, fears, and questions. She has said that she channels these characters and that they arise full blown in her mind, not developed mechanically as tools of an author, and they are dynamic characters because of it, acting instinctively and driven by their needs (Matousek, 112). In writing the story of Louis and Lestat and their vampire daughter, Claudia, who dies at five, Anne wrote out her anguish over all the questions about evil and purpose that Michelle's death had created for her and began her slow recovery from alcoholism and despair.

Another factor in the Rices' recovery was the security they gained through *Interview*'s success. Although the advance for *Interview* was only $12,000, the paperback rights sold for $700,000, and the film rights went for $150,000. Stan was also doing well, publishing another book of poems called *Whiteboy*. They moved and traveled so that Anne could research her next book, *The Feast of All Saints*, and Stan's career got another boost when he won the Edgar Allan Poe Award. And in 1978, they had new reason to rejoice when their son Christopher was born. Christopher was so important to them that they both stopped drinking completely because they did not want him to have alcoholics for parents. This had an added benefit for Anne who has said "My output tripled after I stopped drinking. I've been on a natural high now for years" (Wadler, 134).

In 1979, Anne's second book and first historical novel, *The Feast of All Saints*, was published. *Feast* began as part of Anne's fascination for her New Orleans heritage. In her researches of her city, she found information about the Free People of Color, the freed offspring of African slaves and the French and Spanish traders, many of whom had emigrated from Haiti. While they had their freedom, they had few rights, and so they hovered in a no-man's-land between white society and slavery, and they also tend to slip through the pages of history. Anne called her book *The Feast of All Saints* because that particular feast day is used to celebrate the forgotten dead and saints, and she wanted to celebrate the lives of the almost-forgotten Free People of Color. Her central character is a fourteen-year-old boy named Marcel, the son of a white planter and a free woman of color. The book tells of his yearning for a creative outlet and for a sense of community, since, like so many of Anne's characters, he feels like an outsider, caught between two worlds. He goes to study with Christophe, a novelist, but his father pulls him out of school to become an undertaker so he can support himself. Marcel rebels and is beaten, and in his recovery he refuses to be a victim, choosing to go into the future with hope. *Feast* also has several subplots about other Free People of Color, particularly Marcel's sister, Marie, who is almost destroyed by her own community. *The Feast of All Saints* took two years to write, but it came out to a mixed response by reviewers who did not understand what Anne had attempted.

Anne was devastated by the reviews and poor sales, but not defeated. In 1980, she followed *Feast* with another historical novel, *Cry to Heaven*, this time setting her story in eighteenth-century Italy and writing about the castrati, the choir boys who were castrated so that their beautiful voices would not deepen in puberty and be ruined. She structured her novel as a detective plot, telling the story of Tonio Treshi, an aristocratic boy who is delivered to the great choir master Guido Maffeo by his treacherous older brother Carlo. Tonio's life is full of things that are not what they seem, and he struggles to come to terms with the new insights he has into his life and his new life in general. His journey into self-awareness takes him to the depths, and he descends into greed and sexual depravity as he tries to avoid recognizing what he has always known, that as a castrati, he will forever be an outsider. He meets a woman, Christina, who has rejected gender roles to become a great painter, and through his love for her he moves to an appreciation of himself. Finally coming to terms with his family, he forms a community with Guido and Christina and is at peace.

Cry to Heaven was published in 1982, and although the *New York Times* gave it a favorable review, most of the other reviews were so savage that they devastated Anne, and she began to withdraw. She chose to experiment with sexual fantasies under pseudonyms, writing two books of erotica, *Exit to Eden* in 1985 and *Belinda* in 1986, and three books of erotic fairy tales that explore sadomasochism, *The Claiming of Sleeping Beauty*, which was published in 1983, *Beauty's Punishment* in 1984, and *Beauty's Release* in 1985. These books, written under the pseudonyms of Anne Rampling and A. R. Roquelaure, gave Anne a chance to explore areas of human character without being condemned by the critical press as she had been for *Cry to Heaven*. As critic David Gates has noted, both of these writing alter egos served their purpose: Rampling loosened up her writing and Roquelaure was fun (Gates, "Queen," 76).

While she was writing these experimental novels, she was also drawn back to the supernatural, particularly to her vampires. The helplessness and despair that she had felt after Michelle's death and that had led her to create the helpless, despairing Louis as her narrator had since given way to a more aggressive outlook on life. No longer identifying with Louis, Anne instead became intrigued with the villain from *Interview*, the always strong, never surrendering Lestat. In 1985, she published his story, *The Vampire Lestat*, making him both a rock star and the mythic hero of a biography that spanned more than two hundred years. It hit the *New York Times* bestseller list within two weeks, although critics still missed the point of the vampires as metaphors, labeling her book as a simple horror story.

In 1987, the Rices moved to a new house, and Anne wrote *The Queen of the Damned*, a mythology of the vampires tied to the present by a mythic struggle between good and evil in the vampire community. Their new house was so beautiful that Anne used it as a model for the vampires' compound in *Queen*. But Anne was still drawn back to her old home town of New Orleans, and in 1988, the Rices bought a home there. Following the publication of *The Queen of the Damned* which went to number one on the *New York Times* list, they moved to New Orleans permanently. Anne now began to draw her family around her once again, establishing the connection that all her books emphasize as important. As she puts it, "We are all in a world without parents, and we have to discover who our true brothers and sisters are" (Ramsland, *Witches Chronicles*, 90).

During this time, she had also worked on a screenplay for a mummy movie, one of her favorite kind of films from childhood. But Hollywood couldn't accept the more creative aspects of her screenplay, and so she turned it into a book, *The Mummy or Ramses the Damned*, which was published as a paperback original in 1989. *The Mummy* is the story of a great king who rises from immortal sleep to save a twentieth-century woman. It was intended as pure escapist fiction, but it still asks the questions that are important to Rice, and it adds new twists to an old genre.

Returning home to New Orleans was a psychic awakening for Rice. She told an interviewer, "I'm picking up threads that were totally ruptured by leaving. . . . I feel complete, at peace, less afraid of dying" (Ferraro, 76). In another interview, she talked about the twilight sky and the lush beauty that is found nowhere else, "the romance and the gloom," adding that even if she began a book somewhere else, her characters always ended up in New Orleans (Wadler, 133). New Orleans inspired her second series, the Witches Chronicles, beginning with the epic of the Mayfair witches, *The Witching Hour*, which was published in 1990. Lestat then required another book, *The Tale of the Body Thief*, in 1992, a book in which he finally gets to choose vampirism of his own free will by fighting to get his immortal body back from a psychic thief who has stolen it. But the next year in 1993, Anne returned to her witches, publishing *Lasher*, the story of the demon who has plagued the Mayfair witches and of Rowan, the most powerful witch whom he almost destroys. In 1994, she published *Taltos*, the history of a supernatural race that is part of the Mayfair legacy.

Lestat demanded one final appearance, one in which he argues with God and the Devil, and *Memnoch the Devil* was published in 1995. Anne said on "The Larry King Show" that this is Lestat's final appearance since he has now said all he has to say. For her first book signing for *Memnoch*, she had a New Orleans jazz funeral and rode in a coffin dressed in a white wedding dress. As a symbol of the death of one era in her life and the beginning of a new one, her funeral-wedding assures her fans that while Lestat may have left Rice's stage, there will be more books to come, certainly one about a Hebrew ghost titled *Servant of the Bones* in 1996, and possibly one about the most captivating of all the Mayfair witches, Mona, a character Anne has said she very much wants to write more about.

Whatever she writes, Anne Rice will tackle the big questions of our time, questions critic David Gates has summarized as "What does it mean to be human, and what does it matter?" (Review, *Body Thief*, 62). Rice has spoken of her need to get to the core of meaning, to get closer and closer to the truth, and she has said, "To write something great, you have to risk making a fool of yourself" (Gates, "Queen," 77). Part of Rice's genius is that she's always ready to take that risk to get closer to the core of what she's writing. Whether her novels succeed or fail, no one will ever accuse Anne Rice of taking the safe way to her truths.

2

Supernatural Genres: Horror, Gothic, and Fantasy

To analyze Anne Rice's work by genre or kind of fiction, it's necessary to go all the way back to the beginning of the nineteenth century. It was then that writers developed a fascination with the modern ideas of the supernatural. These writers, the Romantics, rejected the idea that everything could be explained by science and instead insisted that there were many things unexplained and unexplainable, including the individual human spirit. Romantic literature emphasizes strong ties to nature as both wild and true, an acceptance of the supernatural as a real force in life, an appreciation for passion over logic, and a rejection of conventional rules or rituals. The Romantics' fascination with both the importance of the individual and the supernatural led them to explore new areas in the two genres that Anne Rice most often draws on: horror and gothic fiction. But Rice's similarities to the Romantics go beyond the genres they both write, for Rice is a twentieth-century Romantic writer, a throwback to dreamers such as Samuel Taylor Coleridge, John Keats, and Mary Shelley.

Coleridge created one of literature's most famous characters in his poem "The Rime of the Ancient Mariner," and there are many echoes of this tale in Rice's work. The old sailor who is the central character in this poem has committed a terrible sin against nature by shooting an albatross, and as the poem opens, he has grabbed the arm of a wedding guest to tell him his tale, even though the guest wants to go in to the wedding reception. The guest tries to pull away, but the Ancient Mariner stares into his eyes and the guest can't move. Rice used much the same setup in *Interview with the Vampire*: just as the Mariner must tell his tale and the guest must bear witness, so Louis the vampire must tell his tale of how he denied his human nature to become a vampire as the disbelieving interviewer bears witness. At the end of both tales, both listeners are won over by the enormity of the sins their storytellers have committed and the enormity of the price they've paid for transgressing nature. Both Rice and Coleridge end with the same theme—acceptance of the beauty of nature and of life is the only possible redemption—but Rice takes the idea further by returning to it in all of her vampire books. Both Louis and Lestat must recognize their place in nature before they can end their stories.

Other echoes of Coleridge show up in Rice's witch stories. Coleridge wrote another long story poem called "Christabel" about a young woman named Christabel who meets a witch, Geraldine, in the woods. Coleridge's poem is unfinished, but he makes it clear that although Geraldine is powerful, she is unhappy, and that the terrible things she does all reflect her need for love and belonging. In the same way, Rice's Mayfair witches are, for the most part, desperately unhappy, longing for love and acceptance but thwarted at every turn by the evil spirit Lasher that controls them. Lasher himself has strong parallels in Geraldine; the reason he commits such atrocities is that he wants the love and acceptance of the human race. He is, in short, trying to belong. When Rowan Mayfair invites him into her life at the end of *The Witching Hour*, she is doing exactly what Christabel does at the beginning of Coleridge's poem: she is inviting evil into her life in hopes of finding love.

This terrible sadness linked closely with supernatural power, especially female supernatural power, occurs often in Romantic poetry. Keats wrote two poems with the same theme. One, "La Belle Dame sans Merci," tells the story of a faerie woman or sorceress who seduces knights who travel by the forest where she lives. Although she keeps them all under a spell, she weeps for them and for herself, more caught in the spell than the knights, just as the Mayfair witches are more caught by Lasher's supernatural powers than they are made powerful by them. Keats also wrote the poem "Lamia," the story of a supernatural being whose natural form is that of a snake. When she falls in love with a human man, Lamia calls on the help of the gods to become a human female, but she knows that she is not human and lives in fear that she will be betrayed and exposed, which of course is exactly what happens.

In the same way, the Mayfair Witches often lose the human men they love because they are not what they seem and they are helpless to prevent the source of their power from overwhelming them. Claudia, the child vampire of *Interview with the Vampire*, is another of these powerful/helpless women. As Nina Auerbach has pointed out in *Our Vampires, Ourselves*, Claudia's powerful existence as a vampire is actually a degradation because she is forced to remain a child forever, helpless in a tiny body while her mind becomes adult (158). Rice's work often reflects this Romantic idea of the seemingly powerful sorceress who is, in fact, helplessly and tragically caught in a greater magic.

But possibly the greatest influence of all the Romantic writers on Rice was Mary Shelley. Rice's feeling of kinship with Shelley may in part be due to the parallels in their personal lives—both married men who became famous poets (Mary married Percy Bysshe Shelley) and both lost young children—but the similarity in their work is also evident. In *Frankenstein* Shelley wrote of a man who created a monster from the parts of corpses because he wanted to create life; Rice writes of a man who became a vampire and who then makes monsters of others when he gives them the Dark Gift of vampirism. Both writers are concerned with the morality of their central characters' actions. Shelley's scientist Frankenstein first rejects his monster heartlessly, endures great loss, and finally comes to recognize his responsibility to his creation. Rice's vampire Lestat first rejects any sense of community among vampires, and then after great loss, recognizes his responsibility and his need for others.

But Rice wrote another book that is even closer to Shelley's *Frankenstein*. In *The Mummy*, Rice's hero, Ramses, is the mummy of the title, come back from the not-exactly-dead, prepared to be not only a hero but also a man of reason in the unreasonable twentieth century; Ramses is the parallel of Frankenstein and his scientific mind. Ramses also acts like Frankenstein when, midway through the book, he sees the corpse of his lover Cleopatra and reanimates her. Cleopatra returns to life as Frankenstein's monster is born, a horrible mass of decomposed flesh, and Ramses has the same reaction as Frankenstein: revulsion. Ramses runs from his creation just as Frankenstein rejects his, and both are then tormented by the vengeful actions of the creations they disowned. Thus both Rice and Shelley use the creation of monsters to illustrate the great ideas of Romantic literature, especially the idea that emotion and in particular love is the most important act of life.

Romantic literature was not all literary poems and stories, however. It also included popular genres, written not as art but as entertainment. In fact, the Romantic fascination with the supernatural influenced the development of two of the most famous forms of modern popular fiction: the horror story and the Gothic tale.

HORROR FICTION

Rice recognized the relationship between horror and her Romantic ideals and drew on the chilling effect of the ghosts, demons, black magic, witches, possessions, vampires, werewolves, and monsters around which Victorian horror masters such as Edgar Allan Poe and H. P. Lovecraft built their stories. The cornerstone of this genre is the creepy atmosphere that Poe made famous in stories such as "The Fall of the House of Usher" in which a man goes to visit an old school friend in his crumbling ancestral mansion just in time to help him entomb his sister in the family crypt in the basement. Later that night, the sister, not quite dead yet, claws her way out of the tomb to come after her brother, fulfilling the central character's (and the reader's) overwhelming suspicions that there's something terribly, *horribly*, wrong going on. Lovecraft, on the other hand, perfected the Thing story and wrote about horrendous monsters that reached up from the pit and dragged their screaming victims to vicious fates. Both Poe and Lovecraft could scare a reader into sleepless nights, but their horror stories also serve a purpose that Rice capitalized on in her fiction: they make readers reevaluate their ideas of evil.

Flesh-creeping horror such as Poe and Lovecraft wrote is not designed to appeal to the intellect, but it does help to remind the reader of the presence of evil in a world that is so overrun with real horrors that most readers are desensitized to the terrible things around them. As critic David Hartwell puts it, horror fiction "jumpstart[s] the readers' deadened emotional sensitivities" (8). Modern horror novelist and critic Stephen King argues the same idea: "We make up horrors to help cope with the real ones" (13). King argues that, whether or not it appeals to the intellect, horror fiction at its greatest truly is art because it is looking for what he calls phobic pressure points: "The good horror tale will dance its way to the center of your life and find the secret door to the room you believed no one but you knew of—as both Albert Camus and Billy Joel have pointed out, The Stranger makes us nervous . . . but we love to try on his face in secret" (4). Rice takes the horror story to this higher level, and instead of saying "I want to scare you to death," she says, "I want to scare you to think," pushing the horror genre by giving her readers The Stranger in the form of vampires and witches who ponder not only the evil in the world but also the evil in themselves and everyone else. Rice raised the traditional vampire story far above the usual "I want to bite your neck" nightmare by playing with the concept of free will, something that Bram Stoker, the author of the most famous of all vampire stories, *Dracula* (1897), had done a hundred years before.

Although vampire stories reach back into antiquity, the first great vampire novel was Stoker's. *Dracula* was told as a series of journal entries by a variety of Dracula's victims and opponents, and since much of what they write reinforces conventional vampire lore, many critics have seen the book as simply the extension of earlier vampire novels such as Thomas Presket Prest's *Varney the Vampyre* (1847) and John Polidori's *The Vampyre* (1819). But as Nina Auerbach points out, Stoker's *Dracula* actually refutes the themes of the older books which insisted that vampires were only looking for human connection. Dracula chooses to make his only connection to his long dead "race," the noble family that has since died out, not to the humans who surround him. He lives to prey on others, seducing them into his grasp, but if those others get close to him and know him, as Dr. Van Helsing does, he becomes vulnerable and dies. Rice's Lestat shares this aversion to closeness with living; those that Lestat feels attracted to he inevitably makes vampires like himself. Dracula is not a sad and isolated figure; he is a being who freely chooses evil, just as Rice's Louis and Lestat freely choose.

This choice is what gives the stories of these three vampires their power. Stephen King has noted that horror stories which draw strongly on the psychological almost always deal with "inside evil," the choice of evil by a being that has free will. King argued that Bram Stoker's *Dracula* is a remarkable achievement because "it humanizes the outside evil concept: we grasp it in a familiar way . . . and we can feel its texture" (62–63). Rice's vampires do the same thing for the twentieth century. We hear the stories of Louis and Lestat, and we know why they do the evil that they do because we can understand it in terms of our own lives. The texture is familiar, and in many ways, they are like us.

But in many ways, of course, vampires are different, and therein lies the appeal of the vampire horror story. Vampires have supernatural powers, they live without rules, and above all they represent what King calls "sex without responsibility" (66). Rice recognizes these light elements of the vampire novel, but concentrates instead on deeper meanings of the vampire figure, the loneliness and "Otherness" of the outsider, and the meaning of evil in the twentieth century (Ramsland,

"Interview," 34). And she does this, ironically, by making the vampires human—that is, by giving them human regrets and guilt and pain, so that we can relate to them as outsiders in a world that is so fast moving and cold that we are all virtually outsiders.

This is an aspect she shares with Robert Louis Stevenson, author of another great nineteenth-century horror story, *The Strange Adventure of Dr. Jekyll and Mr. Hyde*, the story of a scientist who experiments with a secret potion that separates his evil self (Mr. Hyde) from the good, civilized self he shows himself to be in his everyday affairs. It sounds like a good idea, but Dr. Jekyll soon finds that he can't separate the evil from the good forever because they are both a part of him. Rice shares with Stevenson a fascination with this idea of the evil inside us all. Her vampires anguish over their inability to control their dark desires just as the good Dr. Jekyll agonizes over his inability to refrain from turning himself into Hyde. The success of their stories rests on something Stephen King has theorized about horror fiction: "Horror does not horrify unless the reader . . . has been personally touched" (12). Rice's vampires and Stevenson's doctor personally touch their readers and leave them pondering the real meaning of evil in the world and wondering what their own choices would be if they were offered the Dark Gifts that the vampires and Jekyll are offered.

Rice draws on this combination again when she turns to another classic horror character, the witch, the most powerful supernatural female in the group. In her Witches Chronicles, Rice explores what Stephen King calls the basis of horror fiction: "secrets best left untold and things best left unsaid" (50). King goes on to say that all the greatest horror writers promise to tell us the secret and follow through with varying degrees of success. Rice, however, successfully reveals all the secrets in her Witches Chronicles, and while they are intellectually stimulating and have no easy explanations, they are also more horrifying and enthralling than any reader could possibly guess. Rice's doomed and tortured witch women call into question the power of the family and relationships between men and women while scaring her readers into fits, and in this she has another nineteenth-century forerunner, Henry James and his novel of women and evil, *The Turn of the Screw*. Rice has said that she wrote *The Witching Hour* in response to her reading of James's novel, and the influences are clear.

James's novel is about a governess who comes to a lonely house to care for two orphaned children. Once there, the governess becomes convinced that the children are in danger of possession from two ghosts, and she fights bitterly for their souls, destroying them in the process. James leaves open the question of whether there actually are ghosts, but he leaves no doubt as to the existence of evil. The governess is as determined to possess the children as the ghosts are, and this struggle for possession and power foreshadows the struggle of the Mayfair witches for the possession of their own souls and for the power they crave. Just as it is difficult to determine whether James's governess is evil or misguided, so it is difficult to determine whether many of Rice's witches are actively malevolent or simply caught up in the forces of the demon that drives them. Like James, Rice isn't as concerned with assigning guilt as she is with exploring the idea of evil and morality.

Rice has said, "Horror strikes deep moral chords in us," and *The Witching Hour* and her vampire stories, like *The Turn of the Screw*, are an almost perfect combination of moral questioning and full-out horror (Matousek, 112). Even in a book like *The Mummy*, intended as pure escapist horror fiction, Rice cannot resist making her point about evil and power and the lure of immortality, and this is part of Rice's genius as a novelist: she can combine mainstream moral philosophy and flesh-creeping horror in the same novel and make the reader enjoy both.

GOTHIC FICTION

Rice also draws heavily on another popular genre, the Gothic novel, a combination of horror and romance fiction. The term *Gothic* once applied to anything that was medieval, but the nineteenth century took it as a description for a very popular kind of story that featured supernatural threats in big, dark, old castles and houses that reeked of death and decay. Rice has drawn on this tradition so strongly that critic David Gates has described her as "America's classiest Gothic novelist" ("Queen," 76).

The earliest Gothic tales of Horace Walpole (*The Castle of Otranto* 1764) and Anne Radcliffe (*The Mysteries of Udolpho* 1794) featured mad uncles and monks who imprisoned innocents in gloomy mansions and monasteries filled with secret passages and underground rooms. These early settings became a hallmark of the Gothic story, one that Rice draws on constantly. In *Interview with the Vampire*, Louis de Pointe du Lac is an innocent when he wanders into the clutches of the vampire Lestat. Once bitten by Lestat, Louis's life becomes a Gothic novel full of underground crypts and coffins and sinister houses like the Theatre of Vampires in Paris. In the same way, the vampire Lestat in *The Vampire Lestat* is taken from his bedroom and spirited off to a great Gothic castle by the master vampire Magnus and there made a vampire against his will. Other great houses in Rice's work include a new Gothic castle of redwood in southern California in *Queen of the Damned*, but even though the house is new, the inside is old, cut into the side of the mountain, full of secrets, crypts, and coffins. But the greatest of all Rice's Gothic settings is the Mayfair Mansion in the Witches Chronicles. In this lavish New Orleans house, generations of women are dominated by an evil male spirit who destroys them again and again, the ultimate Gothic nightmare.

Another aspect of those Gothic tales featuring men, particularly those Gothic tales featuring vampires, is something critic Eve Sedgwick has called "paranoid Gothic." Sedgwick uses this term to describe a situation in which "one or more males [is] not only . . . persecuted by but considers himself transparent to and often under the compulsion of another male" (Auerbach, 14). Sedgwick applies this to the vampire story written by the great Romantic poet Byron, but it certainly also applies to Louis in *Interview with the Vampire*, the first of Rice's novels. Louis feels he is completely under the control of Lestat, the vampire who made him. Only when their vampire "daughter" Claudia destroys Lestat can Louis escape. Lestat's return from the undead reinforces the Gothic tone of the novel; Louis, in fact, can never escape Lestat.

Rice also echoes Victorian novelists who drew on the same Gothic aspects for inspiration, most notably Charlotte Brontë's *Jane Eyre* and Emily Brontë's *Wuthering Heights* with their dark heroes who exercise almost supernatural control over the others in their stories. Charlotte Brontë's hero, Mr. Rochester, keeps his insane wife in the attic; Emily Brontë's hero, Heathcliff, becomes a monster in his grief over the loss of his great love and tortures everyone who comes within his reach. Either of these dark, brooding heroes would feel right at home in a Rice novel, where the matriarch of the Mayfair family keeps a long-dead body rolled up in a carpet in the attic and the vampire Lestat becomes a monster in his grief and despair. That both Rochester and Heathcliff inhabit gloomy Gothic mansions just as Rice's vampires and witches only strengthens the comparison. Just as Rice elevates ordinary horror fiction, so does she elevate the Gothic, in much the same way that Henry James (*The Turn of the Screw* is often considered a Gothic work) and the Brontës elevated it, to make the reader question the idea of evil.

FANTASY FICTION

There is one other kind of supernatural literature to which Rice's work can be compared: the fantasy genre. Rice often combines the supernatural aspects of the Gothic setting and mood and the archetypal characters of the horror genre and roots them both in the rich tradition of epic fantasy that veers close to created mythology in the tradition of C. S. Lewis's Narnia books or J.R.R. Tolkien's *The Lord of the Rings* trilogy. Although fantasy may seem too lighthearted a word for Rice's work, the definition of this genre is simply a literary work that breaks from reality, often to make a serious point. And in the twentieth century, fantasy may be the only way to make a serious universal point. As writer and critic Ursula K. LeGuin has noted, our society is now "global, multi-lingual, and enormously irrational." LeGuin suggests that only global, intuitional fantasy can fully describe the aspects of this world, and she uses Tolkien's *The Lord of the Rings* trilogy as an example. *The Lord of the Rings* is a series of three books about the quest of a creature named Frodo to restore peace to his land. LeGuin says of this work that "It may be that the central ethical dilemma of our age, the use or non-use of annihilating power, was posed most cogently in fiction terms by [Tolkien, who] began *The Lord of the Rings* in 1937 and finished it about ten years later. During those years, Frodo withheld his hand from the Ring of Power, but the nations did not" (Introduction, 12). In the same way, Anne Rice tackles issues such as AIDS, free will in a technological society, women's growing power, and the hazards of genetic research, all within fantastic story worlds that allow the reader to see them more clearly.

Rice's creation of these story worlds is impeccable. As critic Betty Rosenburg has noted, "Fantasy strictly follows a set of laws formulated by each author for an imaginary world, rules which need have no congruence with the laws of nature as we know them but which must conform to their own logic" (210). So Rice constructs elaborate mythologies and genealogies for her vampires and witches, giving them supernatural powers with limits and supernatural freedom with boundaries. Each of her supernatural worlds has an internal logic that she never breaks, and because of her careful use of fantasy, her stories rise above simple genre tales of the supernatural to epics of particular worlds where magic makes sense and immortality is just one more thing to deal with.

The creatures in Rice's books are characters from horror, Gothic, and fantasy fiction, not reality, but they move through a real world, and the contrast between their cynical immortality and the innocent and fragile mortality of the humans they encounter gives Rice great scope in arguing her philosophical questions about life, death, evil, and the meaning of existence. As she said in an interview in 1990, "what's important is that you write what's really, really intense, and what gives you the greatest thrill . . . the supernatural gives me that intensity whether I'm reading it or writing it" (Ferraro, 75). Drawing on this intensity, Rice has taken the classic tales of vampires, mummies, and witches and changed them into modern myths, fairy tales, and nightmares in the language of the twentieth century, more fantastic and frightening because the supernatural stories she tells are about us, our own dreams and fears and feelings. Anne Rice's debt to the Romantics and the genres inspired by them is great, but she has repaid that debt by expanding the ideas and forms and deepening their themes.

THE VAMPIRES

3

Interview with the Vampire
(1976)

In 1969, Anne Rice sat down to write a story called "Interview with the Vampire." But once the story was done, the characters would not leave her, and she went back, rewriting and expanding the short story into a novel she finished in January of 1974. The novel, *Interview with the Vampire*, explores the meaning of evil in the world through the thoughts of Louis, a moral vampire struggling with the evil of his existence.

Interview with the Vampire opens as a young man begins to interview an older man named Louis de Pointe du Lac in San Francisco. Louis claims to be a vampire, and at first the interviewer assumes that he is just one of the city's more colorful street people. But as Louis's story unfolds, the interviewer becomes both fearful and fascinated, realizing that Louis truly is a vampire who is telling his life story to warn others of the seductive power of evil and immortality. The interviewer listens through the night as Louis tells him of Lestat, his unholy vampire partner, and of Claudia, the vampire child they created together. It is a tale of guilt, terror, betrayal, death, and above all, terrible isolation, and yet at the end, seduced by the power and the romance of the story, the interviewer begs Louis to make him a vampire, too. This becomes Louis's last defeat. Not even when he tells all the horrors that have been his life can he destroy the lure of immortality. He leaves the interviewer who, as the story closes, makes plans to follow him to learn the last of his secrets.

POINT OF VIEW

One of the most interesting aspects of *Interview with the Vampire* is the way Anne Rice has worked with point of view—the person (i.e., the narrator) through whose eyes (or from whose point of view) the reader sees the story. There are many kinds of point of view, but three are the most common.

First-person point of view is the easiest to identify because the narrator uses the first-person pronoun "I" when she or he tells the story. If a story begins "I am the vampire Lestat," the reader knows the story is going to be in the first person because the narrator uses the pronoun "I" even though he's not reporting dialogue. First-person point of view is an intimate way of presenting a story because the narrator is part of the story, telling the reader directly about events that happened in her or his past. Rice's later book, *The Vampire Lestat*, is told in the first person. (For more information on first-person point of view, see chapter 4.)

Third-person point of view uses the third-person "she" or "he" to identify the narrator. Third person is much more distant than first person because it tells a story about events that happened to other people through a voice that is not part of the story. But the third-person point of view can do things that the first person cannot because of that distance. A story that begins "The boy watched the vampire in the dim light. He could see the furnishings of the room more clearly now" is in third-person point of view because the narrator uses "he" instead of "I."

There are two kinds of third-person point-of-view. First is the third-person omniscient, which means "all-knowing"; thus, in this point of view, the narrator, who is not part of the story, knows what everyone is thinking and everything that is going to happen, and tells it all to the reader. Because it's a very distant point of view, most writers prefer to use the second kind of third person—the third-person limited, which uses the "she" or "he" pronoun. In this point of view, the narrator concentrates on seeing the story through one person's eyes, just as in the first person. The narrator tells the reader everything that the he or she sees, thinks, feels, and does, but only reports what the other characters do or say that can be observed or heard by the narrator. This does not necessarily mean that the narrator is the main character in the story. While some third-person point-of-view characters are indeed the centers of their stories, others are observer characters, characters who watch and comment while the main characters in the story act out their parts. *In-*

terview with the Vampire opens with a third-person limited point of view, using an observer-narrator, the interviewer.

What difference does point of view make? For an author, it's one of the most important choices she or he makes about telling the story. A first-person narrator puts the reader into the action but requires that the author report all events from the narrator's experience and in the narrator's voice. A third-person limited narrator distances the reader from the story, but allows the author more freedom to use a more authoritative voice and to make more detailed descriptions of actions and their meanings. Many novels switch point-of-view characters from scene to scene; this technique is usually too confusing to attempt with first-person narrators, but it can work very well with third-person narrators. (Rice switches viewpoints in *The Queen of the Damned, The Mummy,* and all of the Witches Chronicles; for a further discussion of multiple points of view, see chapters 5 and 8 through 11.) The writer's choice of point of view, then, is the voice that is best for the kind of story she or he has to tell.

In *Interview with the Vampire,* Anne Rice had a tough point-of-view choice to make. She wanted to tell the story of the intense emotional longings of a moral being after two hundred years as a vampire. Louis's story was not interesting to Rice simply because he sucked blood to survive. What fascinated Rice about the character of Louis was that after all those years as an immortal, he still retained his humanity and still anguished over what he had become. Given her interest in Louis's psychology and inner torment, first-person point of view would seem to be Rice's logical choice because it would put the reader in Louis's mind to suffer the torment with him.

But Rice also wanted the reader to feel the seductive pull of the vampire, to see him as the Other, someone who is different from the "normal" people in society, a tragic outcast, inhuman and beautiful. To do that, she needed the distance of a third-person observer-narrator. A third-person narrator who was a "normal" person could see and describe not only the alluring way Louis looked and moved, but also the emotional pull of his story on those he met. In other words, Rice needed to show both points of view so that the reader understood the agony of being a vampire completely and yet was as drawn to it as the interviewer in the story.

Needing both, Rice chose to have her literary cake and eat it, too. The beginning of the story is told in the third-person observer point of view through the eyes of the young man who has asked to interview the vampire. This interviewer is like the reader in every way, ignorant of the ways of the vampire, fascinated by and fearful of the dark figure before him, and finally seduced into the lure of the Other. As the interviewer observes Louis's agony from a distance, the vampire becomes a real physical presence, and the reader listens and is seduced into the vampire's story along with the interviewer.

But the interviewer's role in the story—and the story that the interviewer actually takes part in—is only a fraction of *Interview*. The majority of the story is Louis's, and he tells it to the interviewer as a first-person narrator. That is, most of this story is Louis telling his story using "I" as his pronoun. This means that the reader gets to participate in Louis's agony, becoming one with Louis as the "I" narrator.

So Rice has surrounded Louis's intimate first-person story with the interviewer's distant third-person limited-observer frame story, thereby getting the benefits of both points of view. However, the technical answer to the question, "What point of view is *Interview with the Vampire* told in?," is third-person limited because the story begins and ends with the interviewer—and the reader—watching and listening to the vampire.

CHARACTER DEVELOPMENT

The correct choice of point of view is not enough to pull the reader into the story. For that, the best plots begin with character, and the simplest definition of a character-driven plot is the sequence of events caused by a character who needs something and can't get it. The character who needs something and who is at the center of the book is called the protagonist (pro = for). The protagonist's need is called the goal. The character or force (nature, society, the government) that keeps the protagonist from getting the goal is called the antagonist (anti = against). In the third-person point of view plot that begins *Interview*, the protagonist is Louis, his goal is to tell his story, and his antagonist is the young man who has asked to interview him. At first glance, the interviewer doesn't seem a likely source of struggle and conflict because he fears, admires, and respects Louis and spends the majority of the book listening to him and recording his story. But an antagonist doesn't have to try to stop or hurt the protagonist in order to cause conflict. In the best plots, the antagonist is as strong or stronger than the protagonist in order to set up a strong conflict. In *Interview*, the interviewer asks questions that are at first skeptical and then later curious about Louis's life as a vampire. This makes him a strong antagonist because every one of the questions sends Louis deeper into his confession of his sins and makes Louis try harder to explain the terrible aspects of the immortal vampire life and causes him more anguish.

This struggle of the protagonist and the antagonist toward their final battle becomes the plot, and the question of the outcome of what they're struggling for becomes the central plot question; that is, "Will the protagonist defeat the antagonist and achieve his or her goal?" In *Interview*, the central question is, "Will Louis convince the interviewer of the ultimate agony of being a vampire?" In a character-driven plot, the central question always has tremendous impact on the character of the protagonist because it tests her or his identity, that is, her or his concept of who she or he really is. The central question of *Interview* has impact on Louis's character because he desperately wants to see himself (his identity) as a moral person even though he is a vampire, and so he wants to warn the interviewer of the perils so that he doesn't fall as Louis did. When at the end of the book the interviewer demands, "Make me a vampire now!" the central question is answered—no, Louis won't succeed—and Louis is left feeling evil and damned once again, doubting his identity as a good, moral being but clearly developed as a character.

But the plot of Louis's struggle with the interviewer does not show Louis's character completely. For a fuller development of Louis's character, the reader must turn to the story that Louis tells the interviewer, the second plot of the book. In this story, the protagonist is Louis, Louis's goal is peace of mind and understanding of the thing that he has become, and the antagonist is Lestat, the vampire who made him and who tries to control him by luring him to surrender fully to his vampire nature. Since Lestat is both powerful and seductive, he makes a wonderfully strong opponent. The central question of this plot is, "Will Louis free himself from Lestat and find peace and self-knowledge?" It's an important question because Louis's struggles to answer it and retain his identity as a moral being make him an interesting and complex character.

Louis's character development in this plot begins with a major trauma in his life when he denies his brother something he needs spiritually, and his brother dies. This conflicts with Louis's identity as a good brother and a good human being because he feels the tragedy was caused by his inability to accept the idea of a spiritual world. Half mad with grief and guilt, Louis stumbles into the second trauma of his life: Lestat the vampire, who takes his blood and leaves him weakened to the point of death. When Lestat returns and explains how much above all human things the life of a vampire is, Louis sees him as the representation of the supernatural that he could not accept in his brother and also sees in him a way to reject all the distractions of the world that blinded him to his brother's needs. The answer to his anguish seems clear: he will become a vampire and cast off all human things, which will also release him from the agony of guilt he can't escape as a human. Louis is motivated or given reason to act by the needs of his character, and by acting he begins his own character growth by choosing to become a vampire. At this point, Louis's character is fascinating: active, involved, and emotional. Even more important, his actions, which are motivated by his character needs, drive his plot.

But motivation is not enough: there must also be conflict. Conflict in fiction also comes from character, both the external conflict in the real, physical world and the internal conflict of the mind. Louis's external conflict in the second plot is his clear struggle with Lestat, but he also has an internal conflict that escalates when he realizes that he's made a terrible mistake. He's chosen to become a vampire, but he still has human feelings and he still clings to his human identity, which means that he is now in a hell of his own making: he's a vampire and must drink blood and take human lives even though he still sees himself as a moral human being. This internal conflict makes Louis seem like a psychologically true character because he acts the way a "real" person would act. But his external conflicts are important, too. Louis's resistance causes Lestat to try even harder to make him completely a vampire, and their external battles form the most exciting parts of the book. This combination of both internal and external struggles makes Louis a fully developed character.

As the story unwinds, however, most of Louis's conflicts become internal and dwell on the struggle between his fading human morality and the strong pull of his new vampire nature. The problem here is that his internal struggles make him appear passive, refusing to begin actions himself, always reacting to the demands of others. A lot of Louis's story time in *Interview* is spent sitting and thinking in anguish that eventually begins to sound like whining. Eternally questioning his own existence, he shouts to the human woman he could have loved, "What am I? I am to live to the end of the world and I don't even know what I am!" But rather than aggressively seek out the answers he needs, he allows himself to be driven by Lestat (70). His passivity and hopelessness bring him further into Lestat's power when he finds the child Claudia crying beside her dead mother and feels human pity for her. Louis's character is so passive, however, that he does not act to save her; instead he sinks again into internal despair, deciding that he is forever damned. This leads him to give up and drink from her neck, not as an act of aggression but as an act of surrender. This gives Lestat the leverage he needs. He seduces Louis into making Claudia their vampire daughter, a child by blood of both "parents." After that, Louis cannot leave his Unholy Family and spends the rest of the book following the whims of both Lestat and Claudia. He takes action only when he's pushed to the wall, and such action does not have much impact on his character. Without continued character growth and with most of his conflict internal, Louis often gives up his own story to those characters who are more active and more interesting in their external struggles than he, even though he remains a well-developed character to the end.

One of those characters who is more active and interesting is the second major character in the book, Louis's antagonist or opponent, Lestat. A hot-headed, greedy, cruel, instinctive vampire, Lestat rages through Louis's story, fascinating him and repelling him and always watching over him. Lestat's character growth is revealed gradually as his need for Louis grows. He makes Louis a vampire, he says, because he needs Louis's money and home, but his ties to Louis soon become more complicated. He jeers at Louis but teaches him what he needs to survive. He does things he knows will repel Louis but leads him to create Claudia, the child vampire, to make a family that will bind Louis to him forever. Lestat does these things because he has his own character identity to protect: he sees himself as powerful and respected, and his control of Louis and Claudia reinforces that identity. When the other two try to leave, everything that Lestat believes is true about himself is put in jeopardy. His attempts to keep them tied to him are his external conflict, but his emotional panic at losing them is his internal conflict.

Lestat is the perfect antagonist for Louis because his need to control Louis is in absolute opposition to Louis's need to be free, and the two opposing needs create a wonderfully tight conflict for the story. But their character needs are not the only things about them that are opposites. Lestat's over-the-top emotions make him a foil for Louis, a contrast figure that heightens Louis's moody internal character. Louis is tortured by the idea that he has become evil; Lestat shrugs off the question with "Evil is a point of view" (89). Louis clings desperately to the remains of his humanity, while Lestat coldly but wisely tells him that he is in despair because he refuses to accept the reality of his vampire nature. Standing beside Lestat, Louis looks much more human than vampire, but unfortunately, he also looks much less interesting. Lestat rises much

higher in exultation and falls much harder into suffering and degradation at the end and ultimately becomes the more interesting character,
the passionate opposite of Louis's quiet despair.

Even though Lestat is shown as Louis's opposite, he is not without
emotional growth. Lestat's fall, in fact, is proof that he has changed from
the cold unfeeling creature that he first presented to the reader. Destroyed by Claudia's hatred and need for freedom, Lestat nevertheless
comes back to find Louis again and again, literally crawling back from
the grave in order to retain the most important relationship of his life.
If Louis becomes a vampire through Lestat, Lestat retrieves something
of his lost humanity through his ties to Louis, and so at the end, Lestat
is a fully dynamic character who has changed greatly and learned much.

The third major character in *Interview* is the cause of most of that character change. Claudia, the eternally damned child created by both Louis
and Lestat, is interesting as a character because she begins with none of
Louis's internal moral reservations. Because she is a child, she feeds
when she is hungry without guilt or moral choice, and all her goals are
external: she must drink blood, and she wants pretty things. But as time
passes and her mind and character develop, Claudia recognizes her
growing internal conflict as she yearns for knowledge, freedom, and
physical maturity. Claudia can get some of the knowledge she craves
from her "parents"—from Lestat she learns the glory of the kill, and
from Louis she learns the beauty of life and the questions about their
existence—but freedom is a different problem, and physical maturity is
forever an impossibility. Her frustration sparks the great conflicts that
further change her character.

The first of these conflicts is the struggle with Lestat who wants to physically restrain her to keep her and Louis with him, an external conflict that
seems great because Lestat is so powerful. But the greatest of her conflicts
turns out to be internal: her need to escape emotionally from the passive
Louis. She grows strong enough to defeat Lestat and even to plan killing
him with great enjoyment, but no matter how strong she grows, she cannot escape from Louis because she loves him and he loves her. He holds
her so completely that she cannot even sleep apart from him; when she
asks for a coffin of her own, Louis is so distraught that she reverses herself
instantly, telling him that she doesn't want it if it hurts him and that she'll
stay with him always (103). But Claudia's need for freedom is relentless,
and by the time she has spent sixty-five years trapped in the body of a five-
year-old, her frustration has led her to ask the first great question of her
life: "*Which of you made me what I am?*" (109).

The answer, that she is a child of both, finally alters her life and her character completely, freeing her from obligation to either of them. "I took your life," Louis tells her. "He gave it back to you." Claudia's answer is, "And I hate you both" (116–117). Claudia takes control and plots to kill Lestat, becoming the leader while Louis follows. When she tells Louis they must leave Lestat to find the answers to their questions, Louis tells her that Lestat will never let them go. Instead of agreeing with him as a child would with her father, Claudia smiles self-confidently and says, "Oh . . . *really?*" and becomes at once an equal to Lestat in strength of purpose and far superior to Louis. At this point in her character development, her battle with Lestat for Louis's soul is begun and can only have one outcome: the total destruction of one of them. That Claudia is the one who fails is not so much a failure of her spirit, which remains unquenched throughout, but a failure of circumstance and knowledge. In the end, Lestat wins because he knows more about vampires than Claudia does. Like so many women in literature, Claudia dies because she lacks knowledge she has sought but been denied. But she dies a fully developed character, even though that character is still trapped in the exquisite body of a five-year-old.

Louis, Lestat, and Claudia stand out in *Interview* because they are dynamic characters who achieve character arc during their struggle; that is, the events of the story have such a strong impact on them that their characters change dramatically by the end of the story. Dynamic characters are fully developed and are so psychologically complex that they are capable of surprising the reader with their different "sides" so that the reader says, "Gee, I hadn't seen that side of Claudia before." Dynamic characters drive the plots of their stories with their needs and propel the actions with their problems as they try to satisfy those needs and solve those problems.

But not all characters in a story can be dynamic. Other characters who are identified by one main personality trait and who do not change very much during the course of the story are called static. The static or flat characters in the story never grow or surprise the reader, but they usually play such small roles in the plot that their flatness never becomes a problem. In fact, if they were dynamic characters, they'd probably hurt the story because the details of their characters would mislead the reader into thinking they were about to play more important roles than they were. Most of the vampires' victims in *Interview* are static characters because Rice wants the reader to identify with and sympathize with the vampires, not the victims. But sometimes quite important characters in a novel can be static, and the interviewer in the frame plot of *Interview* is one of those characters.

Rice left the interviewer undeveloped for two reasons. First, his character and story are unimportant in the scheme of the book. He is there merely as a ficelle figure, a character the author has provided to ask the right questions so that the main character can be revealed as a fully developed character. The interviewer is in this book for one reason only: to interview Louis and give him a reason to tell his story. In fact, this character doesn't even get a name in this book, only a function; he is "the interviewer." Second, the interviewer acts as an analog character for the reader; that is, he represents the reader in the story. He feels the emotions the reader feels in the beginning, asks the questions the reader wants to ask, and is finally seduced into the story the way the reader is finally seduced into the story. If the interviewer were developed in more detail, it would be harder for the reader to identify with him. As an essentially blank slate possessing only the emotions the reader possesses, he becomes the reader's place holder in the story. There are many other static characters in *Interview with the Vampire*, but in the end, like the interviewer, they are all employed to test and illuminate the dynamic characters of Rice's Unholy Family, Louis, Lestat, and Claudia.

PLOT DEVELOPMENT AND STRUCTURE

The simplest definition of a plot is the sequence of events caused by a protagonist or central character who needs something and is prevented from getting it by an antagonist. The struggle between the protagonist and the antagonist sets up the central plot question, "Will the protagonist get what she or he needs?" And the plot ends when the question is answered.

But plot is much more than just the events of a conflict that answer a central question. A good plot has a clear underlying structure that promises the reader that the author is in control, that all the events she's telling will combine to make sense and will be causal (one plot event will logically cause the next event), and that these events will build to a final great scene, a climax, in which all questions will be answered. Rice's structure in *Interview*, which is both clever and complex, delivers on all these promises.

Rice's structure can best be analyzed using a plot curve that actually resembles a plot triangle but that neatly diagrams how a plot moves. The most famous plot triangle is called Freitag's Pyramid (see Figure 3.1).

Figure 3.1
Freitag's Pyramid

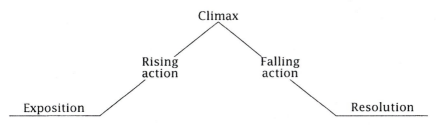

The first part of the plot curve is called exposition, but a more modern term might be the setup. This is life as usual for the protagonist. Things are stable, maybe not great, but calm and safe. Exposition is usually shown as a flat line at the beginning of the diagram. The protagonist of *Interview with the Vampire* is Louis, and his exposition or setup is his stable but unhappy life as a mortal riddled with guilt over his brother's death. At the end of this flat line is a point often called a turning point, when something happens to turn the protagonist in a new direction that leads out of her or his stable life. The turning point is Louis's meeting with Lestat, who makes him a vampire.

After the turning point, there is rising action (which is why the line in the diagram angles up or rises). The rising action is the struggle between the protagonist and the antagonist, which makes the plot more knotted and complicated as the story moves toward the climax. In Louis's case, the rising action or the knotting is the series of events he creates in his attempts to come to terms with what he is and to free himself from his antagonist, Lestat.

At some point in this rising action, the protagonist changes so much in the struggle that she or he is no longer the same person as in the exposition. Usually an act that changes everything occurs at this point in the story, which is why it is sometimes called the point of no return because the protagonist is too changed to return to the life she or he once led. The point of no return in *Interview* is Claudia's murder of Lestat while Louis watches, paralyzed with horror.

After the point of no return, all the events knotted in the first half of the plot must come undone because once the rising action has reached the climax or final showdown, the story is over. By the time the protagonist meets the antagonist in the climax, most of the questions have been answered except the final great question of whether or not the protagonist will succeed at her or his goal. This climax often involves a recognition on the part of the protagonist. In old plays, the recognition was literal because the protagonist would recognize an enemy or a lover in disguise. In modern fiction, the protagonist is more likely to recognize some truth about himself or others. In *Interview*, Louis's last meeting with Lestat helps him recognize that Lestat is not the all-powerful monster Louis had cast him as, and that there are no answers to their questions after all.

After the climax and recognition comes the downward movement of the plot that answers all remaining questions. It's called the falling action, or the denouement (French for "unknotting"), which leads directly to the last flat line of the plot, the resolution, in which the protagonist is once more in a stable situation, although a much different stable situation than the one in which she or he began. Rice's resolution leaves us with Louis alone, all battles done, facing the world of the night.

Freitag's Pyramid shows these plot parts, but it puts the climax or most important scene in the center of the story, and most modern authors put their climaxes at the end. Therefore, most modern plots look like lopsided Freitag Pyramids (see Figure 3.2).

Figure 3.2
Modern Plot Course

But no matter how the plot is diagrammed, the plot parts remain the same. They begin with stable exposition, which is broken by a turning point that leads to rising action, which finally culminates in a climax and recognition, which are swiftly followed by falling action and resolution.

Rice's plot is a classic plot curve because she balances every aspect of the first half of her plot with a matching aspect in the second half, thus neatly setting up reader expectation in the first and satisfying it in the second. Look at the way Rice's events knot their way up to the midpoint and then unknot their way down again:

1. Louis fails his brother and is alone.

2. Louis meets Lestat and is made a vampire; tied to Lestat.

3. Lestat creates Claudia for Louis.

4. Claudia kills Lestat to set them free.

3. Lestat causes Claudia's death by sun.

2. Louis frees himself from Lestat.

1. Louis turns away from his new brother, Armand, and is alone.

Rice's plot is beautifully crafted, which it needs to be because the narrator of her first-person plot (Louis's story) pursues an abstract goal. What Louis needs is peace of mind, something he'll never achieve as long as he's a vampire and something that isn't clearly achievable through action. Since Louis does not have one clear, compelling external goal from the beginning to the end of his first-person story, the reader needs something else to compel her or him through the plot. Rice solves this problem by echoing Louis's first-person conflict in the third-person interview plot which frames his life story. In that third-person story, Louis does have a clear-cut goal: to tell his tale as a warning to others, specifically to the interviewer who will pass it on to the others. Rice makes this double plot work not only through classic structure but also through the brilliant use of two literary devices, flashback and frame.

LITERARY DEVICES: FLASHBACK AND FRAME

Rice goes beyond the plot analyzed in the preceding section because she runs a double plot, a first-person plot in the past and a third-person plot in the present.

Rice's double plot gives *Interview* what Aristotle called the unities. A good plot, Aristotle said, must be united by a single protagonist with a single problem and be played out in a single time and a single place to illustrate a single theme or idea. But Louis's life story can't fit the unities; he rambles all over the world, encountering different problems as he goes, pursuing his internal goal of peace of mind. So Rice imposes the unities on the plot by surrounding Louis's story with another, this one with a clear goal: Louis wants to confess his sins to a younger human man, thereby achieving at least the temporary peace of telling the story of how evil he is as a warning to others. This story has all of Aristotle's unities: character (only Louis and the interviewer), problem (vampirism), place (a single room in San Francisco), time (one night), and theme (the lure of evil and immortality). It also poses a strong central question—Will Louis's story convince the interviewer of the agony and despair of the vampire's life?—and answers it—No. This unified plot pulls the story together because it begins and ends the book, thus framing the story of Louis's life, which is why this literary device is called a frame.

Another aspect of a good plot is that it takes place in the "now" of the story; that is, the reader reads what's happening as it happens to the protagonist. Rice's frame story of Louis and the interviewer takes place in the now of the story. But at times, some characters may need to remember things that are from their pasts. When authors take the story out of the now and into the past, they use the flashback technique. Flashback literally means that the mind of a character flashes back to the past to pick up a memory that the now of the story has evoked. Flashback is the reason small children don't touch hot stoves more than once: after the first burn, when they get near something hot, their minds flash back to the original experience and they pull their hands away. In the same way, characters flash back to early memories when they get near something that causes them to remember. And Louis's reason to remember, the part of the plot that throws him into flashback, is his need to give his warning to the interviewer.

The interesting thing about the structure of *Interview* is that it is nearly *all* flashback, all Louis's life story as it sprawls through time and space. But the flashback is contained and controlled by the frame of Louis, sitting in a darkened room, talking to a writer who has asked to interview him.

Rice extends the frame by dropping pieces of it into Louis's story now and then to remind the reader that the frame is in place and to pull some of the sprawl of Louis's tale together. The frame reminds the reader that Louis is telling this story for one single reason, that there is, in fact, one idea driving this plot although it seems to ramble through time. In this way, once again, Rice gets to have her literary cake and eat it, too. She gets Aristotelian unity and epic sprawl, the human Louis, and the larger-than-life Louis, all through her masterful use of literary device and structure.

THEMATIC ISSUES

Theme is the central, underlying idea in a work of art. In literature, theme is often confused with moral, which in *Interview with the Vampire* would be something like, "Don't hang out with vampires; they'll bite you and ruin your life." But most writers aren't interested in providing their readers with rules to live by. Instead, they're interested in an idea that seems to them to be true but makes no moral judgment, no decision about good or bad. In the best novels, theme is not obvious, but it's always present, embedded in different aspects of the novel. Some of the aspects to consider when deciding on theme are

- Setting
- The central plot question
- The protagonist's internal conflict
- The protagonist's character growth
- The beginning and ending
- The title

The setting of a story is the time and place in which it happens. In the best stories, setting is so much a part of the plot that the story could not have been set any other time or place. The time of *Interview* is the late twentieth century, so that the reader cannot dismiss the story as myth or legend because it's happening right now in the cynical, disbelieving light of modern times. And the story takes place in San Francisco, a city noted for its gay population, adding another dimension to the relationship between two men who meet late at night in a bar and who then go to a private room to talk. This setting adds to the idea of the vampire as the Other, an outcast of society, by making a possible reference to the homosexual's outcast status in our homophobic society. Therefore, the setting seems to imply a concern with the difficulty of acceptance of difference in the twentieth century.

The central question and its answer usually reflect the theme in some way. If the central question is, "Will Louis convince the interviewer of the despair of immortality and vampirism?" or, drawing from the first-person story, "Will Louis escape the curse of his vampire nature?", and the answer to both is "No," then the book becomes a story about the overwhelming power of vampirism and whatever it represents in Rice's story: evil, passion or our own animal natures.

The protagonist's internal conflict, the internal struggle as he or she decides what to do, also often reflects the theme. Louis's internal struggles are over his existence as a vampire and the death and destruction he causes and witnesses. This struggle seems to be tied up in both his revulsion for and his fascination with evil, particularly in his quest for the meaning of evil and the meaning of his own existence. But that quest also suggests that what he sees as evil may simply be the darker side of human nature, and therefore that the theme may have to do with Louis's recognizing a darker side of himself that he must accept to be at peace with himself.

In the same way, the protagonist's character growth also often reflects the theme. By the end of *Interview*, Louis is stronger, acting on his own without Lestat, and while he is no happier, he seems resigned to his vampire nature. Since Rice appears to present this resignation in a mildly positive way, her theme appears to be tied to the acceptance of one's own nature, whatever it might be.

Clues to theme are often placed in the most important parts of the story. The beginning of a story is important because it hooks the reader by showing the main character and the start of the story problems. The ending is important because it's the last thing the reader reads, and so it's the part of the book most likely to be remembered. *Interview* begins and ends with a vampire and an interviewer talking about what it means to be a vampire, so that the interviewer may be convinced that the life of a vampire is to be avoided. The fact that the interviewer begins a skeptic and ends begging Louis to make him a convert indicates that Rice is writing about the seductive power of evil.

Finally, an author's choice of title (if it's a good choice) in many ways can be thought of as a minisynopsis of the book. Think of *Gone with the Wind*, Margaret Mitchell's story of a woman who suddenly loses everything in the Civil War. Think of *Raiders of the Lost Ark*, which describes not only the villainous Nazis who are trying to steal the ark but also the hero who is trying to do the same thing. And now think of *Interview with the Vampire*, which could have been called *The Life of Louis* or *Blood and Death* or *The Unholy Family* or any number of other names. Rice's decision to title her book after the main event of the frame story, the interview, puts the emphasis on the central question and answer of the frame story, which is that even after an evening of listening to Louis's tale of despair, the interviewer still longs to be a vampire. The lure of immortality and power is too strong.

Taking all these things together, it's possible to develop several themes. One might be that the curse of being the outsider or the Other is that no one can understand the isolation unless he or she is an outsider, too. This cuts off anyone who is the Other (like Louis) from being understood by any but his own kind no matter how hard he tries to communicate (as Louis tries to communicate with the interviewer). Another theme might be that the lure of power (immortality) will always overcome the knowledge that the powerful existence is one of isolation and unhappiness. Another might be that, since we can identify with Louis so easily, we are all Others, alone in the night (or as a character says in another of Rice's novels, "Behold the void").

Any of these themes are possibilities. There is never any one right answer to the theme of a work of literature because readers bring their own ideas and psychologies to the book and interpret the theme in a way that best suits their own needs. That's why the determination of theme is almost always a psychological decision, and few novels repay psychological analysis in the way that *Interview with the Vampire* does. In fact, a psychological analysis of *Interview* gives another possible theme hinted at above: that no one is whole until he or she understands and accepts all the aspects of who he or she is, both the good "human" and the bad "vampire" natures.

A FREUDIAN READING OF *INTERVIEW WITH THE VAMPIRE*

Psychological analysis of literature really boils down to three questions:

1. Why do the characters do what they do?
2. Why did the author do what she or he did (write these characters and this story)?
3. Why does the reader do what she or he does (react the way she or he does)?

But as simple as these questions seem, the path a critic takes to their answers can be complex and depends on what form of psychological criticism that critic prefers. One of the most popular kinds of psychological criticism, Freudian criticism, was developed from the theories of Sigmund Freud. To discover why Louis and Lestat do what they do, why Anne Rice wrote what she did, and why so many readers have responded, it's best to begin with Freud and his ideas about the unconscious.

Freud said that while there is a part of us that is conscious of what we are doing, there is also a part of us that is unconscious and that has ideas that we do not recognize in the conscious world (although pieces of them may float to the surface in our dreams). He called the conscious part of our lives the ego, the Latin word that means "I am." The unconscious part, which Freud said was our spontaneous, selfish drive for physical pleasure, he called the id, or instinctive drive. Finally, Freud said that layered on top of the ego by our societies is the superego, or the rules that our societies impose on us through religion, law, and education. The superego and the id struggle for control of the ego like the little angel and devil sitting on the shoulders of the cartoon characters.

For example, you may see a diamond ring in the window of a store and want it badly. Your ego will recognize that you want it and that you can't have it because you have no money. Your id will tell you to smash the glass and grab it because if you want it, you should have it right now so you'll be happy immediately. Your superego will tell you to ignore your id because it's morally wrong to steal and the police will come and punish you if you do. Later, if someone asked you what you were thinking about when you looked at the ring, the only part of the struggle that you'd probably remember would be your ego looking at the ring and realizing you couldn't have it. You'd probably repress or deliberately ignore the memory of your id's urges because your super-ego's disapproval would be so strong.

In Freudian terms, Louis and Lestat's story in *Interview with the Vampire* is the story of the ego's repression of id impulses told by using characters as symbols. A symbol is a concrete representation of a nonconcrete or ab-stract idea, such as a cloth flag representing the emotional idea of patri-otism or a plastic trophy representing athletic skill. Louis, in his ceaseless search for meaning, logic, rules of behavior, and goodness, appears to be a clear symbol of the ego controlled by the superego. Lestat, in his pursuit of selfish physical pleasure and immediate power over others, appears to be a symbol of the uncontrolled id. In their story, Louis the Ego and Lestat the Id play out a battle for supremacy that neither can win because both need the other to be one whole person. Therefore, although the story con-flict is a physical (external) one between Louis and Lestat as physical peo-ple, it's also a psychological (internal) one between a symbolic ego and id, one being's struggle to become psychologically whole.

That conflict takes place because Louis as the ego, driven by the su-perego of his religious background and education, refuses to recognize that Lestat the id is part of him, too, and that he needs to share Lestat's wild embrace of the vampire life to be truly alive. Louis stubbornly in-sists on repressing the instincts of his new nature and clinging desper-ately to his old, no longer appropriate human nature, even though Lestat warns Louis that his repression of his real nature is leading them into the danger of destruction. Lestat, in turn, tries desperately to control Louis instead of accepting him as an equal partner. The truth is that, to survive, Louis must respond to his vampire nature and Lestat must learn to accept Louis's control of his wildness. Or in Freudian terms, Louis must recognize the repressed emotions of the id, and Lestat must re-spond to the control of the ego.

Had Louis and Lestat worked together and become one integrated or combined personality, Rice would have had no plot, but instead they struggle for power and supremacy, until Lestat's creation of Claudia to keep Louis in his power disrupts the balance that has been teetering for so long. For Claudia, born as pure id as the child vampire, coldly matures into her own ego and becomes a strong integrated antagonist to the split Louis/Lestat personality. If she splits them completely, she takes control and destroys their power over her. She does manage to separate them for a while, dumping Lestat the Id in the swamp of unconsciousness to control Louis the fragile ego.

But it's only for a while. Once Claudia has killed Lestat, Louis follows her to Europe to find the truth that was always present within his relationship with Lestat and discovers only more death and destruction until Lestat finds him again, crawling back from the grave to recover the ego half of himself. He tells Louis, "You must come back . . . for only a little while . . . until I am myself again" but he could just as easily have said "until we are ourselves again" because Louis has only grown colder and unhappier without him (504–505). Lestat's indestructibility makes him the perfect symbol of the id. Louis may watch as Claudia hacks Lestat to death and later traps him in a burning building in New Orleans; he may even try to set fire to him in Paris, but he cannot stop Lestat. Eventually, implacably, the id will always come back to join with the ego. A consciousness can only suppress its unconscious self for so long before the dreams begin again.

When they meet again after Claudia's death, Lestat recognizes his mistake in creating her as the thing that came between them and caused their split personality. Even though he refers to himself and Louis as "us," he clearly sees them as one person, one heart: " 'She should never have been one of us, Louis.' And [Lestat] rapped his sunken chest with his fist as he said "Us" again softly" (331). But Louis still does not recognize his need for Lestat. Instead Louis watches him, "remembering things which I had supposed I had completely forgotten. . . . It seemed then I was in a different place, a different time. . . . And I was on the verge of knowing that place and knowing it with a terrible pain, a pain so terrible that my mind veered away from it, said, No don't take me back to that place—and suddenly it was receding" (334). Louis's repression of his unconscious memories, of all the pain and life that Lestat holds for him, takes a terrible toll. *Interview* ends with Louis emotionless and alone, and Lestat insane with uncontrolled emotion and alone, both of them defeated.

Rice does eventually resolve the split personality when she reunites

Louis with Lestat in her next Vampire Chronicle, *The Vampire Lestat*. In this reunion, Louis asks Lestat "Will you take me with you?" Lestat responds, "Of course I'll take you with me," and the reader is left with the sense of a reunited consciousness that has been restored because both beings have learned to accept and admit their need for the other (532).

Literary character isn't the only kind of character illuminated by Freudian criticism. The second great question in psychological criticism is, "Why did the author do what she did (write these characters and this story)?" This criticism is really a combination of two kinds of criticism: psychological criticism and biographical criticism, which compares the events in a story to events in the author's life in order to try to explain her reasons for writing what she did. Critics have long used Freudian criticism to explain Anne Rice's work, in particular the emotional undercurrents in *Interview with the Vampire*, a novel written after Rice had endured one of the greatest tragedies known to human beings, the loss of a child. The most detailed Freudian criticism of *Interview* has been done by Katherine Ramsland in her biography of Rice, *Prism of the Night*. Ramsland explores in particular how Rice first identified with Louis and his despair as a second literary self or alter ego, and then, after the passage of time in her later books, she turned to the far more aggressive and emotionally healthy Lestat as her representative in fiction (152). In *Interview* in particular, Rice seems to be working out emotions that she had to suppress in her everyday life in order to function. Two of the methods of suppression of her unconscious desires that may have had great impact on *Interview* are sublimation and displacement.

Sublimation means taking an unacceptable emotion or urge and putting it into an artistic creation. For example, some people who become dangerously angry and want to hurt someone sublimate the urge in playing strenuous sports or pounding on a piano or writing violent stories. Ramsland, along with other critics, has suggested that writing about the despair that Louis feels was a way for Anne Rice to sublimate the dangerous despair she felt at the loss of her small daughter. Rice herself says that "Louis is based on the lack of strength and will and faith I had while I was writing it" (Ginsberg, 27). Rice has also said that sublimating her pain in writing saved her from the alcoholism she sank into after Michele's death: "The writing eliminated the need for alcohol. I turned my pain into art" (Ginsberg, 26). And finally, Rice has said that she modeled Lestat on her husband, Stan Rice, playing out her frustration and resentment at his controlling nature during their child's long illness, even while she also wrote of the strong attraction they have for each other. Rice clearly acknowledges that she sublimated much of her emotional turmoil from the tragedy of Michele's death and the aftermath into the writing of *Interview*.

Another form of repression that Rice may have used is displacement, the substitution of a safe object of emotion for a dangerous one. Many people who feel angry with loved ones (parents, lovers, children) and can't show that anger take the emotion out on those they work with or those they encounter in everyday life: waitresses, salesclerks, other drivers, the dog. Again, many critics have suggested that Rice displaced her feelings for her dead daughter onto the character of Claudia who is frozen forever near the age at which Michelle, Rice's daughter, died. This is reinforced by the fact that one of Rice's nicknames for Michelle was Claudia. Rice's need to work through Michelle's death by writing Claudia's life is reinforced by the character of Madeleine, the woman who is grieving for her dead daughter and who will become Claudia's surrogate mother. Rice writes of her that "it was guilt [over her daughter's death] that was consuming her, not love" (271). In the first unsatisfactory version of *Interview*, Claudia lived, and Rice has said in an interview that she almost went crazy because she'd "cheated" in allowing her to live when Michelle had died. When she rewrote the end of the book and this time included Claudia's death, she said that the "things that were meant to happen" did. "If somebody is meant to die and you don't do it, you're really risking your well-being at the end of the book" (Ferraro 76–77). Therefore it seems that writing Claudia's death helped Rice recover her well-being as she worked through her guilt through displacement to set herself free. In another interview, Rice spoke of the way writers use their writing to deal with the tragedies in their lives: "Writers write about what obsesses them. . . . You draw those cards. I lost my mother when I was fourteen. My daughter died at the age of six. I lost my faith as a Catholic. When I'm writing, the darkness is always there. I go where the pain is" (Wadler 133).

Finally, Rice may have been projecting her own need to accept the dark chaotic side of her personality onto her characters. In a 1995 interview with Larry King on CNN, Rice described herself as indecisive, brooding, despairing, anxious, and filled with angst and constant worry. In other words, she described herself as Louis. But although it's clear that Louis is not only the protagonist of *Interview* but also her alter ego, Rice never wrote about him again after *Interview* except as a supporting character. In fact, in the Ramsland biography, Rice says of Louis, "At the time [I wrote the book] I loved him. . . . I don't now." Instead she turns to her other side, Lestat, whom she describes in the introduction to the video of *Inter-*

view with the Vampire as her alter ego and conscience. The progress of the Vampire Chronicles taken together reads as Rice's movement away from the guilt and passivity that Louis represents, through the passionate embrace of life and anarchy that Lestat comes to represent in the later novels, and ends with the questions that Lestat is finally integrated enough to ask in the last novels. In *Tale of the Body Thief* and *Memnoch the Devil*, Lestat develops a conscience and begins to question the meaning of life, finally combining both the old Lestat and Louis into one mature consciousness, Rice's true alter ego. Rice has insisted in the introduction to the video of the movie *Interview* that the story is not just about vampires, but about everyone. At the very least, her fictional movement from a passive alter ego to an active one tells us that it is very probably about her.

The final psychological question is, "Why does the reader react the way she or he does?" In this case, why do readers respond so strongly to Rice's stories of murderous supernatural beings? Do Rice's stories intellectualize our own long repressed desires to kill for survival? Do we use Rice's stories to displace our own unacceptable emotions toward society? Does the reading of these stories help sublimate the murderous tendencies that the everyday stress of living create in us? Or do we identify with the power of the vampire outsiders, taking on their glory as our own while we are in their world?

Father Andrew Greeley, a sociologist at the University of Chicago, argues that readers are looking for spirituality in their lives: "It's a hunger for the marvelous" (Ramsland, "Hunger," 33). Stephen King thinks it's due to sexual fears, especially for teenagers who are insecure about their sexual knowledge. With vampires, impotency is never a problem since vampires only have oral sexual urges. And New York editor Stephen Martin proposes that the vampires represent our ids: "They have to do with the darkness and magic that is not given its due. If we ignore the unconscious, it becomes avaricious, voracious" (Ramsland, "Hunger," 33). Rice herself seems to think that catharsis (or getting rid of tensions and fears through living them vicariously in a work of fiction) is involved: "People long to be transported and then brought back safely" (Matousek, 112).

For whatever reason, Rice's vampire stories have become immensely popular with readers everywhere, moving beyond the realm of favorite books into a mythology of their own, and like all mythologies, the only reason that Rice's mythos has lasted is that it fulfills a deep psychological need in those who return to the stories again and again.

The Vampire Lestat
(1985)

Anne Rice wrote six more nonsupernatural books after *Interview with the Vampire*, but in 1984, she went back to the vampire who had been haunting her imagination, Louis's maker, lover, and enemy, the great Lestat. Having worked through the tragedy and helplessness in her life that made her identify with Louis the victim, Rice now wanted to write about Lestat the defiant outcast. She has called Lestat the bad part of her, the character that takes action at all costs ("Charlie Rose," 5). And in his story, *The Vampire Lestat*, he certainly takes action, moving the plot through the sheer energy of his character.

The Vampire Lestat begins with Lestat as protagonist or central character in the twentieth century, determined to become a rock star so that he can call all the world's vampires to one last hellacious showdown at a great rock concert in San Francisco. Having set his plans in motion, Lestat then sits down to write his autobiography, the book that will correct the lies that his vampire companion Louis told about him in *Interview with the Vampire*. Lestat also hopes it will annoy all the vampires left in the world and alert mortals to the presence of evil. The majority of *The Vampire Lestat* is this autobiography, spanning from his youth in eighteenth-century France to the 1980s. Only eighteen pages at the beginning of the 550-page book and thirty-four pages at the end take place in the present or the now of the story. All the rest is flashback of Lestat raging through history, trying to solve the mystery of what he has become, bigger than life and literature combined.

POINT OF VIEW

The point of view of *The Vampire Lestat* is clear from the first line, "I am the Vampire Lestat." The "I" tells the reader that the novel is going to be told in the first-person point of view; that is, the narrator or storyteller is going to be present throughout the whole story, telling it in his voice, using the first-person pronoun. Lestat's confidence is an abrupt switch in voice from Louis, the narrator in Rice's previous vampire novel, *Interview with the Vampire*, and it has a huge impact on the tone of the book. Where *Interview* was a melancholy book, infused with Louis's tortured feelings about the morality of his existence as a vampire, *The Vampire Lestat* is as boisterous as Lestat himself. Louis may feel tortured, but Lestat is fascinated by what he was, what he is, and what he may become in the future. Louis tells the interviewer at the end that he wants to be where nothing is familiar and nothing matters, that he wants to be forgotten and alone. Lestat ends his narrative as a rock singer calling all the vampires in the world to recognize him and to come to destroy him if they can. If Louis's narrative seems exhausted and powerless, Lestat's narrative seems exhausting as he gloats with power. And this change is due entirely to the change in the point-of-view character.

Lestat's flamboyance could have been the downfall of this book. With another point-of-view character, *The Vampire Lestat* might have seemed too dramatic, too over-the-top in its exuberance. Whatever Lestat does, he does better than anyone, so if Rice had reported this through a third-person narrator, that narrator would have seemed either delusional or a vampire groupie gone mad. But Lestat as a character *is* dramatic and over-the-top. The vanity that infuses his character also infuses his voice and makes him an ideal first-person narrator, perfectly comfortable describing himself as a "Rock superstar" with a "continuously animated face," detailing his adventures as a heroic mortal who kills a pack of ravening wolves and captivates audiences as an actor, only later to become a vampire who defeats a pack of vicious blood-suckers and creates his own Theatre of Vampires. Because Rice has chosen to let Lestat speak for himself, the outrageousness of his narrative is perfectly acceptable because Lestat is outrageous. In fact, Lestat's voice is so powerful that the reader knows why Rice chose the first-person point of view: Lestat wouldn't have it any other way.

CHARACTER DEVELOPMENT

The center of *The Vampire Lestat* is always the Vampire Lestat, Rice's greatest protagonist. His flamboyant personality affects every other character in the story. Although many of those other characters are dynamic, that is, fully developed with understandable motives for what they do, many others are static, possessing only one character trait that does not change through the course of the book. Lestat's mother, Gabrielle, for example, is a dynamic character because she's a very different person at the end of the novel than she is in the beginning, but his father, a static character, remains the same selfish, ignorant fool. And even those characters who are dynamic—Gabrielle, Lestat's best friend Nicolas, Armand the leader of the Children of Darkness—are often in the narrative only to act as foils or contrast characters to Lestat. Growing more than any other character, Lestat dominates his book.

But Rice makes it clear through Lestat's autobiography that he was not always the confident showman that he is now. Her development of his dynamic character is psychologically complex and begins with the influence of his parents. His father is a blustering, selfish, insensitive man who can see only the practicalities of life, but his mother, Gabrielle, is sensitive and intelligent and drawn to Lestat as her favorite even though she is remote and unaffectionate. Lestat as a young boy wants to belong and cannot find that connection with his parents, so he goes outside the family. He finds the belonging he needs first with teaching fathers in a monastery and later in a theatre troupe, but both times his father drags him back home for selfish reasons, and Lestat becomes more remote and more bitter. Unable to connect with his boorish father and brothers in any human way, he takes satisfaction in becoming the hunter of the family, making a connection to them by providing for them, seeking warm companionship in the company of his mare and his dogs. But even this connection is broken when, in his role of hunter, he is sent into the woods to kill a pack of wolves that have been terrorizing the neighborhood. The wolves kill his mare and his dogs, and when he has defeated them all, he is left alone once more in a stinking mass of blood and dead bodies. When he returns, his brother mocks him, saying he's lying and that he hasn't killed the wolves, thereby isolating him even more with misunderstanding. This is the final blow to the boy Lestat, and he retires to his room to come out days later a bitter, cold young man. Rice's depiction of this character growth is both horrifying and wonderful because the experience is so vivid that the reader can feel Lestat's character change with him.

Into this barrenness comes Lestat's first real friend, Nicolas, his alter ego, the kind of friend who is so like him and so understands him that they finish each other's sentences. Nicolas in particular understands Lestat's hatred of his father for preventing him from learning with the monks and traveling with the theatre group because his own father has threatened to cut off his hands if he doesn't stop playing the violin. Their bond is a strong one psychologically because they find in each other the connection they both desperately need. When they run off to Paris together and join a theatre company where Nicolas plays the violin and Lestat stuns the audiences with his acting, Lestat believes that he has escaped from the coldness of his childhood and found the community he needs. This desperate need to belong is part of Lestat's identity, that is, his sense of who he is. He sees himself as brave, loyal, and special, but he also sees himself as someone who is a good member of a community. Having been constantly frustrated at home as he tried to be a good member of a family who could not understand him, his joy at being received into the theatre family with Nicolas is unrestrained. Finally, he is at peace with himself.

Into this peace comes a new father figure, Magnus the vampire, who kidnaps Lestat because he has heard he is a wolf killer. Magnus makes Lestat into a vampire against his will and thereby also makes him his son. While Lestat is still lost and confused from the experience, as desperate for knowledge as he was when his first father took him from the monks, Magnus commits suicide by walking into fire, and Lestat is left abandoned by a father figure again. But this time his abandonment is even fiercer because he cannot return to his old biological family or to his theatre family. He is now truly alone spiritually and physically. This act develops his character even more because it isolates him even more.

Because he has grown since the beginning of the story, Lestat can see the pattern of his life: as a mortal he was denied learning when his father took him from the monks, artistic expression when his father took him from the stage, and understanding when he defeated the pack of wolves. As a vampire, he is denied learning when his vampire father kills himself rather than teach him, artistic expression when his only performance as a vampire terrifies the audience, and understanding from the other immortals when he defeats the pack of vampires called the Children of Darkness. His vampire life is a cruel repetition of his mortal life, and in a logical and desperate attempt to achieve the salvation in his immortal life that he had in his old one, Lestat makes Nicolas a vampire at his request, hoping to revive their old friendship, the relationship that saved him in the pattern of his mortal life. But the act only drives his character further into loneliness because he finds that Nicolas was never the alter ego Lestat thought he was, and that in fact he is Lestat's opposite, dark where he is light, craving death as Lestat craves life. The leader of the Children of Darkness, Armand, seems to offer connection only to jerk it away at the last moment in an attempt to control him. Even his mother, now a vampire, leaves him to go back to nature. Lestat is left alone once more and despairing.

Lestat's character by this point in the book is not only well-established, it's also beautifully motivated. How can any being that so longs for connection be so often deprived of it and not despair completely? Whenever Lestat reaches out, he is rejected as the Other, someone too different from the rest of the mortals and the rest of the vampires to live comfortably with them. Combined with Lestat's need for an identity as the good leader of a family, this isolation breaks him, and he goes to sleep in the ground to escape from the pain, staying there until one more father comes to drag him back to life again: Marius, one of the most ancient vampires of all.

Marius gives Lestat the education he has so longed for, telling him of how vampires began with the Mother and Father of all the blood drinkers, Akasha and Enkil, now frozen in immortal beauty in the chamber below Marius's estate. He also gives Lestat the connection to others he has longed for when he tells him that all vampires are connected through the blood to the Mother and Father. Marius has called him out of the ground to give him this connection, he tells Lestat, because he admires and loves him. Marius beyond all the others in Lestat's life gives him what he needs: knowledge, connection, and love. But even Marius sends Lestat away once he finds him with Akasha, drinking her powerful blood at her invitation. Lestat must go to prevent Enkil's anger, Marius tells him, but he must also go to live out one full life as a vampire pretending to be human.

To do this, Lestat goes to New Orleans and finally makes the great connection of his life by creating an Unholy Family with two other vampires he makes, Louis and Claudia. In this second lifetime, he achieves the family he has longed for for sixty-five years, isolated no longer, but it is all ended when Claudia tries to murder him twice, leaving him disfigured and crippled and despairing. He travels to Paris to find them and asks the Vampire Armand for help, but Armand executes Claudia and tries to take Louis for himself, throwing Lestat from his own tower and breaking him once again. Defeated and alone, Lestat returns to New Orleans where he goes to earth again in 1929, determined to end his pain. And there he stays until 1984, when he hears rock music and wakes to the new world.

When Lestat wakes this time, his character is fully formed. He has the knowledge he sought so desperately in the past, he has connections through Marius that cannot be broken, he has drunk the blood of Akasha, the Great Mother, and become almost indestructible, and he has experienced great love with Louis and Claudia. Through the events of his story, he has grown from a lonely despairing boy into a dark god, all-powerful and all-knowing. *The Vampire Lestat* is a triumph of dynamic characterization because Rice makes this growth seem not only possible but inevitable. Lestat was born to be the brat prince of vampires, Rice seems to say. Given his character, this story could not have happened any other way.

But Lestat is not the only dynamic character in his story. Gabrielle, his mother, also has a well-developed character arc, but hers begins in a back story, the events that took place before Lestat's story began. Married to a lout who can't understand her, bearing children who cannot appreciate her, Gabrielle longs for freedom as she walks through the roles of wife and mother. Only in her youngest son, Lestat, can she see herself as she really is, free and wild. She has fantasies, she tells Lestat, of bathing naked in a mountain stream, of going into the town and taking all of the men there into her body, not caring about her reputation or her responsibilities to her husband and family, because by flouting society's rules, she can be free and belong to no one. When she realizes she is dying of consumption, she sends Lestat, her other self, to Paris to be free as she knows she never will be, but when she joins him there for her last days, he frees her in turn by making her a vampire.

At this point, Rice has set up Gabrielle's character so completely that it is inevitable that she will go back to nature as a vampire, preferring to travel the rooftops instead of the crowded streets, preferring to sleep in the earth instead of the manmade coffin. Gabrielle's lust for freedom is greater than her lust for human blood; when Lestat protests that there will be nothing to drink in the wilderness she wants to take him to, she tells him there will be animals. Having spent her whole mortal life repressing her nature, Gabrielle is not going to spend eternity the same way. In fact, Gabrielle's only conflict is an internal one: she loves her son and doesn't want him to be alone, so she stays even though the wilderness calls her. When he rejects her for trying to keep him safe from the family responsibilities that weighed down her mortal life, she leaves him never to return, according to Lestat. Although she shows up in his next book *The Queen of the Damned*, at the end of *The Vampire Lestat* Gabrielle is free in nature, a fully developed character.

Another fully dynamic character, Nicolas, Lestat's best friend from the village, has no such happy ending. Raised by a father who threatened to cut off his hands if he didn't give up his beloved violin, Nicolas broods and turns bitter, his central identity his need for revenge, his only salvation his friendship with Lestat. But when things go wrong and Nicolas is made a vampire, he has none of the goodness in his heart that keeps Lestat from becoming a beast in nature. Even their trip to Paris came from different motives, he tells Lestat. Lestat left their village to be free and find joy; Nicolas left to infuriate his father and to leave him shamed. The darkness in Nicolas's soul combines with the blood lust he feels as a vampire until he reels out of control, endangering the rest of the Theatre of the Vampires, not to mention the rest of humanity. Their vampire leader, Armand, cuts off his hands to stop him, and Nicolas is confronted with confirmation of his suspicions of fate: no matter what happens, whether mortal or vampire, he is doomed to be handicapped by the disapproval of those he lived with. Despairing, he walks into fire to end it all.

Nicolas's character, while fully developed and motivated throughout, also exists in the plot to serve as a foil to Lestat; that is, he is part of Rice's plot in order to show Lestat's character by contrast. Nicolas and Lestat come from the same village, have similarly abusive fathers, feel the same outcast nature in their communities, and share the same fears and questions. They are almost the same person as they head off to Paris. But when the great change comes and they are made vampires, the differences in their souls are revealed. Watching Nicolas, the reader knows how strong and moral Lestat is because if he weren't, he'd have fallen into the abyss in the way that Nicolas falls.

Not all the characters in this novel are dynamic, however. Armand, the leader of the Paris vampires, is a follower, and thus a static character because he is defined by one character trait. Having been a victim all his life, he blindly follows the Rules of Darkness. When he attacks Lestat for

breaking the Rules, Lestat laughs at him, tells him the rules are mean-
ingless, and frees him. But when Armand then tries to join Lestat and
Gabrielle to make a new family and become a follower once more, Lestat
rejects him even though they are both powerful, intelligent immortals
because Armand is too different from him. "You've always been a
slave," Lestat tells him (309). The contrast between Armand and Lestat,
both dealing with years of rejection and isolation, again underscores how
strong Lestat's spirit is because the reader knows that no matter what
happens, Lestat will never be a slave.

Like Armand, Marius, Armand's maker and Lestat's teacher, is also a
static character. Although he speaks of his despair at seeking the reason
for vampirism, his awe at finding Akasha and Enkil, and his love for the
courtesan Pandora, he is not a dynamic character because he doesn't
change. He stands for knowledge and fairness and justice, and he is there
to provide Lestat with the knowledge he seeks and the father figure he
needs. There are many other static characters in *The Vampire Lestat*, but
they all revolve around the central figure of Lestat and are put into the
story to inform and illuminate his character. This concentration on the
central character above all others is also reflected in the plot structure of
Lestat which, like Lestat, is very different from others of its kind.

PLOT DEVELOPMENT AND STRUCTURE

At first glance, the only structure that Lestat's narrative has is the
structure imposed on it by its frame story (or surrounding setup story)
set in 1984. The frame story identifies the central conflict as Lestat's need
to assert power over the other vampires by drawing them to his rock
concert. Therefore, in the frame story, Lestat is the protagonist and his
goal is to draw the others to him. His antagonists are the other vampires,
and the central plot question is, "Will Lestat succeed in calling all the
vampires to him, causing a showdown that will assert his power?" He
needs to succeed because it will reinforce his identity as the most powerful of the vampires. Lestat works out the rising action of his frame plot
in cause-and-effect steps, first becoming a rock star, which leads to his
publishing his autobiography, which leads to his welcoming all the vampires from his life as they gather at his concert. This leads him to the climax of his frame story, where he appears onstage, and, true to his
wishes, all hell in the form of Akasha, Queen of the Damned, breaks lose.
The end, or resolution, of *The Vampire Lestat* is in many ways a teaser for

the next novel in the Vampire Chronicles, *The Queen of the Damned*, but it also satisfies the needs of classic plot structure by answering the central question posed by the frame: the answer is yes, with some surprises.

The vast majority of the book, however, is Lestat's autobiography which acts as a huge flashback, giving the reasons that Lestat feels the need to cause this showdown. And that autobiography, like all autobiographies, is more episodic than causal. That is, it's more a collection of episodes or stories about what happened to Lestat than it is a string of logically connected events that lead to the protagonist's achievement of a clear goal. Even the narratives of other characters like Armand and Marius become events in Lestat's life more than their own life stories. Anne Rice is not the first to structure a novel this way; the episodic picaresque novel and hero go back at least five hundred years.

A picaresque novel is the autobiography of a picaro or a rogue hero who "lives by his wits, gets into trouble and out of it, but always interests the reader" (Holman, 330). That's Lestat, the brat prince, exactly. Lestat's autobiography follows the picaresque definition in other ways, too, because

- It tells the entire life of its picaro protagonist.
- The protagonist is an unconventional character who breaks rules.
- It's episodic.
- The character is static, not changing in the story; that is, the character starts as a picaro and ends as a picaro. (Lestat's character does develop in great complexity, but he's a picaro at the beginning and a picaro at the end.)
- The story is presented realistically, not as a joke or a farce, and it's made even more real through its details.
- The picaro flaunts the law but is never an actual criminal. (Lestat is careful in his selection of his victims in this book, choosing only those who are criminals themselves, essentially acting as a freelance executioner.) (Holman 331)

Given that the majority of *The Vampire Lestat* is a picaresque novel, the usual analysis of central question developed through exposition, rising action, point of no return, falling action, and climax is turned inside out. The exposition and rising action which should be at the beginning are Lestat's life story in the center of the novel. The point of no return which should be at the center is at the beginning when Lestat issues his challenge to the other vampires. The climax, falling action, and resolution come at the end as usual when Lestat recognizes his connection to those he loves and the danger he has put them in. Like Lestat himself, the structure of *The Vampire Lestat* defies the rules, goes its own way, and gets away with it.

LITERARY DEVICE: METAPHOR

Lestat's defiance and independence help make him not only a great literary character but also a great literary metaphor. A metaphor is not the same as a symbol. A symbol is a solid, visible representation of an abstract idea; a metaphor is an object that calls to mind the qualities of another object or idea. A symbol means only the idea; a metaphor means a lot of things but can also represent an idea. An example of a symbol is a flag; it represents a country and loyalty to that country, but it means nothing on its own because it's simply a piece of cloth. An example of a metaphor is leaves falling from the trees in autumn; this image is often used as a metaphor for death, but leaves have an existence and a meaning all their own and can call up several ideas besides death. In the same way, Lestat the vampire has an existence and meaning of his own, but he and his vampire companions also serve as a metaphor. Among the ideas that the vampire can stand for are sexual freedom, power, and independence as the Other in society. Rice's use of the vampire as a metaphor for these concepts is one of the reasons why her books appeal to so many people.

All of Rice's books are full of sensuality, and her vampires, in particular, are very much lovers of fine things and of each other. But because vampires have given up the life of the body aside from drinking blood to survive, they are not physically sexual creatures; that is, they cannot have genital sex. At first this seems a loss, but Rice makes it clear that it's actually a gain because freedom from genital sex also means freedom from sexual taboos since almost all our cultural restrictions on sex are based on what we *do* to each other, not on what we *feel*. And vampires, Rice makes it clear, get glorious sexual feelings out of drinking blood. Clearly, the drinking itself is sexually satisfying, particularly in the making of another vampire because it involves the mutual physical exchange of body fluids, the most intimate of bodily acts and the most dangerous in our AIDS-plagued society. So Rice has created a creature that can act as a metaphor for complete sexual—and by extension, complete physical—freedom. Vampires have no fear of pregnancy or disease since they're dead. Therefore they act as metaphors for the absolute pleasure principle, safe sex at any time of night (day is a problem) with no repercussions and no guilt.

But vampires are more than just metaphors for sexual freedom. They're also representatives of the power of the rule-breaker, the being that can flaunt all the rules of society and still flourish. Vampires break major social rules when they drink blood and kill, but they also flaunt smaller rules. Vampires live by night, for example, and do not need to work, support a family, invest in pension plans, or worry about global warming. Their immortality gives them plenty of time to do the things they've wanted without worrying that their dreams will be cut off by old age and death. Vampires, therefore, represent complete freedom from the superego of Freud's mental universe (rules, guilt, and restrictions) and from the physical restraints of being human.

Finally, Rice's vampires are a clear metaphor for the Other in society, the one who is different, who is cast out because he or she cannot conform. When Lestat tells Louis in *Interview with the Vampire* that evil is a point of view, he's merely making his case for the Other as a way of life. In society's scheme of things, drinking blood is evil. In the vampire scheme of things, it's dinner. The vampire is the Other in spades, creating his or her own reality outside of society's limits and still managing to flourish, triumphant and enviable.

Since so many of us see ourselves as the powerless Other, hopelessly out of step with the world we live in, the popularity of Rice's vampires is easily explained. We read her vampires, and we see not murderous blood-sucking immortals but sexually free, societally free, powerful beings who live life to the fullest. Lestat, the great vampire/rock star, is our metaphor for social anarchy and sexual freedom, the ultimate powerful Other. As readers, we see Lestat, and we wish we were him, so we read to be him for just a little while, to have his power and his freedom in the world.

THEMATIC ISSUES

The central, underlying idea in *The Vampire Lestat* is a little more difficult to determine than usual because of the picaresque nature of the plot. Since there is no one clear external goal in Lestat's autobiographical story, it's harder to pinpoint the idea that Rice was trying to communicate. Still, an analysis of several parts of the story such as setting, central plot question, the protagonist's internal struggle and character growth, the beginning and ending, and the title give hints to the theme. Rice also uses allusion to another literary work to help get her point across.

The setting of Lestat's frame story is in 1984 in New Orleans and San Francisco, essentially the same setting as the frame story in *Interview with the Vampire*. Again, the setting seems to imply that, in the twentieth century, only a place as accepting of the Other as San Francisco would make possible the vampire concert, a public showing of the Children of Darkness. But Lestat's autobiography ranges through eighteenth-century rural France and Paris, Egypt, Greece, and New Orleans, with additional settings in ancient Rome and Britain provided by Marius and Armand. This vast span of times and places seems to imply that whatever theme Rice is working with this time, it is universal, not just a comment on life in the twentieth century, but an idea about the human condition that is for all time and all places.

The central question of the plot is harder to determine because Lestat's picaresque narrative seems to have no real goal inasmuch as he has no real external goal. Yet all of his adventures taken together seem to add up to a craving for knowledge about his vampire self and for connection to others. When this generally vague internal goal is combined with Lestat's clear external goal in his frame narrative to call all the vampires together, the central question becomes, "Will Lestat ever achieve the connection he needs and the knowledge he seeks?" Louis's return at the end seems to guarantee the connection again, but the knowledge is only foreshadowed by the cold hand of Akasha on Lestat in his coffin in the last lines of the book. Therefore, the theme of *Lestat* seems to center on connection with others more than on knowledge.

Lestat's inner conflict in part is the war between his need to be "good" and his defiance of a world that has shut him out over and over again. In essence, Lestat wants to be a good vampire, a holy Child of the Dark, a famous secret, and a loving and loved bringer of death. Lestat knows what he is and he knows what he wants to be, and his struggle is to bring the two seeming opposites together while retaining his identity as a good person. One of the ways he tries to reconcile these opposites is by forming connections with other vampires who understand his problems and his needs. Once again, connection seems to be part of Rice's theme.

Lestat's character growth moves him from a bitter, powerless, unloved boy to a cynical, powerful, adored rock star/author/vampire. He has achieved great character growth, but his needs are constant: he wants knowledge and connection to others, and his willingness to do anything to get both has only changed in that by the end of the book he truly has the power to do anything. This seems to imply that the things that Lestat needs are universal to all beings, young or old, powerless or powerful.

The beginning of the story tells of Lestat's being awakened in 1985 by the sound of rock music. Rice has said she chose rock music deliberately because to her it symbolizes outrageousness, independence, and surprise, all aspects of Lestat's matured character (Ramsland, *Prism*, 250). Thus the music of 1985 wakens Lestat because he hears it as his music, and the ending of the book reinforces this by making it literally his music. At the end, he's onstage at the Cow Palace in San Francisco driving crowds to a frenzy with his vampire-rock lyrics and Jim-Morrison-like rock star voice. He has found the connection he was seeking with others, complete acceptance of his outrageous, independent character. But it's a distant emotional connection, and the people screaming his name cannot really know him. As a rock star, he's still an Other, an outsider, even though the crowds adore him.

Finally, the title, *The Vampire Lestat*, is both fitting (after all, the book is Lestat's life story) and frustrating since it gives little clue to the theme of the novel. It does reinforce the idea that whatever theme is at the center of this book, it's definitely Lestat's idea.

While all of these clues give some direction, there is another method authors sometimes use to help communicate theme that sheds more light on this novel. Occasionally, authors will either directly or indirectly allude to other famous stories, and if there are clear parallels, many times the two books will share a similar theme. In the case of *The Vampire Lestat*, Lestat early on makes a direct reference to a similar story in the modern movie *Apocalypse Now* (1979). In doing so, he also indirectly refers to the story the movie was based on, a turn-of-the-century British novella called *Heart of Darkness* written by Joseph Conrad. In this book, a British sailor named Marlowe journeys up the Congo River into the heart of Africa to meet a man named Kurtz, a man everyone has assured him is much like himself. Since Kurtz has become a legend through his intelligence, hard work, success, and goodness, Marlowe is eager to meet him and to see for himself if they are alike. But when he finally meets Kurtz, he finds that the man has given himself over to the darkness inside his heart and become a murderous tyrant, appearing as a god before the people he abuses. Face to face with Kurtz, Marlowe knows that he is capable of these things, too, and vows never to give into the heart of darkness inside him. The movie tells the same tale, moving the setting from turn-of-the-century Africa to the Vietnam War, but once again the protagonist sees how far into savagery it is possible to fall.

Taken in context with Lestat's picaresque story, Lestat's fascination with the movie seems to show that he, too, is concerned with his own possible fall into the heart of darkness. And so in *The Vampire Lestat*, he tries to show mortals through his music just how evil vampires are so that they won't fall. In a way, Lestat is trying to do the same thing with his rock music that Louis was trying to do with his interview—warn people of the evil that they represent—and they both fail because the lure of evil is too strong. But Lestat at least acknowledges the presence of evil in himself, just as Marlowe does in *Heart of Darkness*, thereby achieving a sort of victory through self-knowledge.

Taking all these things together, it seems clear that Rice's book is in some way about finding out who we are and what we are so that we can know ourselves and connect with other people. No matter how far Lestat ranges in time and space, he always hungers to know about the meaning of his life as a vampire, and he always feels the need to connect. When he finds out from Marius that vampires were created by accident, that there is no grand plan in which the vampires play a part, he does not despair but instead tries to form his own plan by calling all the vampires together, a plan that will either lead to a great connection and a great new plan, or to the destruction of all that he knows. For Lestat, it seems, destruction is better than chaos; at least he'll know what's going on. So the theme of his story may be: Self-knowledge brings strength, or All beings need to connect with each other, regardless of their origin. This last theme is supported not only by the events of Lestat's struggle, but also by the mythological references Rice has chosen to use in her book. By using mythology, Rice has made her story part of a long line of stories that ask the same questions and use the same characters, regardless of the culture, thereby repeating old themes that will always be new because they are universal.

A MYTHOLOGICAL READING OF *THE VAMPIRE LESTAT*

The universal ideas that Rice draws on are revealed in a mythological analysis of *The Vampire Lestat*. The most famous myth critic is Carl Jung, a psychologist and a student of Sigmund Freud, who agreed with Freud that all human beings have an unconscious life of the mind. But when Freud said the ideas of the unconscious were only repressed memories of pains and desires from childhood, Jung disagreed, adding that there is another kind of unconscious that comes from a racial memory, a collective unconscious that all people are born with and share. In that collective unconscious, Jung argued, are certain mythological images such as the Great Mother, and he supported his theory by pointing out that figures like the Great Mother show up in all literatures in all cultures, which is why he called them not just types but archetypes. Therefore, an archetype is a figure or a symbol that appears over and over again in the art and literature of all cultures.

One of the most common mythological and literary archetypes is the romantic hero, the central figure who saves society, such as Hercules in Greek mythology, Beowulf in British literature, and Indiana Jones in modern adventure films. Another archetype is the monster that threatens the well-being of society, such as the Cyclops and the Minotaur in mythology, dragons in fairy tales, and the homicidal maniacs in modern slasher films. Whether these figures are the product of a collective unconscious as Jung asserted, or the result of the passing of the ideas across cultures by the telling of myths and stories, or simply a result of the universal human experience, they definitely appear in the stories of all cultures. Thus a comparison of literary characters to great mythological archetypes can often shed light on the characters' psychology. Lestat, part hero, part monster, is also the perfect representation of the mythological archetype of the Trickster.

The Trickster figure shows up as African folk characters like Brer Rabbit and Anansi the spider, the Greek god Hermes who was a shapeshifter and guide to the land of the dead, the Native American Coyote who helped make the world, and the giant Loki who was the prankster and antagonist of the Norse Gods. They are all the same figure, as Joseph Campbell points out in his great work, *The Masks of the Gods*. The Trickster, Campbell says in Volume 1, subtitled *Primitive Mythology*, represents "the chaos principle, the principle of disorder, the force careless of taboos and shattering bounds" (274). This is the perfect description of Lestat who defies the rules of the Children of Darkness by entering churches and living as a human, disobeys Marius to drink the blood of the Mother, and finally flouts the most sacred rule of vampirism, Don't Tell Anybody. Rice calls Lestat "the brat prince," and Lestat lives up to his nickname. As he himself says after he has begun to break the Dark Commandments, "It gave me great satisfaction to do it. And after all, I had never been very good at obeying rules" (320).

Campbell points out another interesting aspect of the Trickster: he's androgynous, having aspects of both male and female. For the Trickster in mythology, this often means cross-dressing and sometimes adding female organs so he can give birth. For Lestat, it means bisexuality, not simply in the romantic sense of loving men as well as women, but also in the sense that his nature is both male and female which increases both his understanding and his strength. Rice says that her ideal of the androgynous male comes from her Roman Catholic upbringing, full of feminine saints, priests, and choir boys, but she's also drawn to androgyny as a symbol of power because of the combination of opposites, the best of both worlds (Ramsland, *Prism*, 30, 310). She has written that "the end of gender isn't the abolition of the masculine/feminine. Rather it is the abolition of the gender tyranny that would divide us into armed camps" ("David Bowie," 498). Lestat possesses both aggression and tenderness, which makes him all the more mythic in his emotions and in his accessibility to both genders.

But there is more to the Trickster character than just an androgynous rule-breaker. Jung saw the Trickster as only a foolish shadow figure, but Campbell disagreed, arguing that the Trickster is also "the archetype of the hero, the giver of all great boons . . . the epitome of the principle of disorder [yet] he is . . . the culture-bringer also" (274). Campbell uses Prometheus, the Greek who defied the rules of the gods to bring fire to men, as an example of the Trickster-hero. Prometheus breaks rules not just to break rules but to free people and bring knowledge. And Lestat is this figure also, breaking the rules of the Children of Darkness to set them free from superstition, giving them the knowledge that they can live their lives in the open as he has done. And they do free themselves, forming the Theatre of Vampires to live as human beings once again. He breaks the rules and frees Akasha from her vegetative state—not the best move he could have made, it turns out—but still an act of freedom and giving of knowledge that will not be fully understood until *The Queen of the Damned*, the book that tells of the final release of all knowledge and a new dawn for the vampire family. And finally he calls all vampires to meet, breaking the rules of silence in order to let them know of the possibilities of their lives. Those who cannot embrace the new order (and Lestat) die, but those who accept Lestat move into a new era of freedom and wisdom. Lestat is the liberator of the vampires because, as the Trickster-Hero, he breaks their rules and gives them life. This also explains much of his appeal as a literary hero. Because Lestat evokes unconscious memories of other Tricksters, he's recognized as part of the tradition of the great rule-breaking Heroes at the same time that he's seen as a brand-new literary figure. By drawing on myth memories, Rice both makes Lestat familiar and creates a new legend.

But the Trickster is not the only strong archetype Rice has used in *The Vampire Lestat*. She also used the most primal of all archetypes, the Great Mother or Magna Mater or Mother Earth or Great Goddess, the goddess who gives birth to the earth and all living things. She is Demeter in Greek mythology, Ishtar in Babylon, Durga in India, and Isis in Egypt. She is in every culture, without exception. And she is embodied in Lestat's mother, Gabrielle.

Gabrielle is a woman caught by her culture. She is strong, fiercely independent, sexual, and intelligent, but she's stuck in a society that can see her only as a sex object, wife, and mother. When Lestat frees her by making her an outcast from the society that stifles her, she returns to the earth as the place where she can be most free. She tells him that she wants to leave humanity because "I care less about these creatures than I do about the trees in this forest or the stars overhead. I'd rather study the currents of the wind or the patterns in the falling leaves" (253). While Lestat's search for knowledge leads him to people, Gabrielle's leads her to nature: "I want to know . . . why beauty exists . . . why nature continues to contrive it, and what is the link between the life of a lightning storm with the feelings these things inspire in us" (288). Gabrielle becomes the complete earth goddess when she leaves Lestat and humanity to go back to the earth, at one with the world that inspires her. Because she represents the Great Mother, however, this reads as a natural move and not a desertion. And by giving Lestat a Great Mother as his mother, Rice also increases his myth status as the son of a goddess figure.

But the Great Mother also has another side. Along with giving life, she gives death because no society can exist without it. When Gabrielle leaves Lestat, she tells him, "I will be a goddess to those I slay" (348). In this guise of a death goddess, the Great Mother is part of the great circle of life. Life comes from the earth, grows to maturity, withers and dies, and goes back to the earth. This is why the Great Mother is often seen as a Triple Goddess, Maiden, Mother, and Crone, or Birth, Life, and Death. In India the goddess that represents death is Kali, and she brings death not only as a part of life but also as part of the religion she inspired. Kali's followers, the Thuggee, like many followers of the Great

Mother, demanded human sacrifice, and that sacrifice was always male. Like Kali, Rice's other Great Mother figure, Akasha, has followers who take blood sacrifice; they are her children, the vampires. She will also demand another sacrifice, the sacrifice of all men, in Rice's next book, but even in *The Vampire Lestat* she brings death to those who oppose her and who oppose the male she has chosen as her new consort, Lestat.

Akasha's need for a consort is part of her identity as a Great Mother who must mate not only to produce children but also to make the world fertile for crops and all other growing things. Thus the goddess Ishtar has her lover Tammuz, Durga has Shiva, and Isis has Osiris. This last couple becomes most important because Rice uses their myth to explain Akasha and her king-consort's story. Akasha and her king, Enkil, Rice explains, adapted the Isis–Osiris legend in order to explain their own origins as great leaders who opposed cannibalism and were mutilated for their efforts.

But the king-consort of the Great Mother also has another role to play: he must die. In many cultures, the companion to the Mother is the Dying God. When he dies, she weeps and in her grief forgets to tend to the earth. While the Mother mourns, the earth lies fallow and in many parts of the world, winter comes. When the lover returns from the land of the dead, or when the Mother takes a new lover, she returns to caring for the earth, and the world blooms again. The lover is now known as a Vegetation God, the one who makes the earth's vegetation grow.

Thus many cultures sacrificed a male representative of the Mother's lover every fall to ensure that she would mourn and then return again. And many legends present heroes with the problem of the Mother's love. The good news is, the Mother loves you and wants you. The bad news is, you're going to die. For this reason the great Babylonian hero, Gilgamesh, rejects the Great Mother Ishtar when she propositions him, by saying, "Which of your lovers have lived forever?" Since the answer is "none," Gilgamesh obviously has a point. But rejecting the Mother is also not a good idea since she tends to be destructive in her rage, as Gilgamesh finds out when Ishtar sends the Bull of Heaven after him and destroys his best friend. Rice therefore draws on the universal myths about the Great Mother destroying heroes and weeping for her dead lovers to add a feeling of foreboding to Akasha's presence in Lestat's story. Even though she has few scenes and does very little in them, the reader's unconscious recognition of her as a destroying Great Mother makes those scenes ominous.

But Akasha is not Lestat's only myth-link to death. The god he most identifies with is another Vegetation God, Dionysus, the Greek god of wine, revelry, and darkness. Dionysus also dies in his myth, torn to pieces by his screaming female followers. When Rice titles the last section of Lestat's story "Dionysus in San Francisco," she sets the scene for Lestat the rock god to be met by his screaming followers and also by vampires who have come to kill him. Lestat has already had one experience with being hacked to pieces by a dark goddess in *Interview with the Vampire*, when his daughter/sister/lover Claudia drugs him and then slashes him to ribbons with a knife. In *The Vampire Lestat*, he tells the reader that while he lay dying at Claudia's hands, he remembered Dionysus and thought that if there was not meaning in his death, at least there was the tradition of "the same old theme" (502). Clearly, Lestat knows his myth criticism.

All of this conscious and unconscious tradition gives incredible power to the last scene in *The Vampire Lestat*. Lestat has gone to his coffin for the night, a hero to the remaining vampires, master of his story at last, only to feel the cold hand of Akasha, the Queen of the Damned, the Great Mother of the vampires. She has joined him, choosing him to replace the consort, Enkil, whom she has just rejected and killed. Lestat's last thought is of great joy that she has chosen him, and that he has a happily-ever-after ending at last, secure in knowledge and connection to the Mother of All. But as any myth critic knows, things are far from over, and Lestat the brat prince has not won a princess; rather, he has just accepted a role as a great sacrifice in somebody else's epic. Since Lestat is not the type to play a sacrifice in anybody's story, the struggle in Rice's next book, *The Queen of the Damned*, is already clear. Either the myth of the Vegetation God will be overturned, or Lestat will die trying.

5

The Queen of the Damned
(1988)

Anne Rice had much more vampire mythology that she wanted to explain in *The Vampire Lestat,* but she ran out of room. So she typed "The Vampire Chronicles WILL CONTINUE" at the end of the book and then returned in 1988 with *The Queen of the Damned,* once more featuring Lestat the vampire. The end of *The Vampire Lestat* shows all of the vampires that Lestat loves returning to him on a night when most of his enemy vampires die horribly in spontaneous combustion. The beginning of *The Queen of the Damned* steps back in time to tell the stories of Lestat's friends and supporters—Armand, Daniel, Gabrielle, Khayman, Marius, Pandora, and the human woman Jesse—journeying to him while having horrifying dreams of red-haired twin witches being tortured and maimed. When the friends finally gather at Lestat's concert, they are all reunited briefly, but shortly after that, Lestat is taken by Akasha, the Great Mother of all the vampires. While Lestat encounters wonders and horrors in his travels with Akasha, the others learn from Maharet, one of the twins, the ancient myth that explains the origin of the vampires. A composite of many stories, *The Queen of the Damned* finishes Rice's vampire mythology by tying all story threads together in one great showdown between good and evil.

POINT OF VIEW

The Queen of the Damned opens with the same line that opened the previous book in the Vampire Chronicles: "I am the Vampire Lestat." Then Lestat adds "Remember me?" and the reader is once again in the vivid, overwhelming first-person point of view of Rice's most famous character. But Rice then goes on to try something risky: she splits her narrative into multiple third-person limited points of view, losing Lestat entirely to tell the story she wants to tell. This technique gains her much in setting free her story, but it also costs her a great deal. The individual stories she tells are fascinating, but they are broken apart by their various voices which confuse the reader, and none of those voices can compare with Lestat.

Rice's aim in *Queen* is to create a history of the vampires, and she begins by telling the stories of all the vampires (and one mortal) who are hurrying to Lestat's rock concert, the climax of *The Vampire Lestat*. She could have done that from Lestat's point of view if she had set up a dozen mini-interviews with vampires, echoing the method she used in her first book in the Vampire Chronicles, *Interview with the Vampire*. But Rice wants to tell *their* stories, not the story of Lestat listening to them tell their stories. She wants nothing less than a global view of the vampire world. So she splits the point of view, once again trying to have all the benefits of both first person and third person without any of the drawbacks of either. What works well in *Interview* does not in *The Queen of the Damned*, in part because the multiple narrators or storytellers become confusing and leave the reader with no one voice to connect with as a protagonist or central character in the story, and no clear thread to tie all the narratives together.

Rice begins with Lestat's first-person prologue which sets up the framework for the story by having Lestat himself announce that he's giving up his first-person voice for most of the rest of the novel: "So we will move out of the narrow, lyrical confines of the first person singular," Lestat announces to the reader. "[W]e will jump as a thousand mortal writers have done into the brains and souls of 'many characters.' We will gallop into the world of 'third person' and 'multiple point of view' " (*Queen*, 6). Lestat is now going to be the author instead of Rice, reporting distantly what other people have told him by casting their stories as third-person narratives. But Lestat sees some of the drawbacks to making this believable, so he tells the reader that when the other characters think or talk about how beautiful or irresistible he is, he is only reporting what they told him later or what he took from their minds with his "infallible telepathic power" (6). Even for Lestat, this is pushing the envelope of reader acceptance.

This manipulation of point of view is so mechanical that it clunks, but the clunkiness of the literary method is not the only drawback to the scattering of point of view in this book. The great benefit of a single point of view, whether first or third person, is that it gives the reader a character to identify with. Lestat is a great character to identify with: who can resist a hypnotic rock star/vampire who wrestles wolves and earns the admiration of all he encounters, even those who hate him? But Rice follows Lestat's brief seven-page introduction with 425 more pages of one narrator after another in sixteen different fragments of story, some admirable, some horrifying, some just confusing.

The first section after Lestat's first-person narration is one of the more puzzling. It's called the Proem, which means a brief introduction. This is a little confusing since Lestat just introduced something on the previous pages, but the confusion mounts when the Proem opens with a long section of graffiti found on a wall in the back room of a bar. Since this graffiti is four pages long, the reader is left wondering just how big that back wall is, but even more important, the reader is left wondering who's reading the graffiti. After four pages, the obvious conclusion is that no one is; Rice must be employing an omniscient narrator, one who sees all but does not participate and is not a character in any way. This narrator is also objective in not passing judgment. Although omniscient objective narrators have their place in literature, their best place is not following the flamboyant Lestat.

But then, on page fourteen, the reader finds out that it's not an objective narrator after all when Rice writes, "the blond-haired figure in the red velvet coat read the declaration over again from his comfortable vantage point." So the previous four pages have been in the point of view of a "blond-haired figure," but the reader needed to know that four pages ago. Now the reader has to consciously rearrange her or his thoughts instead of being drawn into the story. This means that in the first fourteen pages of the book, Rice's readers have adapted to three very different narrators, one of whom is a mistake and the last of whom she hasn't given a name to yet. The question most fiction writers want their readers to ask is, "What happens next?" The question at this point in *The Queen of the Damned* is, "Who's in charge here and what's going on?" Readers will deal with not knowing what's going on if there's some guarantee that there is one voice guiding the story that will make everything clear in the end. But with multiple voices, Rice's readers don't have that guarantee.

And those multiple voices continue to multiply. The next fifteen sections give the reader more narrators to identify, understand, and connect with. They include Marius the ancient Roman vampire, a dying archeologist, a drug-crazed delinquent vampire named Baby Jenks, an ancient Greek vampire named Pandora, the boy who interviewed Louis in *Interview with the Vampire* (now identified by name as Daniel), an ancient Egyptian vampire named Khayman, and a woman named Jesse. Then abruptly we are back in Lestat's voice, but this is not the Lestat of the beginning, the Lestat who said, "I'm going to tell this story in a lot of different viewpoints." This Lestat is simply another viewpoint, another one of the gang. All this hopping from character to character is confusing enough, but the next section includes an internal point-of-view shift, too. This section, called "The Story of the Twins, Part 1," begins in Marius's point of view but then becomes a first person narrative told by a character named Maharet to whom Marius only listens. It's the same technique Rice employed beautifully in *Interview with the Vampire*, but adding it to a narrative that is already under indictment for mugging the reader with point-of-view shifts is not a good idea.

Rice switches point of view more than thirty-one times in *The Queen of the Damned* using nine different narrators. Of all the weaknesses of the novel, the most damaging is this uncontrolled use of point of view. Point of view is the reader's doorway into the story. By providing so many doorways, each opening into a different story, many of which turn out to be false entrances, Rice has made it very difficult for the reader to fully become a part of her novel. And that is unfortunate because her novel is filled with fascinating characters doing remarkable things.

CHARACTER DEVELOPMENT

After two books, one would think that Lestat's character must be fully developed, but as Rice demonstrates in *The Queen of the Damned*, one would be wrong. Lestat as the central character or protagonist has even more to learn in his latest story because he is ripped from his friends and forced to confront what he is and what he might become by his antagonist or opponent, Akasha, the Mother of All. Akasha is a worthy opponent for Lestat because she is seductive, immortal, and much more powerful than he is. She takes him as her lover, and she also offers him the opportunity to become a god with her, but while that seems to be everything he's ever wanted, it also wars with his identity of himself as a good vampire, leading to a central character question of, "Will Lestat forget his human origins and turn into a monster like Akasha?" Internal struggles like these make for great character growth, which creates dynamic or changing characters. Lestat's growth, like everything else in his over-the-top life, is truly great.

At the beginning of the novel, Lestat calls all the vampires together at his rock concert in a final battle, but Akasha steals the fight from him, defeating his enemies before he can reach them, taking him away with her to fulfill her dreams, not his. She promises to teach him much, and she does, giving him the knowledge he's been looking for in his two previous books, but she also offers him what he has wanted since he was a small child. She tells him that she will show him how to do great "good" in the world.

The only problem is that Akasha's definition of "good," while affording Lestat immense power, conflicts with what he knows to be good. Her plan is to end all war and suffering by killing 99 percent of the men in the world, a plan that is both beautiful and stupid in its simplicity. Lestat follows her as she begins to work her new religion, but he's repelled by the death and he knows she's wrong. When Akasha tells him that she is the Goddess of All and that therefore what she says is good *is* good, Lestat is forced to choose between not just his vampire nature and his human nature, but also between the overwhelming love he feels for the beautiful lonely woman that Akasha is (not to mention the absolute power she offers him) and the instinctive recognition that humanity is not theirs to reorganize and massacre. "We are not gods," Lestat tells her, rejecting her plan and her power and thereby retaining his humanity and growing as a character from a vampire who would do anything for power to a vampire who turns away from power to stop evil. Rice shows Lestat's character growth beautifully in the passages in which he first falls into Akasha's plan, and then gradually rejects her until finally, when she lies dying at his feet and he knows he loves her and has the power to save her, he does nothing and lets her die so that humanity will be free of her ghastly plan. For Lestat who has always been the selfish, impulsive brat prince, this is huge character growth.

Akasha, Lestat's psychological sister in selfishness and impulsiveness, cannot make this character leap and is therefore a static or unchanging character. As a human, she too wanted to be good, but in her narrowness, she could see goodness only as she defined it. Since her people did not practice ritual cannibalism, she saw it as her duty to stop the practice in other cultures, even though it meant killing everyone in the culture to "save" them from themselves. Her high birth and her great beauty combined to give her the power she needed, and she never hesitated to act as she saw fit, even if she had to rationalize her own actions to fit her identity as a "good" person.

When her selfishness and her cruelty bring on the wrath of the demon Amel who enters her dying body, she is horrified and fascinated by the power she now has. But like everything else in her life, this too can be rationalized as a force for good, for now she is a goddess, and she will rule the world as she sees fit. But others rise up against her and trap her, leaving her helpless while they feed from her, and her body turns to stone while only her mind burns brightly alive. For six thousand years, she grows stronger but not smarter. The inflexibility she had as a human is magnified as the years pass. When she is finally awakened by Lestat's rock music, she is convinced of her divinity and goes to claim her place, as she explains to him later, as the Queen of Heaven.

Even though she remains essentially the same character, intensifying over time, Akasha is a fully developed character who retains her emotions and her need for others while her will solidifies into godlike assumptions. Her love for Lestat makes her almost human, while her contempt for life and the loyalty of others like her husband (whom she drains of blood so that she may move again) and her loyal keeper Marius (whom she imprisons in ice so she may escape) make her the Death Goddess she wants to be. Because Akasha does have feelings for Lestat and because she is outraged at the treatment of women throughout history at the hands of men, it's impossible to dismiss her as simply a cold Bitch Goddess. When she dies at the end, the reader heaves a sigh of relief along with Lestat, but it's Lestat's sigh of regret, too. She had to go, but she won't soon be forgotten.

If Lestat is similar to Akasha, the twins Maharet and Mekare are her static opposites. Loving and disdainful of power where Akasha is cold and controlling, the twins are no match for her power or her ambition. Tortured, mutilated, and separated by Akasha's blind rage, the twins sorrowfully and patiently pursue their lives, Maharet minding the Great Family descended from her daughter Miriam and Mekare evidently brooding on rage and revenge in a South American jungle. Maharet, in particular, becomes Akasha's opposite, fostering life as Akasha plans to obliterate it. But they also share the detachment from humanity that many of Rice's female characters have. Both have been alive for so long that their humanity has seeped away, leaving them remote and focused on the single goal of their lives. Maharet seems to recover some of her old humanity when she is reunited with her sister, but in the end she is too analytical and too emotionless to achieve any kind of character growth. She is simply awesome in her knowledge and detachment, a force of nature more than a fully developed character.

The other characters in this story are even less well developed, in part because there are so many of them, but also in part because they're vampires, essentially emotionless creatures who are removed from humanity. Marius does move to stop Akasha before she destroys the world because he cares deeply about humanity, but Marius has always cared deeply about humanity. Essentially, Marius remains Marius, the good, wise vampire who's a little ticked off about being put in the ice for ten days but is willing to repress his anger if he can talk Akasha out of murdering the world's male population. Even more static is his old lover, Pandora, who rescues him and then withdraws mentally, becoming a sort of vampire wallpaper for the rest of the story. Daniel, the interviewer from the first in the series of Vampire Chronicles, is also static: he has one desire, to be made a vampire by Armand, and when he gets it, he's happy for the rest of the book. Khayman, one of the First Brood who longs to see Mekare's curse carried out, moves through the plot like a sulking figure of fate, becoming emotional only when Mekare shows up and does what he's been waiting for for six thousand years, which is to send Akasha into oblivion. Louis makes his appearance as Louis unchanging, still too beautiful and sensitive for his own good. Gabrielle shows up, still Gabrielle, so tied to nature that she's almost unconscious, her only human attribute being her undying love for her son, Lestat. New vampires appear, but they, too, become vampire wallpaper, part of the backdrop for the final struggle between Mekare and Akasha. Only Jesse, Maharet's youngest direct descendant, remains mortal for most of the book, but she is also curiously emotionless, excited only by the pursuit of supernatural knowledge. When she is made a vampire at the point of her death, there is none of the anguish that others have experienced in previous books because Jesse never really had much humanity to give up anyway. Rice leaves all of these characters static to simplify her narrative and to focus on the people who are important to it, Lestat and Akasha.

This panorama of characters intensifies the great problem of the book touched on before. Because there are so many stories and so many characters, it becomes difficult to truly identify one character whose goal propels the book. The only character with one strong goal from the beginning of the book to the end is Akasha, the vampire who wants to dominate the world. But she is also one of the very few characters in this book who never tells her own story; that is, the Queen of the Damned tells none of the narratives in *The Queen of the Damned*. Instead, she becomes a universal *antagonist*, the one everybody else obsesses over and wants to stop. Lestat becomes an observer character here, caught up in his love for Akasha but essentially passive, his greatest act in the novel being his decision *not* to act and save his lover. Maharet acts as a power behind the scenes, but even she is passive, doing most of her fighting by trying to talk the problem to death. The character who does act to defeat Akasha, Mekare, shows up for the first time only seconds before she kills her. Rice's narratives in this book are strong, full of action, passion, and violence, but they are also difficult to understand in their entirety because of this lack of one protagonist and one central voice.

PLOT DEVELOPMENT AND STRUCTURE

All the problems created by the fragmented points of view and multiple viewpoint characters in *The Queen of the Damned* are repeated in Rice's fragmented plot structure. Rice wants to construct multiple back stories for all her characters as well as an entire mythology of vampires, but all of these narratives are episodic, composed of stories that do not lead to one another but only exist in the same imaginary world. Modern fiction generally demands that a plot be causal—that is, that one event lead logically to the next event, each event increasing the tension of the rising action. *The Queen of the Damned*'s multiple narrators and stories cannot be causal, but this is not necessarily a drawback since Rice has already proved she can pull off an episodic plot; she did it in *The Vampire Lestat*. In that book she held the scattered events of Lestat's life together by reporting them in the order they happened (chronological order) and even more important, reporting them in Lestat's strong first-person voice.

But in *The Queen of the Damned*, there is no one powerful voice to bind the narrative together, and the stories told are not chronological but are drawn from many places and many times, held together for the most part because their point-of-view narrators have all had dreams about the twins. That's enough to convince the reader that Rice has a plan, but it's not enough to help keep the narrative clear and flowing, and it doesn't give the book a clear protagonist or central character throughout, although Lestat finally becomes the protagonist by default. And because there are so many narrators or storytellers besides Lestat, Rice has a lot of explaining to do. Therefore, the first two hundred pages of the story are exposition, back stories or events that happened before the now of the story which begins when Akasha snatches Lestat. The next fifty pages repeat events already covered in *The Vampire Lestat*, adding crucial new details but still not beginning the story. Not until page 247 does Akasha take her prince and rise through the air, beginning the central conflict. That's a lot of exposition, and a long time for readers to wait while gathering information they're not sure how to use.

Once the rising action begins, it's terrific storytelling, but at this point, Rice divides the narrative into two alternating stories. One is Lestat's story, and he is a vivid protagonist as he is tempted and loved by his antagonist, Akasha, the beautiful and the damned. The rising action of his plot begins when Akasha takes him, his point of no return comes when he realizes he must stop her insane plan and asks to return home, and the climax occurs when he sees his beloved dying and does nothing to save her, recognizing that she must die if the world is to be saved. Although this is a vastly simplified description of Lestat's agonizing narrative, it does show how tightly Rice has constructed his story.

There's also a second story in this last half of the book, a story that has been hinted at throughout the first half. It's the struggle between the protagonist twins and the antagonist Akasha, and it begins six thousand years earlier. Maharet tells most of the tale to the other vampires; this static method of storytelling is nevertheless riveting because Rice's mythology is riveting. The rising action begins when Akasha orders the kidnapping of the twins and the desecration of their mother; it reaches the point of no return when she has them mutilated and separated; and it attains its climax when the twins reunite to face Akasha again, six thousand years later, to defeat her once and for all, recognizing as they consume her brain that someone must take her place in the world of the vampires. This plot is also beautifully developed, a tribute both to Rice's imagination and her craft.

The problem comes in the way the two narratives are presented in alternating sections. Since Lestat's narrative is taking place in the "now" of the story, and most of the twins' narrative is flashback, the reader is jerked from immediate adventure to mythic horror and back again, never really getting the chance to enter into either reading experience. Rice has used the first half of the book to introduce characters, develop back story, and hint that something terrible is coming without ever telling the reader anything concrete, so the reader really needs a clear narrative as a payoff in the last half of the book. Instead, the clarity and impact of the story of the twins is diluted because every time the reader becomes invested in the story, Rice shifts to Akasha and Lestat, arguing about the future of humankind. The terrible poignancy of Akasha and Lestat's love is also diluted because every time the reader becomes emotionally invested, the story switches back to ancient Egypt.

This could have been avoided had Rice set the story of the twins at the beginning in order to set up the conflict of the plot. Instead, she doles out the twins' story in pieces to tempt the reader, and in so doing she sacrifices true suspense for false suspense. False suspense is based on the idea that if readers don't know what is happening, they will be more intrigued by the plot and surprised by the ending. In the case of *The Queen of the Damned*, Rice does this by withholding the story of what happened to the twins, the events that cause all the action in the story. But in actuality, suspense is heightened if readers know what has happened, in this case what Akasha has done in the past.

For example, if a character is walking through the woods, and a murderer jumps out with a knife in his hand, the reader is a victim of false suspense and is left wondering (after the first shock) "Where did he come from?" But if the author lets the reader know there's a murderer in the woods with a knife, and then sends the character into the woods, the reader is in the grip of true suspense, and screaming "Don't go in there, there's a guy with a knife!" for the entire action of the tale. In *The Queen of the Damned*, if the reader gets the story chronologically (the events are told in the order they occurred) from the beginning and therefore knows that Akasha, the Queen Mother of the Vampires, is selfish, power-mad, and haunted by an ancient curse (in other words, waiting in the woods with a knife), then her progression through Lestat's modern world is even more terrifying because the reader knows this woman will do anything. Because Rice waits until the end to let readers know just how big Akasha's knife is, she sacrifices suspense.

The point of all of this shifting about is to get all of the characters (and the reader) to that final showdown between the two Queens of Hell, Akasha and the mutilated Mekare, the scene in which all the characters recognize their ties to humanity in their rejection of Akasha's plan. Once the reader gets there, it's quite a showdown, neatly tying up all the loose ends of the quest plot and saving all the major players even though the reader is sure that the entire race of vampires is doomed. It is, in short, a terrific climax. Rice's vampire mythology is wonderful when it's finally puzzled out, but the structure of her material weakens the myth she creates.

LITERARY DEVICE: FORESHADOWING

Foreshadowing simply means hinting at what's to come. It's a wonderful technique for building suspense and reader expectation, and Rice uses it to great effect in the first half of *The Queen of the Damned* as she moves through a variety of narrators, all of whom have had nightmares about red-haired twins. The dreams grow in horror: the old archeologist dreams of sadness and someone walking in the jungle, Baby Jenks dreams of two red-haired women about to eat the heart and brain of their mother, Akim sees the two women raped, Daniel hears their screams and sees them abandoned and tortured by heat, thirst, and pain in the desert, and Khayman remembers them mutilated, one by having her tongue cut out and the other by having her eyes put out. All of these dreams are fragments of the story only, but they make it impossible for the reader to leave the narrative until they've been assembled into one great story, all mysteries solved. This is exactly what foreshadowing is supposed to do, create a sense of things to come, important things that the reader must see and know, and at the same time make those events plausible when they do happen. Rice's myth is no less violent for being foreshadowed, but it is more understandable because the elements have been introduced ahead of time.

Rice also foreshadows other events, most notably the gathering of the dark power of Akasha that will destroy all the vampires. She does this with the story of the twins and by showing vampires such as Baby Jenks being burned while trying to escape, but she also gives her narrators feelings of doom, as when Armand tells Daniel that he must go to Lestat's rock concert because he feels that it may be the end of all of them. Combined with the dreams of the twins, these premonitions add so much weight to the foreshadowing of the first half of the novel that it almost overwhelms the narrative by becoming more interesting than the events actually happening on the page. Thus the foreshadowing that Rice has woven through the first half of her novel increases the reader's feelings of dread and anxiety to the breaking point. Fortunately, the narratives that follow the foreshadowing are more than disastrous enough to support the weight of the buildup she gives them.

THEMATIC ISSUES

The usual clues of setting, central question, internal conflict, character growth, beginning and ending, and title are not as great a guide to theme in *The Queen of the Damned* as they have been in the previous Rice books. This is because there are really two major narratives instead of one major narrative framed with a minor narrative. Each of these narratives has its own protagonist or central character: the twins oppose Akasha in the great myth story of the vampires, and Lestat opposes Akasha in their great love story. This means there are at least two sets of internal conflicts, character growth, and so on. Therefore, the best place to begin looking for theme in this divided narrative is in the things they share, their antagonist, Akasha, and their goals and central question, "Will Akasha be defeated?"

Whatever concept is embodied in Akasha, the theme will oppose it since all the protagonists (and virtually everyone else in the story) opposes her. Akasha's great plan is to stop rape and war by killing 99 percent of the men in the world, keeping the last 1 percent as restrained pets. While her motives are good, her plan is not, denying the humanity of men (which she argues they have forfeited through their brutality to women), and the importance of both genders in the great human scheme of things. She is the only one who cannot see the horror in what she is doing because she's lost whatever humanity she may once have had. Even when she was human, she had no empathy for others. In fact, this blindness to humanity is what got Akasha into trouble and began vampirism in the first place. Because she refused to open her mind to others' thoughts and feelings, she destroyed the lives of the twins and earned the wrath of the demon who took possession of her body and made her the mother of all the vampires. That same blindness causes her to lose Lestat when he finds himself opposing her on the grounds that he is too connected to humans to see them as insignificant pieces in the game she wants to play. The other vampires, inhumans all, object for the same reason. As Lestat tells her when he refuses to follow her any more, "We're not angels, Akasha. . . . We are not gods. To be human, that's what most of us long for. It is the human which has become myth to us" (451).

Therefore, Rice's theme in this novel may be connected to the idea of being able to feel for others even though they are different. The beginning of the novel seems to reinforce Lestat's claim that after the events of the story he is about to relate, not only is he more powerful and wiser, but "the human in me is closer to the surface than ever" (1). And the ending of the story has him breaking the rules of the new vampire coven by contacting a human being and encouraging him to remain in contact. Thus the idea that Rice uses in the introduction and conclusion of her book is that Lestat is a better person because he understands and reaches out to humans as he has not done before.

Taking these clues into consideration, we see that the title does finally shed some light on the theme. Akasha is Queen of the Damned not only because she is the Mother of All the vampires, but also because she is damned by her own blindness and lack of connection to others, not just to her own vampire children whom she destroys but also to the humans she sees as bugs in her great plan. Akasha dies defeated, not because she's the Mother of All the vampires, but because she's damned by being unable to make the connections that might have saved her.

Another clue to theme in literature is motif, an idea or image that is repeated throughout the work. *The Queen of the Damned* is full of reunions between people who have loved each other very much in the past and who reestablish those connections, who reach out to others without jealousy, and who band together to defeat what seems to all of them to be overwhelming evil. When this reunion motif is combined with all the other evidence in the text, one theme that becomes clear is the importance of maintaining connections among all people, no matter how alien they may seem. Rice has offered one other suggestion for theme, that "the flesh teaches all wisdom and when we become too unanchored and get into abstract thinking that betrays compassion for the individual, that's where the real danger lies" (Ramsland, *Prism* 295). Thus the strength of those vampires who survive the climax of *The Queen of the Damned* is that they can see past Akasha's abstract ideas to connect with the human hearts they gave up long ago.

A FEMINIST READING OF *THE QUEEN OF THE DAMNED*

Feminist criticism is often misunderstood because people assume that what feminists want are stories full of strong, wonderful women. That is, of course, terrific, but if those were the only portrayals of women in our stories, literature would be boring. What feminists ask for instead is that the reader be aware that the portrayals of women in literature are often unfair stereotypes and not reflections of women's reality. In order to understand a work of literature, then, feminist critics do not ask, "Are all the women in this story wonderful people?" Instead, they ask more open-ended questions, designed to analyze how the images of women work in the story. Stephen Lynn, in his book on literary criticism *Texts and Contexts*, suggests several questions that feminist critics might ask:

> Where are the women in this story?
> What role does gender play in the story?
> What image of women is conveyed?
> How is the relationship between women and men depicted?
> How is the relationship between women and women depicted?

When these questions are asked of *The Queen of the Damned*, several troubling aspects become clear, not the least of which is that most of the depictions of women show them to be cold and passive.

Where are the women in this story?

For once, there are plenty of women in a Rice book, and for once they're center stage, playing out most of the conflicts. The most obvious is Akasha, the Queen of the Damned, cold, stupid, selfish, power-hungry, and deadly, and altogether a wonderfully developed female character. She is the epitome of the Feminist Gone Mad, a woman enraged at the brutality that men have shown women for centuries. This antagonism against men who victimize women is something many women share. Rice herself told interviewer Charlie Rose that she had fantasies of going around in a black limousine and shooting every pimp she could find ("Charlie Rose," 10). Driven by a motivation that most women can understand, Akasha is by far the most vivid of all the female characters in the novel. Unfortunately, her plan to make the world safe for women by killing 99 percent of the men is insane. Murderous Akasha is hardly the ideal way women would like to see strong women portrayed, but this is not a problem as long as there are other women in the text who are warm, active, and strong to balance her. Unfortunately, there aren't.

There are the twins, Maharet and Mekare, obedient and respectful to their mother; victimized by Akasha; tortured, raped, and mutilated; left to survive throughout the centuries to wait for (but not seek) revenge. Maharet describes her inability to choose between killing the monster that Akasha becomes and saving the vampires of the world by saying "and so I did nothing," a fairly apt description of many female decisions in the text (268). There is Gabrielle, Lestat's mother, so gone to earth and part of nature that she seems half asleep throughout the novel, her only emotion the vague concern she has for her much-loved but rarely embraced son. There is Jesse, born prematurely when her mother dies violently, asking questions her remote surrogate mother won't answer, raised by foster parents with love, and yet still inexplicably cold and cut off from humanity. Jesse only achieves a spark of animation when she finally meets Lestat seconds before she is killed and made into a vampire. She then passes into the pale ranks of those who seem to merely follow Lestat without any real interests or questions of their own. There is also Pandora, the vampire consort to Marius who is rarely with him and who wanders the earth in quiet despair, disconnected from all other people, not really interested in anything until Lestat calls to her along with all the other vampires. And there is Baby Jenks, drug-addled, vicious, and stupid, who murders her extremely religious mother, a woman who accepts her murder and forgives her daughter even while she's being battered to death. Even Akasha has spent a large part of her existence passive. As one critic has noted: "Akasha [is] the embodiment of the maternal in patriarchal culture—aligned with . . . silence, and paralysis" in her centuries as a rigid stone mummy (Doane and Hodges, 432).

This division of women characters creates an unfortunate pattern. Women, this novel seems to say, come in two flavors: passive, remote, and cold, *or* active, warm, passionate, and murderous. There is no female counterpart to Lestat or even to Louis, no intelligent, well-rounded figure who has both good and evil impulses and who moves the plot through her motives and actions. Akasha moves the plot through blind, death-dealing, power-hungry ignorance, and the other women either withdraw from actively taking part in the narrative or oppose Akasha ineffectually until the final great climax when she is defeated by the twin who is more avenging animal than human.

What role does gender play in the story?

The most important aspect of being a woman in Rice's stories is motherhood. Gabrielle is Lestat's mother and she loves him, but she rarely shows him affection, and Marius describes her as having a coldness that Lestat can never understand (279). Akasha is the Mother of All the vampires, but she becomes an anti-mother, the Goddess of Death, murdering her offspring. Jesse's mother dies as she is born and leaves her to Maharet, who becomes a loving but absent mother, allowing Jesse to see her only three times in her life. Maharet provides Jesse with every possible material thing while denying her the only thing she really wants, knowledge and connection, by writing her that she loves her too much ever to see her again or tell her of her family (142). This is the kind of love that denies that Jesse is a person in her own right, able to make her own decisions, and is therefore a limiting, controlling love, not a truly nurturing motherly love. Baby Jenks's mother is completely powerless, a victim who forgives her daughter even as her daughter clubs her to death with an iron. All of these maternal characters are flawed mothers, remote or murderous or powerless.

Another usual role for women, that of passionate lover, is almost completely absent from this story. Marius loves Pandora passionately but prefers not to be with her, which appears to be just fine with Pandora who wanders the earth in a semi-comatose state. Lestat loves Gabrielle passionately but cannot overcome the coldness in her nature that sends her away from him and back to the passionless earth. Mael loves Jesse passionately, but she doesn't understand, experiencing instead brief unsatisfactory love affairs with other mortals that have no sensuality to them. The only truly passionate woman in the entire novel is Akasha, who loves Lestat with a burning need that she does not bother to disguise. But even this need is cold in the end, when she tells Lestat she will destroy him, too, if he opposes her. She loves him, but she loves her power more.

Looking only at Rice's female characters, a reader might assume that she simply does not write many passionate people into her books. But her male characters refute that idea immediately. Lestat and Louis are filled with tenderness and passion when they meet. Marius's hands tremble when he touches Armand after centuries apart from him. Armand adores Daniel with all the fiber of his being. These men try to share that tenderness and passion with the women in their lives but are usually turned away. The great love story at the heart of the Vampire Chronicles will always be between Lestat and Louis, and part of the reason for that is the fact that the women in Rice's world are curiously unloving people in either of their gender roles as mothers and lovers.

What image of women is conveyed?

Most of Rice's women are distant, unemotional, and unhappy. Most of them desert, betray, or deliberately remain remote from their children. Most of them are caught up in the surge of events and respond passively to what happens instead of creating their own stories through action; that is, they react instead of acting. The one who does act, Akasha, does so brutally in order to grab all power for herself. She creates chaos by spreading death and despair, becoming the epitome of the antifeminists' nightmare, the "femi-nazi" out to exterminate all men and rule the world. The general image seems to be that most women are passive, and the few that are powerful and active will try to destroy the world.

How is the relationship between women and men depicted?

Lestat's parents are miserable together. His mother, Gabrielle, is shackled to a man who lacks her intelligence and sensitivity until Lestat sets her free at the point of death by making her a vampire, whereupon she immediately leaves her husband forever without a backward glance. Pandora is a prostitute, and her relationship with Marius is one of a valued possession that he prefers to keep remote from himself. The twins' closest female/male relationship is with Khayman, the man who raped them in public on the orders of his queen. Baby Jenks has sex without conscious thought, and her relationships with men are as vicious as everything else in her life. Jesse's few relationships are dismissed as unsatisfactory, and she exists for most of the book as a loner. Akasha drives her husband into damnation because he is so mesmerized by her beauty that he becomes her slave, and when he is no longer of use to her, she sucks his blood and leaves him an empty husk.

In fact, there is no male/female relationship in *The Queen of the Damned* that can in any way compare with the tenderness of the relationships between Lestat and Louis, Louis and Armand, Daniel and Armand, Marius and Armand, and Lestat and Marius. This is not to suggest that these relationships should not be in the novel. The strength of the bond that these men share not only reflects Rice's great characterization, but also gives the Vampire novels the sense of love and joy they possess. But when these close, warm male/male relationships are put in contrast with the sterility and distance of *all* the male/female relationships in the books, it seems to be clear that in the world of Rice's novels, only relationships between men can be warm and supportive.

How is the relationship between women and women depicted?

Akasha sets out to destroy the twins because she is jealous of their power. Maharet mothers Jesse and truly loves her but keeps herself remote to protect her secret of immortality and the secret of the twins. When Jesse is dying, the spirit of her mother appears before her and watches her choose vampirism "with a cold unmerciful expression," disapproving of her daughter from beyond the grave (239). Baby Jenks kills her mother. Pandora and Gabrielle have no relationships with other women, although the novel says later in one line that Gabrielle begins to spend time with Jesse after she is made a vampire.

The one strong bond between two loving women, the sisterhood of the twins, is broken for centuries by another woman's tortures. When the twins are rejoined, Mekare seems more monster than woman, dragging herself up out of the desert like an avenging beast, barely human. Maharet joins her to feed her the brains of Akasha, but all their actions are instinctive. Their entire reunion consists of the split-second killing of Akasha. And although Rice says they are together at the end, centuries of martyrdom and isolation have made Mekare less than human, and Maharet is caught up in the administrative duties of minding the Great Family. Their reunion has none of the tenderness of the Lestat/Louis reunion in *The Vampire Lestat*. There is one intensely passionate moment between two women when Maharet makes her many-times-great-granddaughter Jesse a vampire, but the scene is entirely sexual, an erotic masterpiece that makes all tenderness physical. Once Jesse is made immortal, their relationship returns to the remoteness of before. Essentially, there are no strong, openly loving female relationships in *The Vampire Chronicles*.

Having answered these questions, the feminist critic does not demand that Anne Rice be burned at the stake for being antifeminist. One of the great things about literature is that there is room for all arguments and points of view, and Rice's stance on women is one point of view that is often fascinating. What the feminist critic does ask instead is, "Why is the story so cold in its female characterizations?" and "What impact does this have on the reader?"

But to answer the "Why?" requires another kind of criticism, psychological criticism, the criticism that asks, "Why did the author do that?" and looks into her biography to find her motivations. Rice herself has noted that she has difficulty identifying with the feminine: "I think I have a gender screw-up to the point that I don't know most of the time what gender I am, in terms of anybody's thinking" (Ramsland, *Prism*, 149). Rice's biography, as already noted, includes a distant, undependable mother who died of alcoholism while Rice was young, disapproving nuns in her Catholic schooling, and a daughter who "left" her at age six by dying of leukemia. Her biography also includes feelings of powerlessness, guilt about her sexual desires, and ambivalence about her woman's body as a sexual entity, all brought on by her Catholic upbringing. All of these events and aspects could combine to make Rice familiar with and most comfortable with cold female characters.

Rice's linking of passivity with the female is also supported by her biography. Although Rice recreated her lost daughter in the character of Claudia in *Interview with the Vampire*, she said later that Claudia, the woman trapped in the body of a child, was also "the embodiment of my failure to deal with the feminine. . . . She's the person robbed of power" (Ramsland, *Prism*, 154). This echoes something Lestat says about twentieth-century women in *The Vampire Lestat*: "For the first time in history, they were as strong and as interesting as men" (7). Given that history has plenty of strong and interesting women, Lestat's statement is more a reflection of Rice's perceptions of women as powerless and uninteresting than it is a reflection of the twentieth century. All of these aspects taken together go a long way toward explaining why the women of *The Queen of the Damned* are so passive.

Even more important than the impact of Rice's life on her fiction is the impact of Rice's fiction on the reader. For much of the time, Rice's distance from the women in her books isn't a problem because Lestat is her first-person narrator and so her distance becomes Lestat's distance. Lestat is a wonderful character, but no reader ever listened to him and said, "Here is the voice of unbiased reason." He is, after all, an arrogant, power-mad vampire, charming, intelligent and fun, but not a terrific role model. It's only when Rice comes to *The Queen of the Damned* with its multiple viewpoints that real problems arise. The multiple viewpoints create the assumption that many characters' opinions will be presented and that those viewpoints taken together will present a complete worldview. And the complete worldview of women that Rice presents here is that they're cold, passive, and occasionally murderous.

Even taking the depictions of women into consideration, however, *The Queen of the Damned* can still be considered ultimately a feminist novel because of Rice's view of men and women in the world. Although Akasha's plan to kill men in retaliation for crimes against women sounds like something a feminist would love, in truth, it's antifeminist. A better name for feminism might be "humanism," the idea that all humans are equal regardless of their gender. Akasha's condemnation of men goes against basic feminist theory that both sexes are equal and needed for balance and harmony in the world, and so Rice's rejection of Akasha's plan is actually a feminist act. In the same way, although many of her female characters are remote and cold, they are also strong, enduring, and intelligent, and none of them are antifeminist stereotypes like the dumb blonde. Rice's female characterizations may be limited, but they are not ultimately antifeminist.

Feminist criticism of *The Queen of the Damned*, therefore, emphasizes the images and ideas of equality that Rice promotes, while pointing out that her female characters are limited in ways that her male characters aren't, so that the reader will be aware of the author's uncertain feelings about female power and female sexuality. Pointing out these limitations does not suggest that they should be "fixed." No good feminist critic would ever suggest that Rice's books should be changed to make them politically correct. One of the glories of Rice's work is that it is so often politically and socially incorrect and therefore liberating. All that feminist critics would ask is that the reader be aware that in Rice's world, women inhabit a particular reality that does not reflect all women's experiences.

6

The Tale of the Body Thief
(1992)

Anne Rice had thought the Vampire Chronicles might be over with *The Queen of the Damned*, but Lestat the vampire had another story to tell. Having almost achieved godhood in *The Queen of the Damned*, Lestat journeys in the other direction in *The Tale of the Body Thief* and almost recovers his mortality. Haunted by dreams of Claudia, the lost daughter he made a vampire but did not save from death, and by visions of David Talbot, the older mortal man he longs to make a vampire and save from death, Lestat tries to escape, first by exposing himself to the sun which burns but does not kill him and then by agreeing to switch bodies for twenty-four hours with a mortal body thief named Raglan James. James disappears with Lestat's body and part of Lestat's fortune, and it's evident that he has no intention of ever coming back. With David's help, Lestat tracks James down. But when they recover Lestat's body, James grabs David's old body so that he can take his respected reputation and his fortune, leaving David in a new young form. This game of musical bodies turns out to be much more serious than any of the players had realized, leading not only to the deaths of two, but also to greater self-knowledge for all of them, unwelcome though it is. At the end of *The Tale of the Body Thief*, Lestat is back in his body, older, wiser, and surprised at the things he now knows about himself.

POINT OF VIEW

The Tale of the Body Thief opens, as did the previous two Vampire Chronicles, with the narrative point of view firmly in the first person of Lestat: "The Vampire Lestat here. I have a story to tell you." But while in two of the previous three vampire novels, Rice played with point of view, here she returns to the classic first-person narration that made *The Vampire Lestat* so powerful and sticks with it throughout. It's a wise choice. Staying with Lestat as first-person narrator or storyteller not only makes the book easy to understand, but also contributes to the tightness of the plot and the sense of control that makes this book so readable. And since *The Body Thief* is once again about the emotional anguish of the central character, Rice's choice of first person is a smart one from an entertainment point of view; it is also the best one to communicate Lestat's pain, fear, and confusion. In choosing the first person for Lestat's experiences as a mortal again, Rice ensures that the book will draw the reader in and keep her or him spellbound to the last page.

CHARACTER DEVELOPMENT

The tightness of Rice's plot in *The Tale of the Body Thief* is also demonstrated in the tightness of her character relationships. Her protagonist is once again Lestat, and his goal this time is to get his body back so he can once again be immortal. Lestat's antagonist, the character who wants to prevent him from reaching his goal, is Raglan James, the Body Thief. James is a worthy opponent because he is clever and ruthless and because he's walking around in Lestat's deadly, immortal body while Lestat is stuck in a weak, mortal body. The plot is the struggle between Lestat and James to control the body and get immortality, and the central question is, "Will Lestat get his body back?" Lestat's identity or idea of who he is rests on this question because he sees himself as all-powerful and immortal, not as the weak and vulnerable mortal man he has become. Therefore his motivation to regain his body is directly tied to his identity; that is, he must defeat James and regain his body in order to see himself once more as himself. The central question also provides his external conflict because he must physically fight with James to get his body back. But because Lestat is also a dynamic character who changes and grows throughout his story, the central question also intensifies his internal conflict, the struggle inside his mind over the fact that he is a vampire and he has killed, which therefore makes him evil.

Lestat's internal struggle is one that he's been dealing with in both *The Vampire Lestat* and *The Queen of the Damned*. In these books, obsessed with the idea that he is doomed to be evil when all he ever wanted as a mortal was to be good, Lestat decides to be "good at being bad," flaunting his evil as a rock star and calling all the vampires to him. But in *The Queen of the Damned*, he learns that he is not completely evil and that he does have ties to humanity when he refuses to help Akasha with her massacres. In the beginning of *The Body Thief*, Lestat is still reeling from this new insight. He is also haunted by visions of Claudia, the child he made a vampire and whose death he inadvertently caused, and these visions represent the guilt he cannot escape. Torn between his human impulses and his vampire nature, Lestat cannot deal with his guilt any more. Motivated by his internal conflict, he goes into the desert to die by sun, "in heat, as Claudia had died," where he is tortured and burned but still survives (43).

Lestat recovers and is then confronted with the second great opportunity of his life when Raglan James, the Body Thief, offers to trade bodies with him for twenty-four hours so that he can once more experience the mortal life. Motivated by the temptation of food and drink and sunrises and all the pleasures of mortal flesh, Lestat agrees. But he is also tempted by more than these external things. James has offered him his internal desire, too. Lestat's suffering in the desert may have served as a penance for all the suffering he committed before since long ago he had not chosen to become a vampire but had the Dark Gift forced upon him. But if he stays a vampire, he will have to continue to kill and drink again, and this time his evil will be from his choice because he has refused to become a mortal when James offered. If he takes James's offer, he will never have to kill again and he will be saved. So when James offers him the clean mortal body for his newly cleansed soul, Lestat grabs it, wanting to be completely good as he was when he was human.

Once in the body, tortured by sickness and confusion, Lestat comes face to face with the person he really is, and that person is the Vampire Lestat, not the mortal Lestat. He wants the power and the immortality, even though it means he must be evil. Confronted with this clear view of himself, Lestat accepts himself as a flawed creature and goes to get his body, this time deliberately choosing the Dark Gift. Through both his external struggles with James and his internal struggles with himself, Lestat changes and grows as a dynamic character and reaches the end of the book wiser and more self-aware than ever before.

In contrast, Raglan James, Lestat's antagonist, is a static character because he does not grow. He begins and ends as the same character, a born thief. James is a psychotic who has perfected his thievery to the point where he can steal bodies. He tries to take Lestat's body by force because he wants to be a vampire so he can experience sucking and stealing someone's life, but Lestat is too strong. James then resorts to trickery, stealing Lestat's body through lies and his money through cunning, and takes his new form to the site of a former disgrace, the luxury liner *Queen Elizabeth 2* from which he was fired for theft. There he takes his revenge by killing the passengers on board and disembarking at every port to kill again and again, experiencing the greatest theft of all by taking life. James's only identity is as a thief. He lives to steal, and as long as he can steal, he has no inner struggle and therefore no character growth.

But although James is a static character, he serves as more than just Lestat's antagonist. He is also his foil. A foil is a piece of shiny metal placed under jewelry to reflect its brightness; in the same way, a foil character is one that is placed beside another more important character to reflect it and make it clearer by contrast (Holman, 187). James is enough like Lestat that readers can compare them easily, but the ways in which he is different emphasize Lestat's strengths and personality.

Lestat and James are both body thieves. James steals bodies and throws the souls out of them so he can inhabit them, and Lestat steals bodies and draws the blood out of them so he can live. They are both clever, cocky, aggressive, and immoral, and they both want to be vampires. But when they change bodies, their differences become apparent. James had clumsily used the body he leaves Lestat in, and at first, Lestat stumbles in it, too. But then through sheer strength of will, he masters his new form as James never could, successfully defeating a life-threatening illness and other dangers. Lestat's personality infuses the new body, and he becomes at once both stronger and more vulnerable as he becomes human. James, on the other hand, was less than human when he was human, but it is not until he becomes a vampire that his true depravity is revealed. Although Lestat has often thought himself a monster, James disproves him by showing him what a monster really is with his indiscriminate kills that descend into mindless butchery.

James, therefore, gives Lestat an antagonist like no other because he gives him the possibility of defeating the evil he has seen in himself. In *The Vampire Lestat*, Lestat's mother talks of the possibility of a being so evil that he destroys simply for the sake of destroying. And Lestat's answer there foreshadows what happens in *The Tale of the Body Thief*: "I almost hope someone does. . . . Because I would rise up against him and do everything to defeat him. And possibly, I could be saved, I could be good again in my own eyes" (335). By defeating James, Lestat defeats the evil he could have become, and for at least that one moment, he also becomes good again in his own eyes before he returns to the vampirism that has become his real nature.

Unlike Raglan James, David Talbot is a dynamic character. As Lestat's only mortal friend, he stands by him even though he knows Lestat wants to make him a vampire to keep him with him forever. If David did this simply because he was a good, loyal friend, he'd be a static character, characterized only by steadfastness in the way that James is characterized only by his need to steal. But David has another motive for wanting to stand by Lestat. David is old and will soon die, and he's not ready because there are still so many things he has wanted to do. The obvious solution is for David to take the Dark Gift from Lestat, but that he can't do because choosing vampirism would conflict with his identity as a good man. Therefore, while David helps Lestat with the external struggle of the plot, he also struggles internally with his desire not to die, and the external struggle makes the internal one even more difficult.

The external struggle takes David to the South America of his youth and increases his desire to live longer, but it also provides him with a way out when James grabs his body in the final confrontation so that he can escape, leaving David in a strong, young mortal body. The David at the beginning of the book would have tried to do the "right" thing by regaining his own body to live out his allotted years as part of God's plan. The new David, tested and tempted by the struggle, tells Lestat that he doesn't want his old body back and goes out to experience life again. These experiences help him achieve his final character growth when Lestat makes him a vampire by force. The old David would have rejected and mourned when the deed was done, but the new David has recovered his lust for life and can tell Lestat, "It took you two hundred years to learn that you wanted [immortality] . . . I knew the moment I woke from the stupor" (433).

Gretchen, the woman Lestat meets as a mortal, is also a dynamic character, not because she changes but because she resists change, and that resistance drives her mad. Gretchen is a nursing nun on leave from her nursing mission in South America, working in the hospital where Lestat is taken when he collapses with pneumonia as a mortal. She is sure that she was born to relieve suffering, simple in her faith, "a virtuous woman, a believer in old and merciless deities, drunk on the blood of martyrs and the heady suffering of a thousand saints" (240). She takes him home and heals his body with both medicine and sex, and she then offers to heal his soul by taking him back to the mission with her. There, she thinks, he can save lives and repent for the guilt which has driven him to the delusion that he was once a vampire. Lestat, however, has recognized by this time that he chooses the evil of being a vampire, and he leaves her, rejecting her offer of salvation. When he recovers his body and goes to find her in the jungle, the sight of him as proof of the existence of the supernatural drives her mad because it challenges her identity of herself as a rational, moral human being. If Lestat is what he says he is and what he appears to be, she has slept with the devil. She turns from him to cry out to God, retreating into insanity, her madness driving her body to bleed from the palms, creating the stigmata and making her a living saint. Gretchen's growth is involuntary; that is, she does not choose to become the different person she is at the end of the book, but it still makes her a dynamic character, one whose personality is changed by the events of the book.

Therefore, while James begins and ends a static thief, and Gretchen "grows" from a repressed nun to an insane saint, the real character growth in the novel is in Lestat and David. Lestat grows from a haunted vampire made without free will to a guilt-rejecting vampire by choice, and David grows from a dying mortal afraid of immortality to a vampire who exalts in his limitless life.

PLOT DEVELOPMENT AND STRUCTURE

In *The Tale of the Body Thief*, Anne Rice destroys any doubts that readers might have had about her ability to construct a tight story. *Body Thief* is beautifully structured along classic lines, making it easy to understand and a joy to read. If it does nothing else, *Body Thief* shows that Rice not only knows how to write fiction, she knows how to craft it.

Body Thief begins, as usual, with Lestat as the protagonist or central character, this time briefly sketching in his biography for the benefit of those readers who haven't read the earlier Vampire Chronicles. "I have to tell you about my life," he says in the exposition, "because I've been having these dreams, and the dreams led me to make a mistake, and the mistake and its aftermath is my story." Lestat's mistake is that he wants to be human again, but only for a little while, only for the experience, and so he trusts a man called Raglan James who will turn out to be his antagonist. James assures Lestat that he is a body thief and can teach him to switch bodies and become human again for a day and a night. Lestat falls for James's pitch and changes bodies with him, the first turning point in the story that begins the rising action.

Lestat's experiences as a human in the rising action of the story teach him much, pulling him back from the brink of godhood he seemed poised on in *The Queen of the Damned*, but all his learning seems to have been gained at too great a cost when the time comes for him to return to his body and he finds that James has never intended to switch back. Not only has James stolen Lestat's immortality, but he's become a rogue vampire, killing indiscriminately. After this point of no return, the second half of Lestat's rising action unwinds as he tracks James down to recover his body and end the bloody spree that James has begun. The final showdown brings protagonist and antagonist together in a classic climax, tying all ends neatly off and answering all questions as Lestat recognizes his need for immortality in spite of the evil it requires of him.

But at this point, Rice adds a final chapter that even Lestat is ambivalent about. "Did you think the story was finished?" he asks in Chapter 33. "Well, the book should be ended . . . you can quit now if you like. You may come to wish that you had" (411). In this chapter, Lestat does something that seems gratuitous and out of character given the time he's spent as a human being learning to understand human emotions again: he takes another human by force and makes him a vampire against his will. His motivation for this seems purely selfish. He wants the man as a companion, a third in one of the Unholy Trinities Lestat insists on constructing for himself throughout his life. This final chapter violates the tightness of the previous story, and yet in its own way, reinforces Lestat's character. It is intrinsically Lestat to refuse to play by the rules. By breaking the tight plot of *Body Thief*, Lestat returns to his brat prince self, and once again Rice has the best of both worlds, classic structure and Lestatian chaos.

LITERARY DEVICE: ALLUSION

An allusion is an unexplained reference to another literary work or to a literary or historical character, event, or object. Authors use allusions to create instant connections between the works they are writing and the works they are alluding to. They don't stop to explain because that would destroy the immediacy of the connection between their stories and the allusions. In *The Tale of the Body Thief*, Lestat makes several allusions, but the most important is to William Blake's "The Tyger." This poem is a particularly good example of an allusion because it works in so many different ways.

One of those ways is the time period in which it was written. "The Tyger" was written in 1794, three years after Lestat makes Louis a vampire. This means that Lestat chooses this allusion not only because of the meaning in the poem, but also because it was written during the time he first lived as a vampire. This time was the Romantic period in literature, when most literary themes dealt with the individuality of man, the importance of feelings and emotions, the use of the imagination, the value of spontaneity and impulse, and the existence of the supernatural. Obviously, Anne Rice's Vampire Chronicles are strongly in the Romantic tradition, and Lestat, himself a Romantic character, deepens that characterization by quoting Blake.

Another way in which "The Tyger" works as an allusion is in its connection to the author. Lestat may be quoting Blake because he feels a kinship with Blake who was an Other, an outcast like Lestat. Blake's Otherness came from his sensitivity to the spiritual world. When he was four, he screamed because he saw God at his window, and at eight, he saw angels in trees (*Literature*, 618). No doubt he would have accepted Lestat as a vampire without a second thought since his world was already full of visions of angels and demons, and Lestat is a little bit of both. Blake lived in poverty for seventy years, misunderstood as he worked on his poetry, which was always concerned with the human spirit. Lestat is also misunderstood, and he is obsessed with the human spirit and with his own inhuman one. Lestat and Blake are thus analogs, parallels to one another.

But the strongest way that "The Tyger" works as an allusion is in the meaning of the poem. "The Tyger" is part of Blake's anthology of poems, *Songs of Experience* (1794). This book was a companion to his *Songs of Innocence* (1789). Blake's poems in *Songs of Innocence* praised the innocence of newborn things; the openness of a child, he said, was necessary to fully understand the human spirit. In one poem, "The Lamb," he asks, "Little Lamb, who made thee?" and then answers his own question by comparing the lamb to Christ who "became a little child" in order to save humankind (620). We should all become like little children, Blake suggests, so that our eyes will be opened to the miracles of our existence. But Blake felt that innocence was not enough to truly understand the human spirit. For full understanding, innocence had to be combined with experience. And so he wrote *The Songs of Experience* as a companion volume, matching all the poems in the new book to poems in his *Innocence* book. The poem that he matched with "The Lamb" he called "The Tyger."

"The Tyger," like the rest of the poems in *The Songs of Experience*, argues that until we face the realities of our lives, the evil and the danger in them, we cannot truly know ourselves. Just as we have to recognize the Lamb in ourselves, we must also look within and recognize the Tyger. Blake begins his poem by asking the same question of the Tyger that he asked of the Lamb, but he frames the question differently: "What immortal hand or eye/Could frame thy fearful symmetry?" In other words, what creative force could possibly have made something so dangerous? Since this is a question that Lestat has often asked about himself—that is, how could a good God have made anything as evil as vampires?—his quoting of the poem reflects his own questions about his existence. Blake never really answers this question, ending instead with another: "Did he smile his work to see?/Did he who made the lamb make thee?" (623). Since this is the great question of Lestat's life, whether he is part of God's plan and if God is pleased with his creation, Lestat's choice of this poem for his allusion is obvious.

Even so, Lestat does not quote "The Tyger" with these questions in his conscious mind. He quotes it because he has been reading David Talbot's mind, and David has been dreaming about shooting a tiger that is menacing him. This image recalls Blake's poem to Lestat's mind, and he makes the connection between the Tyger and himself, unconsciously seeing himself as an evil animal who will leap for David's throat if he is given the slightest encouragement. When he sees the tiger skin in David's house later, he tells David that he saw him kill it in a dream. David tells him that the dream was true and that he had to shoot a tiger long ago because it was a child killer. This instantly brings to Lestat's mind Claudia, the child he made a vampire, and it cements his connection to the tiger (44). He makes the connection even stronger when he tells David that he had to kill the serial killer he'd taken the night before because the man was his "brother," a "man-eating tiger" (72).

Riddled with guilt about making Claudia a vampire as a child, about his desire to make David a vampire, and about his own vampire nature, Lestat wants to be mortal, to be a Lamb again, to regain the innocence he had before he was made a vampire by force. To regain that innocence, he chooses to make his deal with the Body Thief, but once he is a mortal, he looks inside himself and sees the Tyger that he will always be. Embracing the dark side of himself, he decides to regain his immortal body, choosing to become a vampire once more, a symbol of evil and experience like the Tyger, but this time he will become evil through free will.

Blake's poem has one other aspect that strengthens Lestat's allusion. Although it would seem logical that if the Lamb is good, the Tyger must be bad, Blake describes him as having great beauty and dignity in his evil, beginning his poem "Tyger, Tyger, burning bright/In the forests of the night." Like the Tyger, Lestat burns bright in the wilderness of the nights that he hunts, his eyes glowing with the supernatural incandescence of the Tyger, of whom Blake asks in what skies "burnt the fire of thine eyes?" Lestat can never return to being a Lamb of a mortal again, but by alluding to Blake's great description of the Tyger that he sees within himself, he shows that he is struggling to see himself as part of God's plan, as the Experience that is required by Heaven as much as the Innocence.

THEMATIC ISSUES

Because *The Tale of the Body Thief* is so tightly characterized and plotted, its theme is much easier to analyze than the themes of the three previous Vampire Chronicles. Taking into consideration setting, central question, protagonist's conflict and character growth, motif, beginning and ending, title, and comparative literary works, it becomes clear that *The Body Thief* is about self-discovery and self-knowledge.

The settings provide the first clue. Lestat stalks the streets of the city of Miami looking like a gentleman and killing like a monster, much the same way that Miami looks like a paradise but is also the home of vicious crime. Miami therefore becomes a metaphor for Lestat, for both his bright and dark aspects. Lestat then goes to England, a place of reason and tradition, to meet with the reasonable and traditional David Talbot in order to discuss all the unreasonable things that have happened to him. Later David leaves England (and logic) for South America (and emotion), and once in the south, he responds to the part of himself that he's repressed for years. In all cases, setting shows that these characters have dual personalities that they are refusing to recognize.

Lestat's character also gives clues to the theme. His character drives the central plot question, "Will Lestat get his body back?" Although this question describes the external conflict, it also leads to the question that describes the internal conflict: "Does Lestat want his body back?" If Lestat chooses to take back his vampire body, he will be freely choosing vampirism for the first time in his life, therefore choosing evil and damnation. The obvious choice is to refuse to take back his old body, but through living as a mortal Lestat comes to realize that he is a vampire in his soul, and that he must regain his body or lose his identity. This also reflects his character growth because he has attained enough self-knowledge not only to recognize the evil within himself, but also to embrace it as part of himself. Therefore Lestat's characterization also supports the idea of self-knowledge as theme.

Motif also supports this theme. One motif is the use of gold chains throughout the story. Lestat sees one around David's neck in the dream of the tiger, he sees a real chain with a gold cross around Gretchen's neck when he visits her in the jungle, and finally he is haunted by a chain with a locket containing Claudia's picture. All of these chains are metaphors for emotional chains that bind characters from achieving growth and self-knowledge. David's chain represents his mortal life in which he kills the tiger Lestat to protect himself, even though immortality would give him the time to achieve everything he's ever wanted. Gretchen's chain with the cross represents the blind faith that prevents her from seeing Lestat as he really is and from growing spiritually with that knowledge. And the chain with Claudia's locket represents the guilt that prevents Lestat from accepting himself as he is and living his life to the fullest. All of these chains must be discarded if the character is to achieve self-knowledge. Gretchen protects her chain and goes mad, but David and Lestat escape their chains and achieve freedom through self-knowledge.

The other motif that runs throughout *The Body Thief* is the vision of Claudia that Lestat sees. He is haunted by Claudia because he has betrayed her twice, once when he made her a vampire as a child and forever imprisoned her in a child's body and again when he followed her to Paris and inadvertently caused her execution by sun. The manifestation of Claudia that his mind calls up is really a manifestation of his own guilty conscience, come to make him suffer for what he has done. Lestat tries to escape his guilt by committing suicide by sun only to have the vision appear to him and say "Not yet" (48). You cannot escape guilt by running from it, his conscience seems to be telling him.

You must face it and know it. Over and over again Claudia appears to him, reminding him of his dark side, forcing him to face the thing that he is.

Claudia is so important that Rice put her in the beginning and in the ending of the book, the two strongest places in her narrative. In the beginning, Lestat tells of dreaming of Claudia more and more, the dreams gaining in intensity, as if whatever it is that she has to tell him is growing more important, propelling him into his story. At the end, he holds her locket and recognizes that the Claudia he has been seeing is neither a ghost nor a real memory because the real Claudia had never been a part of his conscience. Instead, she has been a dream, and he recognizes that the visions have been reflections of his own unconscious, of "the greedy wicked being" that formed "the horror at the core" of his identity. The vision Claudia has led him to see the real Lestat.

The title also reinforces this theme of self-knowledge because it refers not only to Raglan James, the Body Thief, but also to all three main characters. Lestat is also a Body Thief because he steals bodies to drink their blood and because he takes the human body James leaves him to try to steal back his innocence. David is a Body Thief because once inside the young body that does not belong to him, he decides to keep it. Their stays in their stolen bodies show both men what they've been ignoring about themselves, their deepest desires and fears. Thus even the body thieving brings self-knowledge.

Taking all of these clues into consideration, it becomes clear that the theme of *The Tale of the Body Thief* must deal with achieving freedom through self-knowledge. This theme is reinforced by another similar work of literature that involves the temptation of a tortured man by an evil being who lures him to give up a part of himself in exchange for knowledge. This work is Goethe's poem *Faust*, and Lestat refers to it several times in the story, thus reinforcing the parallels. Whereas Lestat gives up his immortal body to the Body Thief to taste the pleasures of mortal life once more, Faust, an old scholar, gives up his immortal soul to the Devil to taste the experiences that have passed him by in life.

Rice has made sure the parallels between the two are clear. Faust seduces and impregnates a woman named Gretchen who goes mad and drowns her child. When Faust visits her in prison and offers her escape, she turns from him and puts her trust in God. Lestat sleeps with a mortal woman named Gretchen, and when he goes to help her with her mission work, she goes mad and turns to God, becoming a saint. Faust accepts his desire for human pleasures and experience and continues through his story, trying to be good and to do good, just as Lestat accepts his own desire for his vampire nature but continues through his story, trying to stop the evil James. In their acceptances of their own natures, both Faust and Lestat (and to some extent David Talbot) come to terms with who they are in the world and accept that they can only be as good as their natures will allow. Both are resigned to eternal damnation at the ends of their stories, but Faust's soul is received into heaven by angels who sing, "He who exerts himself in constant striving,/Him we can save" ("Faust," 329). The implication is that Lestat, too, has a chance at salvation as long as he exerts himself and constantly strives to be good, and he will be tested this way in the next book of the Vampire Chronicles, *Memnoch the Devil*.

Like Faust, then, Lestat and David look into their souls and see their deepest desires, freeing themselves by gaining self-knowledge. This theme is evident in the story clues and is reinforced by a psychological analysis of the novel.

A FREUDIAN READING OF *THE TALE OF THE BODY THIEF*

The unconscious plays a greater role in the motivation of character in *The Tale of the Body Thief* than in any other book in the Vampire Chronicles. All of the major characters—Lestat, Raglan James, and David Talbot—are moved to act by desires that they are not aware of, desires from the part of the mind that Sigmund Freud called the unconscious. As Lestat promises at the beginning, *The Tale of the Body Thief* takes the reader into the mind and soul of its characters "for the discoveries" (4). And the discoveries show that in this book, the unconscious is calling the shots.

Lestat's unconscious fuels his actions in two ways, through guilt and through his desire for mortality. His guilt comes to light in his dreams and visions of Claudia, the child he made a vampire in *Interview with the Vampire*. He sees her when he has collapsed, deathly ill, and is terrified of dying. Her memory comes to him then like a ghost, and he asks her if she was afraid when the sunlight came to kill her. He calls out for the other vampires to help him, but only the vision of Claudia remains (209). Rice makes it clear that the vision of Claudia is not really a ghost. Instead, it is a memory that Lestat's unconscious has reconstructed so that he can project his guilt onto it. Claudia has not come back to haunt him with accusations, but his own conscience has.

Lestat deals with the guilt and the visions of Claudia by turning away from and repressing the experience, refusing to admit that the feelings or the visions are important. But as he spends more time as a mortal, he comes to terms with his vampire nature. After all, if he was really conflicted about being a vampire, he wouldn't be moving heaven and earth to get his body back. Only when he has finally accepted himself for what he is, does Claudia and the guilt she represents disappear from his consciousness.

But Lestat has more in his unconscious than guilt feelings about his nature. He also has a deep desire for mortality which is evident in his seeming stupidity in agreeing to Raglan James's body-switching plan. David Talbot warns Lestat not to trust James, and by that time, the reader is positive James is up to no good, too. How can Lestat not see the danger? The answer, of course, is that he can, but he's ignoring it, using denial to repress his unconscious need to be mortal again. When James does indeed take off with Lestat's body, leaving him helpless, sick, and alone, Lestat experiences mortality again in all its beauty and horror. This is what he has missed for two hundred years, and now he finds that having experienced it, he's ready to be immortal and all-powerful again. Too bad his body is gone.

Lestat achieves more than just a visit to mortality by denying the danger and handing over his immortality to James. He also gets the chance to change something that has unconsciously bothered him for the three previous novels, the knowledge that he was made a vampire by force. He mentions this briefly during the earlier books without emphasis, but the fact that he continues to mention it shows that unconsciously it is important to him. For Lestat clearly believes in free will, that we choose our destinies on earth and are not simply pawns in the hands of fate. Over and over again, Lestat chooses his own path and boasts that he does so, yet in the back of his mind is always the knowledge that the greatest adventure of his life was begun by force and not by choice. Having given up his immortality knowing unconsciously that James would never give back his body, Lestat now gets a chance to consciously choose. Will he remain a mortal or actively seek to be a vampire again? And the clear answer for Lestat is that he wants his immortality back. By wresting his body back from James, Lestat makes himself a vampire by free will, finally laying the old problem to rest. Thus in many ways, *The Tale of the Body Thief* is really the tale of Lestat coming to terms with who he is and what he feels about it unconsciously by becoming somebody else for awhile.

Lestat is not the only character whose actions are fueled by his unconscious. Raglan James makes himself vulnerable by choosing to establish himself as a vampire guest on the *Queen Elizabeth 2*, the ship that was the scene of his father's disgrace. James sails on the ship, killing each time it makes port, and this gives Lestat and David Talbot the chance to track him down and take the vampire body from him. Since James is obviously a clever man, only an overwhelming but unconscious need for revenge could make him choose such a stupid plan. Like Lestat, he doesn't know what it is that he wants, but his unconscious does and gets it for him.

Finally, David Talbot also has unconscious needs that are fulfilled through his actions. David is seventy-four and will soon die because his human body is wearing out. Lestat offers him immortality through the Dark Gift, but David refuses, choosing mortality over the evil of vampirism. But as the book progresses, David's choice becomes clearly the choice of his superego, the part of his consciousness formed by religion and upbringing, not of his id or unconscious desires. David's ego or conscious self can recognize some of those unconscious desires, if they are pointed out to him, as when Lestat in his human body tells David that he feels sexual passion for him. David can admit he feels the same for Lestat, but the superego intervenes again, and he refuses to make love.

Clearly, David's superego is standing in the way of what he wants. But the closer he comes to death from old age, the weaker David's superego becomes. There are too many things David has wanted in this life that he's never had a chance to accomplish, or that he has accomplished and is going to miss when he dies. So when he accidentally ends up in the young body that Raglan James had stolen before he took Lestat's, David chooses to hold on to it, to become young again in this new body. That choice betrays his unconscious desire to live forever. And that betrayal leads Lestat to his betrayal: he makes David a vampire by force, the same crime that was done to him two centuries before. Although David leaves him, they meet again, and David tells him what Lestat already knows: "You've given me the gift . . . but you've spared me the mortal defeat. You took the decision from me and gave me what I could not help but want" (433).

Thus *The Tale of the Body Thief* becomes truly the Tale of the Body Thieves, the story of three men who consciously or unconsciously choose the bodies of others to fulfill their own deepest desires. What appears to be an external quest for missing physical selves is really an internal quest to heal the missing parts of their unconscious selves. In doing so, James cannot understand his inner motives and dies because they make him vulnerable, but Lestat and David recognize their unconscious selves— the id part of themselves that Lestat describes as "my greed and my evil and my lusty little heart"—and accept those parts even though they aren't the ideal selves they were hoping for (435). By doing so, both men achieve self-knowledge and are stronger because of their psychological victories.

Memnoch the Devil
(1995)

A year after his adventures as a human being in *The Tale of the Body Thief*, Lestat the vampire is in New York stalking a new victim, Roger, a drug dealer and vicious murderer who is also a great collector of religious art and the father of one of the few truly good humans Lestat has ever encountered, Dora Flynn. Lestat plans to kill Roger but not until Roger has said good-bye to Dora, who is returning to New Orleans where she has her own religious cable TV show. Roger deserves to die, but Lestat has no wish to cause Dora any suffering at all because he has come to love her for her goodness and her belief.

In the back of his mind he has another problem: something's stalking him. He's had the feeling for months, something dark behind him, watching him, waiting for him, something like the Devil. Shrugging off the thought, Lestat kills Roger and then dismembers him, scattering his body parts throughout New York. But when he goes into a bar to rest, Roger sits down beside him, the first of his victims ever to return as a ghost. Roger holds Lestat spellbound as he tells him the story of his life and entrusts his daughter into Lestat's hands. His only regret is that he never found Dora the Veil of Veronica, the woman who wiped Christ's face on the way to the cross and thereby imprinted His picture on the cloth. While Lestat is still dealing with this, Roger fades away into death, and Lestat encounters the next being who wants to tell him a story, his supernatural stalker, Memnoch the Devil, come out of Hell to recruit

Lestat as his prince. Lestat follows Memnoch and learns how the world was created, how Memnoch fell, and what Memnoch wants him to do: help teach the souls in Hell to repent and believe so that they may rise into Heaven. Along the way, Lestat witnesses not only the great suffering inflicted on humanity in the name of Christ, but also Christ's suffering on His way to the cross during which Christ entrusts the Veil of Veronica to him. Once in Hell, Lestat is appalled at the suffering that "teaches" the souls to reach Christ, and he runs from Memnoch, losing his eye in the struggle, finally managing to reach home and Dora with the Veil. Dora takes the veil into the streets and proclaims a miracle, thereby revitalizing Christianity to Lestat's horror, and the last message he receives is a thank-you note from Memnoch. Lestat has done exactly what he wanted, becoming his prince after all, by revitalizing a religion that has caused untold bloodshed throughout history. At the end of the book, a sadder but wiser Lestat says that he has told all that he knows, and so he will now pass from fiction into legend. The Vampire Chronicles are finished.

POINT OF VIEW

Memnoch the Devil is written in Lestat's first-person point of view (using the pronoun "I" and only reporting what Lestat thinks, says, hears, sees, feels, and does as the narrator or storyteller), and the choice is an excellent one. As in *The Tale of the Body Thief*, this story is about Lestat's mental anguish—this time over the meaning of good and evil, God and the Devil, and Lestat's relationship with both—and only by experiencing the story in his mind and his voice can the reader fully appreciate the spiritual struggles that Lestat endures. This is made even clearer when Lestat hands the story over to Memnoch at the midpoint of the book. The book is still firmly in Lestat's point of view because he is listening to Memnoch, but the passion and the life of Lestat's story slow to a crawl while he listens to someone else's story, even though it's the story of the Devil.

One of the reasons Memnoch's story is so much less interesting is that, since it is not in Memnoch's point of view, the reader gets none of Memnoch's emotions and motives. The reader only hears what Lestat hears and sees what Lestat sees. But Rice must keep the point of view with Lestat, not only because it makes for a tighter, more unified narrative, but also because part of the great mystery of the book is Memnoch's motives for calling on Lestat, a vampire who has killed thousands, to be part of his plan for redemption from hell. If Rice moves to Memnoch's point of view, she'll have to tell what he's thinking, and that will give away the mystery. Therefore the narrative stays firmly in Lestat's first-person point of view, and as long as Lestat is acting and not listening, it is as fascinating and colorful as Lestat himself. Rice's masterful control of point of view once again helps ensure that her novel is tightly written and engrossing.

CHARACTER DEVELOPMENT

There are really two casts of characters in *Memnoch the Devil*, one worldly and one spiritual. The worldly cast includes Lestat, center stage as usual; David, his fledgling vampire companion from *Body Thief*; Roger, Lestat's latest victim; Dora, Roger's evangelist daughter; and several vampires from Lestat's past including Louis, Armand, Mael, and Maharet. The spiritual cast is Memnoch the Devil and God. Once again Lestat is the protagonist, or central character, independent but always seeking knowledge and connection, and this time his goal is to discover the secret of the universe while staying out of Hell so he can return free to earth to take care of Dora. His antagonist is the Devil himself, equally determined to make Lestat a prince to his king in Hell, driven by his need, which he tells Lestat is to stop human suffering and prove God wrong. The central question is, "Will Lestat beat the Devil?" and Lestat's identity, or concept of himself, as a good vampire is at stake.

Therefore, Lestat's character, introduced in *Interview with the Vampire*, explained in *The Vampire Lestat*, made godlike in *The Queen of the Damned*, and returned to his sense of humanity in *The Tale of the Body Thief*, becomes a dynamic character because he is tested in the fire of faith. In every book in the Chronicles, Lestat has pondered the nature of God and evil, boasting that he's not afraid of Hell, wondering what the hell Hell is anyway. At the beginning of *Memnoch*, he is the typical confident Lestat of the previous books, stalking his victim, exulting in his power, loving his companions, and planning to live forever. He even tries to shrug off the feelings he has of being stalked. After all, he is the Vampire Lestat.

But his concept of who the Vampire Lestat is soon comes under pressure. First, he kills Roger only to meet him again as a ghost and grow to like him. When Roger dies again in front of his eyes by fading into Hell, Lestat is appalled. When he meets and falls in love with Roger's daughter, Dora, he is even more appalled. Both of these events attack Lestat's sense of identity; that is, they make him begin to doubt himself as all-powerful by making him vulnerable because now he cares. Into this vulnerability comes the next impact on Lestat's sense of identity, his antagonist, the Devil named Memnoch. Memnoch lectures to Lestat on the great problem of the universe, telling him that there is suffering in the world and God doesn't care. While he tries to convince Lestat to come to him and help him save the souls in Hell, Lestat's ideas of who he is and what the world is and—most important of all—what good and evil are attacked and challenged until Lestat is on his knees, battered by emotion and horror. Lestat's character emerges from the fire of experience greatly changed as he swears he will never kill again because now he knows the extent of the evil he has done. But he is still Lestat, so he shoves the Devil away and bounds out of Hell, losing an eye in the process but regaining his concept of self as a renegade prince. He may be a vampire, but he's not going to help the Devil.

The final blow to his character comes when Memnoch lets him know that everything that happened was part of his plan for revitalizing a religion that has caused suffering and bloodshed for centuries. Lestat's rebellion was actually Lestat's obedience, and he has become the Devil's right-hand man simply by being Lestat. This drives Lestat into madness because it is at odds with everything he has ever known about himself. From the beginning of his life, all Lestat has ever wanted was to be good. Confronted with incontrovertible evidence that he has helped the Devil achieve his ends, Lestat must go mad with rage and guilt because he has lost his idea of who he is. When he screams that if he was tricked, it must have been by God, never by the Devil, he is screaming that he's willing to be God's dupe in the pursuit of good, but never the minion of evil.

Comforted by David, brought to peace by Louis, Lestat recovers but he is not the same. The sense of his own humanity that he gained in *The Queen of the Damned* and *The Tale of the Body Thief* is now merged with a sense of fallibility and humility. He has testified to others of the great plan of the universe, but he can never be sure it wasn't just a show put on by the Devil to convince him to fall. Now he wants to go in peace, no longer the great antihero who boasts of his adventures but the sadder but wiser hero who has survived the Great Adventure and, having reported back, is now done with his tale. In a brilliant combination of character development and story structure, Rice has made the conclusion of this novel (which becomes the conclusion for the entire series) part of

Lestat's final character development. Since Lestat's dynamic character has reached final knowledge and closure, so has his tale.

Unlike Lestat, the other worldly characters are static characters, arranged around Lestat to comfort, serve, and challenge him, but not to grow themselves. Roger comes into the story as a man driven to protect his daughter and to collect religious artifacts, trying to find a pattern in the world while he destroys those around him. Both Lestat and Roger are murderers, and they're both obsessed with the idea of good and evil in the universe, but Roger has one thing that Lestat doesn't, a human connection, his daughter, Dora. Although it seems that Roger's character is transformed by his stay in Hell, Lestat makes it clear that Roger is still Roger when he says that Roger will go to heaven because he's clever and has figured out how to get there (330).

Dora, Roger's daughter, is also static. Her character is infused with her faith, but it's a blind faith. She truly believes in God and therefore admits no disbelief to her life, although she can curse God when her father dies and wonder why He permits suffering in the world. She asks God for an angel, a vision that will bring the cold world back to belief, and when Lestat brings her the Veil of Veronica from Hell, she takes it as a sign. Lestat warns her that it may all be a setup planned by the Devil, but Dora doesn't want to hear. Now jubilant, she takes the veil to the people in the streets and then into the church, achieving the goal that she has sought from the beginning, the revival of faith in Christ and His suffering.

The others in the worldly cast—David, Louis, Armand, Mael, Maharet—are also static characters, exactly the same people they have been since they were introduced into the Chronicles. They serve a purpose in Lestat's world, but they are backdrop characters only, and therefore Rice does not develop them so that they will not distract the reader from Lestat's character growth. But when she gets to the spiritual world and Lestat's antagonists, she can't rely on static characters. If a character is going to oppose Lestat, he's going to have to be dynamic to hold his own. And in making her spiritual characters dynamic, Rice has a big problem on her hands. It's not a new one—Milton encountered it in his epic about the fall of man in the Garden of Eden, *Paradise Lost*—but it's a big one. The fact is, writing the character of the Devil is easy. He's conflicted, torn from his home, filled with raging emotion, and full of purpose. But writing God. . . .

The big problem with writing God is that He's God. He sees all, knows all, plans all, controls all. Nothing can stop Him, nothing can damage

Him, nothing can *change* Him, so He's always a static character. The creators of Superman finally invented Kryptonite because they realized what every writer of fiction knows: if your character isn't capable of being in trouble, you don't have a story. There's not a lot Rice can do with God as a character, so she keeps Him offstage for most of the story, showing Him mostly through Memnoch's eyes. This turns out to be a brilliant move because Memnoch does not see God as perfect; he sees Him as flawed for ignoring human suffering. Therefore, Memnoch's God *is* an interesting character, and by the time Lestat meets God in the flesh as Christ, he is seeing Him through the eyes of Memnoch, and therefore is also seeing Him as someone who is potentially flawed and not to be trusted. This suspicion of weakness makes the conflict between Memnoch and God possible and solves Milton's problem. If God the all-powerful is in a struggle with the Devil, always bet on God. But if it's possible God is flawed, then the odds become more even. And with a Devil like Memnoch, the odds are very even.

Rice's Memnoch is a beautifully developed and therefore dynamic character. As he enters the story, he's the Lestat of Heaven, questioning, impudent, blazingly intelligent, and passionately concerned with life and goodness. But long ago, he tells Lestat, he was an innocent, existing on a spiritual plane only. When God made matter for the first time, he watched with the rest of the angels as the evolution of life occurred, fascinated until he realized that some of the creation was dying. When he realized that it was *all* going to die, he questioned God, and when he realized that there was not only death but also suffering, he threw a celestial fit. Striving for a way to make God see that suffering is unnecessary and wrong, he went to earth to live as a man, impregnating human women and earning the anger of God who told him that if he loved humans so much he could stay with them. When Memnoch protested that he was only trying to find a way to convince Him that the souls of humans should go to Heaven, too, God issued a challenge. If Memnoch went into Hell and found ten souls worthy of Heaven, He would admit them and Memnoch back into His graces. Memnoch immediately took the challenge. He had to. After all, he was the Angel Memnoch.

Memnoch is indeed Lestat all over again. He rebels against authority, breaks rules, lets his physical desires overrule his logic, throws temper tantrums, and cares passionately about human beings. One of the reasons why Lestat loves him so much is that he sees himself in Memnoch, even though Memnoch is the Devil. But what Lestat sees is actually more Fallen Angel than Devil, and that also coincides with how Lestat sees himself. When God finally erupts and throws Memnoch permanently from Heaven, sentenced to spend part of the year on earth and part in Hell, Memnoch's reaction is the same as Satan's in Milton's *Paradise Lost*, and the same that Lestat's reaction would be: All right then, I'll go to Hell. But I'll make it mine.

Memnoch's plan is to use Hell as a sort of finishing school for the soul, teaching the lost what they need to become the saved, and he wants to hire Lestat as part of the Faculty of the Damned. By the time he makes his offer, he's gotten Hell in order, and his character has evolved completely from innocent spirit through rebellious angel into God's Adversary, the ultimate antagonist. Although Memnoch's goal, as he tells it, is first, last, and always to get human souls into Heaven past his uncaring God, he now swears he will get more people into Heaven through the Gates of Hell than God will through religious belief on earth. He's going to be a better savior than the Savior. And to do this, he tells Lestat, he needs help. Only Lestat just isn't sure if it's a good idea to sympathize with the Devil.

Once again, Rice has developed her characters so carefully that the actions of the plot are inherent in the characters' psychology. For if the reader (and Lestat) were not dazzled by the sights and sounds that Memnoch shows them, it would be obvious that the Devil needs no help, and that he must know that unpredictable, rebellious Lestat would be terrible as the Guidance Counselor from Hell. Therefore, any reader who pays attention must know that Memnoch has a different plan, which is why when it turns out that he does have a different plan, the reader has no sense of being cheated. This brilliant use of characterization shows how strong the truly character-driven plot is. Because of who Lestat is and because of who Memnoch is, their struggle can only play out one way, but because their characters are so fully developed and because those characters continue to develop while the plot plays out, the reader doesn't see the logical end coming. Therefore at the end, the reader cries out with Lestat, "It can't be!" only to reflect on Memnoch and realize, "It must be."

PLOT DEVELOPMENT AND STRUCTURE

The logical plot events dictated by the characters of the protagonist Lestat and the antagonist Memnoch are reinforced by Rice's tight plot structure. This is fortunate because Rice has a built-in weakness in her narrative. She wants Lestat and Memnoch to discuss creation and the problem of human suffering, but they must hold that discussion in the abstract, that is, without ever making it the story of one particular character or characters. And abstract discussions are death to rapid plot movement. The first half of *Memnoch the Devil* moves so rapidly and wonderfully that it seems to crash into a roadblock when it stops for Memnoch to tell Lestat things. The pace picks up again when Memnoch takes Lestat traveling, but not until Lestat gets into Hell and breaks free of Memnoch does the story also break free.

Rice begins her exposition or setup with Lestat in New York, meeting his friend David in a bar and telling him about his latest victim and his feelings that he's being stalked. This sets up the information that the reader needs to understand the story: Lestat is a vampire, David is his friend, Roger is a drug dealer who collects religious artifacts, Dora is his evangelist daughter and a true believer, and something is out to get Lestat. Then Lestat kills Roger and sets the plot in motion.

In the rising action, Roger's ghost talks to Lestat and makes him regret the murder and wonder about the afterlife. Lestat plans to go to comfort Dora, but he's waylaid by Memnoch the Devil. Being Lestat, he tells Memnoch he'll have to wait because he has things to do. When he meets Dora, he loves her for her innocence, her bravery, and her faith, and having seen her safely stowed away in an apartment in New York, he leaves to keep his date with the Devil.

The point of no return is therefore halfway through the novel when Lestat calls to Memnoch to take him to see Heaven and Hell. Once Lestat begins that journey, he is never again the same. Unfortunately, the beginning of that journey is Memnoch talking and Lestat listening to a very long recounting of the beginning of the universe. Since nothing hangs on this story—that is, since Lestat is not in jeopardy or even actively participating in the conversation—the plot bogs down here, only to pick up speed again when Memnoch takes Lestat on a spiritual tour that includes the birth of humankind, Heaven, Christ on the way to the crucifixion, and finally Hell, which is horrible enough to send Lestat screaming for the gates even while Memnoch claws out his eye in an attempt to capture him. The climax comes not when Lestat escapes from Hell although it's an exciting scene, but when Lestat recognizes that all that he's done has been part of Memnoch's plan, even his rejection of Hell and all it stands for. The resolution of the story is Lestat working through his mad rage to come to a new stability, sadder and infinitely wiser. Rice's plot is tightly structured and completely character-driven, which makes the ending not only satisfactory but also inevitable. And this tight-ness and clarity helps keep afloat a story that is heavy with theme, meta-phor, and mythic significance. Lestat moves the story with his actions, but Rice grounds the story with her questions about belief and meaning.

LITERARY DEVICE: METAPHOR

One of Rice's most common metaphors is blood. In any vampire story, blood is going to have meaning, but in *Memnoch the Devil*, blood takes on different meanings in different contexts, finally all combining into one great metaphor, the idea that blood represents life.

The first blood metaphor is the blood that Lestat spills as a vampire. As he drinks from the neck of his victims, he takes not only their blood but their lives, both physically as they die and emotionally as their mem-ories are sucked into his mind as the blood is sucked into his mouth. When he kills Roger, he not only takes his blood, but he takes all the memories that gave Roger's life meaning, including his love for his daughter, Dora. And when he sucks in the memory of Dora, he also sucks in Roger's love for her, taking that part of Roger's life into his own. Thus the blood that Lestat takes represents more than just physical death; it also represents the taking away of the memories of life.

The next blood is an even more crucial metaphor for life. In past sto-ries, Lestat has made himself almost invincible by taking the blood of the most powerful vampires, thereby taking their wisdom and power into himself. But in *Memnoch the Devil*, he takes the most powerful blood in Christian lore when he accepts Christ's invitation to drink from Him on His way to the cross. This blood has been the universal Christian symbol for the gift of eternal life for centuries. What Christ offers Lestat is a literal sacrament, not the wine and wafers of communion but the true body and blood of Christ. Christ's offering of Himself is His invi-tation to Lestat to choose life and God, not damnation and Memnoch.

But Christ's blood, the symbol of eternal life bought with sacrifice and suffering, can't shield Lestat from the horrors of Hell, a place full of sacrifice and suffering. When he escapes, he runs to Dora and to the last of the blood metaphors that Rice uses, menstrual blood. Long a taboo in most societies, menstrual blood is actually the most innocent and life-affirming of all blood, a sign that a woman is fertile and that life is ever possible. If any blood represents physical life, it's menstrual blood. Lestat acknowledges this when he drinks from Dora, knowing that the blood he is taking is a natural gift of life, involving no pain and no sacrifice.

Thus Lestat's taking of blood represents not only the taking in of life, but also a progression in Lestat's understanding of life. Roger's blood gives him an understanding of human life and possessive love; Christ's blood gives him an understanding of eternal life and sacrifice and pain in the name of unselfish love; and Dora's blood gives him an understanding of the first things of life, of innocence and redemption without sacrifice and pain. When Lestat runs from Hell to Dora's blood of life, he runs from suffering to rebirth and freedom, vowing never again to take blood or life from any living thing. Thus Rice's metaphor shows Lestat's rebirth as a good being, the good vampire he has always wanted to be.

THEMATIC ISSUES

Theme is much easier to sort out in *Memnoch the Devil* than it has been in any of Rice's previous books. When the setting is earth, Heaven, and Hell, the central plot question is, "Will Lestat succeed in outsmarting the Devil?," the protagonist's internal conflict is whether or not he should trust the Devil, and his character growth comes about through a study of the origins of the world and the idea of evil, it's fairly clear that the theme is going to deal with God's plan for the world and how evil works within it. That the evil aspect will be more important is indicated by the title which is not *Lestat Goes to See God*, but *Memnoch the Devil*. And since the beginning of the book shows Lestat walking toward a victim and the ending of the book shows Lestat walking away from all victims forever and choosing never to kill again, the theme certainly will have something to do with the idea of free will—that is, that we are not destined to be evil, even if we are vampires. We always have a choice.

All of this is also reflected in a similar work of literature that involves a protagonist who is taken on a tour of the creation. In Milton's *Paradise Lost*, Adam is shown the creation and the fall of Lucifer in order that, as Milton puts it, the author might "justify the ways of God to man." In Anne Rice's *Memnoch the Devil*, Lestat is told of the creation and fall so that the Devil can justify the ways of the Devil to Lestat. In both books, the character of the Devil is far more interesting than the character of God, and in both books the Devil argues passionately that the reason he rebelled was that God was a tyrant, failing His subjects. In *Paradise Lost*, those subjects are the angels; in *Memnoch*, they're the humans on earth and the souls in Hell. In *Paradise Lost*, an angel tells Adam that his fall, caused by eating from the fruit of the tree of knowledge of good and evil, was a fortunate fall, a good thing because it led to God's Son volunteering to go to earth and die so that all souls might be saved if they believed in Him and His suffering. In *Memnoch the Devil*, Memnoch argues against this notion, saying that suffering is unnecessary and that God has based his plan for human salvation on a myth that has ensured human suffering for ages before Christ's death and certainly will do so in the ages after. Since both books are concerned with the effect of temptation by the Devil on an inhabitant of earth, the Devil's arguments in both become central to the story and theme. And in both cases, the arguments support a central question in human philosophy which is, Why do bad things happen to good people? Why is there suffering in the world at all?

It's in answering this question that the two books differ significantly, which gives another clue to theme. At the end of *Paradise Lost*, Adam and Eve leave the garden of Eden, sad to be going but full of hope and faith in God's plan because they now know that suffering brings them closer to Christ and salvation. At the end of *Memnoch*, Lestat leaves behind his audience (since this is the last vampire book) and his concept of earth as a Savage Garden, a place where evil triumphs in the survival of the fittest, to choose a life without killing, even though he has little faith in God's plan since he's still not sure it isn't Memnoch's plan. After all, who can trust what the Devil says?

Therefore, if Milton is arguing that everything that happens is part of God's plan for salvation, Rice seems to be arguing that everything that happens may also be part of the Devil's plan to win his cosmic battle with God, and that we will never know for sure. In the end, the only comfort Lestat can take is that when it came to the moment of decision in Hell, he chose to escape and return to humanity. When he is faced with the possibility that that choice may have been exactly what the Devil had planned on, he still chooses to be good because it is the only choice he has. That Lestat walks away a sadder but better vampire, now deliberately choosing not to be evil, may mean that the theme is that, although we cannot know God's plan or the Devil's, we can choose to rise above our natures and be good, even if we are being good in the midst of madness and evil.

A MYTHOLOGICAL READING OF *MEMNOCH THE DEVIL*

Some books draw on archetypes, characters or ideas that are often found in mythology. Anne Rice drew on one very strong archetype in *Memnoch the Devil* when she has the Devil argue that God has made a mistake because he has chosen as his path to redemption an ancient idea that has caused suffering for centuries, the Dying God myth. This Dying God story is found in cultures throughout the world where it forms part of the myth of the Vegetation God, the god that dies so that all things might grow.

The Dying God or Vegetation God is almost always the partner of another archetype, the Great Mother. Their union makes the world fertile (makes vegetation grow), but since all land must lie fallow for a season to recover, the god is often accidentally killed or murdered in the myth. Then the Great Mother weeps, refusing to fertilize the earth. In this period of time after the harvest, the earth rests, and then in the spring the Vegetation God returns from the dead, welcomed by the Great Mother, and their reunion once more makes the world fertile.

Memnoch bases his accusations that God has chosen his myth badly on the fact that the death of the Vegetation God has always caused suffering in the world because it was usually celebrated with human sacrifice. As Joseph Campbell has reported, cultures that worship the Vegetation God often sacrificed the king or the king's representative in brutal rituals that sometimes included companions for the king. Some of these sacrifices therefore took hundreds of lives (164). Excavations of sites in Denmark, for example, have uncovered bodies with the marks of ropes around their necks and spear wounds in their sides that mimic the death of Odin, the God of the Tree, who gave up an eye and hung for nine days and nine nights in order to learn the mystery of the runes so that he could pass the power on to his people. And in one royal tomb in the Middle East, the bodies of dozens of women were found buried with the king (409). Clearly, the rituals associated with the Dying God have led to many more deaths than just the god's. And this, Memnoch tells God, *this* is the myth you've chosen to start your new religion. Bad choice.

But Memnoch's argument goes beyond the suffering that religion imposed through sacrifice. He also points out to Lestat the great massacres perpetrated in the name of God's version of the Dying God myth, Christ's crucifixion. He shows Lestat the butchery of the Crusades and then offers to show him the Inquisition, the Protestant massacres in France, the burning of witches, the martyrdom of the Anabaptists, Queen Mary's burning of those who embraced the Church of England, the slaughter of the Jews, and the modern atrocities committed in the name of religion in Bosnia, Herzegovina, and Iraq. This suffering is all done by the People of the Book, he tells Lestat. They're all arguing over the meaning of the Christ's Dying God sacrifice and making more sacrifice as they argue. That's too much suffering, the Devil says, especially since it's all unnecessary because the whole thing is just a mythological symbol anyway.

The importance of the myth of the Vegetation God in Rice's book goes beyond the literal suffering, however. The myth also has impact on her theme in the meaning of the sacrifice. The ancients believed that the suffering of the sacrifice was important for the health of the country because the king represented the country, and therefore the stronger he was and the longer he took to die, the stronger the country was. Also, the more blood that poured into the ground from the king and those sacrificed with him (or the more life force poured into the community from the dying), the more fertile the land would become. Therefore, the depth of the suffering becomes as important as the sacrifice itself. In the same way, Memnoch tells Lestat, God has justified the suffering of humanity. According to God, the more they suffer, the closer they will come to Christ. Suffering, in fact, brings people to God; therefore, according to God, it is good and necessary. But Memnoch disagrees, and what he tempts Lestat with is not gold or power or eternal life, but the chance to do good. He tempts him by asking him to end suffering, which he tells Lestat is evil even though God says it's part of his plan.

This is a tremendous temptation for Lestat for two reasons. First, Lestat above all wants to be good. Even though he knows he's damned for killing in order to drink blood that keeps him alive, he continually tries to work out a morality for himself, taking only criminals as his victims, refusing to harm the innocent. What Memnoch offers him, therefore, seems to be a way of expiating his sins—that is, a way to make up for all the things he's done to survive. Surely if he can help end suffering, it will in some way compensate for the suffering he's inflicted on others. For Lestat, a way out of his guilt is worth infinitely more than power or money.

The other reason why Lestat is tempted by the chance to reduce human suffering and save others is that he, in his own way, identifies strongly with the Dying God who suffers and dies to save others. In *The*

Vampire Lestat, he links himself with Dionysus, a Greek Vegetation God who is pulled apart by his followers and whose blood then fertilizes the earth. Rice says that she did not realize that vampires were closely connected to the Vegetation God myth until she began looking for mythological connections while she was researching *Lestat*. When she found the legend of Osiris and his coffin and the legend of Dionysus, she knew that she had found the key to the mythology of the vampires (Ramsland, *Vampire Companion*, 502). She also makes it clear in the section on Marius in *The Vampire Lestat* that the Celtic Vegetation Gods were, in fact, vampires, and she has Marius tell Lestat that. Having consciously identified himself with savior gods who sacrifice themselves, Lestat's temptation to sacrifice himself and go to Hell to serve the Devil is overwhelming.

But he doesn't. In the end, he rejects the myth, which is ironically what the Devil has been asking him to do. The Devil has asked him to reject Christ as the Dying God; Lestat instead rejects himself as the Dying God, refusing to sacrifice himself to help the Devil. In so doing, however, he acts out an old Dying God ritual, the suffering of Odin, when he loses an eye as he gains something that he thinks will help a human, saving an important religious relic, the Veil of Veronica, for Dora, an evangelist who is looking for a sign from God. Seemingly, Lestat has once again finessed fate, saving humanity without sacrificing himself. But when Lestat returns to earth and gives Dora the Veil, she uses it to spark a revival of the Christian religion which the Devil has shown Lestat to be the cause of great suffering throughout history. Lestat's uneasiness over this is reinforced when he gets a thank-you note from the Devil with his eye enclosed, telling him that his rejection was all part of the Devil's plan.

The obvious implication of all this is that if Lestat had chosen to sacrifice himself as the Devil asked, he might have defeated him. Instead, by rejecting the Devil, Lestat accidentally causes a strengthening of the Christian religion, thereby ensuring that the atrocities committed in its name will continue. And the return of his eye reinforces the idea that he didn't make a sacrifice after all; he has failed as a Vegetation God. When he ends his story with "This is what I saw. This is what I heard. This is what I know. This is *all* that I know," he seems to be saying that finally he has accepted that the ways of God and the Devil are unknowable and that not even myth can explain them.

THE MUMMY

The Mummy or Ramses the Damned
(1989)

Anne Rice has always been candid about her love for horror movies, especially mummy movies. One of the dedications for *The Mummy* is to her father, "who came more than once to get me from the neighborhood show, when 'the mummy' had scared me so badly that I couldn't even stay in the lobby with the creepy music coming through the doors." In 1988, she wrote a screenplay for her own mummy movie only to find that Hollywood wanted to mangle her story. She refused the revisions and instead turned the screenplay into an action-adventure book that pays homage to all the clichés of the mummy movies and then adds twists and turns that make it a Rice original.

The Mummy begins in Egypt when an archaeologist opens the tomb of Ramses the Damned and awakens him from his immortal sleep by accident. While Ramses is stirring, the archaeologist's villainous nephew, Henry, comes in and poisons the archaeologist. Ramses is shipped back to England as part of the archaeologist's great find and awakens in time to prevent the archaeologist's daughter, Julie, from also being murdered by Henry. Julie falls in love with Ramses and follows him throughout London as he learns the modern world. Then she takes him to Cairo, along with her ex-fiancé and his father and the archaeologist's assistant and the ever-present Henry. Once back in his native land, Ramses makes the mistake of using the elixir of immortality to rejuvenate the mummy of his long dead lover, Cleopatra, creating a mindless monster that begins to break necks all over Cairo. This act changes the lives of all the characters. By the end of *The Mummy* which features the fiery death of the now fully human Cleopatra, all the characters have been transformed and are reestablishing their lives, sadder but wiser people, unaware that Cleopatra has resurrected herself and is coming after them.

POINT OF VIEW

For *The Mummy*, Rice chose the third-person point of view, but she also chose to use more than one narrator. Rice's use of multiple points of view was dictated by the fact that the book originated as a screenplay. Most films have multiple viewpoints as scenes shift from character to character to round out the plot. In the same way, Rice quick-cuts from character to character in short punchy scenes, all of which are told in third-person limited narration. These multiple viewpoints could be confusing, but Rice keeps them tied to only two settings in a chronological plot (one in which all the events logically follow one another in time). Therefore, all the reader has to keep in mind is who all the voices are, not where the scene is taking place or what year it is or whether or not the story is in flashback. And since Rice has introduced all the characters as types the reader will easily recognize, all the reader has to do is identify Ramses as the Hero, Julie as the Girl, Henry as the Villain, and so on, to keep the characters straight. This clear plot structure and carefully controlled use of point of view make *The Mummy* one of the easiest of all of her books to read.

CHARACTER DEVELOPMENT

All of the characterizations at the beginning of *The Mummy* are static; this is a major shift since Rice's books always begin with at least one carefully drawn, continually developing character. This shift may have been due in part to the book's origins as a screenplay, an homage to the mummy movies Rice loved as a child. But it may also be that, once Rice entered into the classic mummy plot, her own personality and talent demanded that she stretch the genre, so that she shifted everything again halfway through, making most of the characters dynamic to challenge people's perceptions and expectations.

In the beginning, the main characters of *The Mummy* are not only static or unchanging, but they're also stereotypes, characters that show up so often in literature, or in this case horror films, that their physical characteristics and their actions immediately tell the reader or viewer what role they play and what the outcome of their plot will be. Essentially, the protagonist or central character of *The Mummy* is the Hero whose goal is to defeat the Villain and marry the Girl. The central question is, "Will the Hero succeed in stopping the Villain?" And he must because if he doesn't he will have lost his identity as the Hero since the Hero always wins.

Ramses the Damned is the Hero. The Hero is tall, dark, handsome, strong, young, honest, sexy, intelligent, blue-eyed, and gentlemanly. The only part of the stereotype that Ramses doesn't fit is "young" since he's three thousand years old. On the other hand, he's immortal, so he's always going to look like he's in his thirties, which is the perfect Hero age, old enough to be experienced, young enough to get the Girl. Ramses is not only supernatural, but he's super at adapting. After one day in the world of the early twentieth century, he has studied language, dancing, the Industrial Revolution, and Marx, visited a museum to see the coffins of his friends, foiled a murder attempt by the Villain, and kissed Julie more than once. His part in the plot is to defeat the Villain and get the Girl.

Julie is the Girl. The Girl is beautiful but not vain, intelligent but not obnoxious about it, passionate but pure, loyal to a fault, and nice. Julie is so nice she even gives the Villain, Henry, money after she knows he killed her father rather than make a scene and hurt her Uncle Randolph, Henry's father. Her part in the plot is to tell the Hero to be careful, help him defeat the Villain, and then marry him.

Henry is the Villain. The Villain drinks too much, gambles and loses, embezzles, forges, lies, cheats, murders, and generally demonstrates himself to be a menace to society. Henry, for example, kills his uncle, stabs his loan shark, and tries to poison Julie. He's also nasty to his mistress, Daisy, and he thinks the world owes him a living. His part in the plot is to lose and die.

Daisy is the Dumb Blonde, also known as the Floozy. The Dumb Blonde is cheap, selfish, and stupid, but she does have big breasts and blonde hair. Daisy is all of these things, plus she has a brother who can get Henry a gun. Her part is to make the Villain look even more disgusting.

Julie's father, Lawrence Stratford, is the Absent-Minded Professor. The Absent-Minded Professor is old and distinguished, and his life is his research. In Lawrence's case, he's an absent-minded archaeologist who opens Ramses' tomb. His part is to unearth something inexplicable and then get killed by the Villain.

Samir is the Noble Native Assistant. The Noble Native Assistant is intelligent, hard-working, cautious, loyal, and courageous, but he is always seen as not only the Other but also as less sophisticated. In the case of Samir, this is pretty ridiculous since he's an adult expert on Egyptology, but even so, Ramses the Great, the Father of All, calls him his child (144). Samir's part is to stand one step to the right and one step behind the Hero, giving him respectful assistance in defeating the Villain.

Alex is the Nice Guy Who Isn't Going to Get the Girl. The Nice Guy is tall, thin, sweet, loving, limited, and nice. Alex has been waiting for months to marry Julie, but she keeps putting him off. He's understanding about it. His part is to not get the Girl.

Cleopatra is the Monster. The Monster is horrible, disgusting, grotesque, and mindless, a thing that kills because killing is its nature. Cleopatra is simply a thing when Ramses pours the elixir over her, a moth-eaten mummy missing several vital chunks of flesh including her eyelids and part of her mouth. Her part is to scare the daylights out of everyone in the story, and she does a very nice job in the beginning, shambling down the corridor of the museum, mindless and disintegrating, mumbling Ramses' name.

The surprise in the early characterization comes in two of the minor characters, the older generation of Lawrence's weak brother, Randolph, whose love for his son Henry has led him to cover up his crimes and to embezzle from his niece himself; and Elliott, Alex's father, who was once Lawrence's lover and then later, Henry's lover. Randolph and Elliott are not stereotypes. If they were, they'd be fuddy duddy uncles or saintly advisers. Instead, they have their own tortured souls and emerge as individuals. Randolph's anguish over his son and Elliott's unhappy resignation both motivate their actions and raise them far above the level of the stereotypes. Elliott continues to grow throughout the novel, sleeping with Cleopatra, sinking to blackmail to try to get the elixir from Ramses, bluffing the government to get them all released, and finally making the choice for immortality, not grabbing at it as soon as it is offered, but taking it only when confronted with the evidence of corrupting death when he sees Henry's mummy.

The rest of the characters all fit the stereotypes of the horror movie genre until Rice reaches the halfway point in her script. At that point,

Ramses does something very Hero-like and incredibly stupid, and everyone is thrown into rapid character development. For the rest of the novel, most of Rice's characters become dynamic, changing because of the impact of events on their lives.

On arriving in Cairo, Ramses goes to the museum and sees the rotted mummy of his great love Cleopatra. On impulse, he pours the immortality elixir over her, bringing her mummy back to life with bones showing and only half a mouth, a horrible shambling thing that reaches for him, crying his name. Ramses immediately realizes his mistake, but it's too late. He's thrown away a life in the future with Julie because of an impulse to reach back to his past. For the rest of the story, Ramses, once the blue-eyed Hero, is now truly Ramses the Damned as he tries to undo the damage by killing Cleopatra, the woman he once loved. Torn between responsibility to two women, beset by those who want the elixir of immortality, and trying to resolve his own feeling about immortality, Ramses suffers throughout until he returns at the end as the Hero to rescue the Girl who has now grown into a woman. Although Ramses remains the hero type throughout, his mistakes and his efforts to correct them make him a dynamic character.

Julie changes, too, sparked by the fact that her Hero has just resurrected a Thing from the dead because he loved It. In true Girl fashion, she vows to remain at his side no matter what, but when Cleopatra corners her in a restroom and tries to kill her, her resolve is shaken. After the climax of the story, she rejects Ramses and his offer of immortality as immoral, which is the right move for a good Girl. Then she sails for London, only to despair on the trip home. Having tasted the ultimate life with Ramses the Hero, she sees only the grayness of everyday life ahead of her. Rejecting her role as the good Girl, she throws herself overboard but is caught at the last moment by Ramses who tells her she must choose life over death. Then he makes love to her. The next morning she drinks the elixir, having moved beyond the rules of morality and being good to choose life forever with her lover.

Henry, on the other hand, is static, not changing except by deteriorating. Never much of a man to begin with, he loses his nerve and disintegrates into a mass of temper, greed, and fear. He dies as violently as he lived, shooting at the second mummy who has come to kill him. This one succeeds. Henry's character change is not really growth; it's static decay. So in essence, he remains the Villain until a better Villain shows up and makes him unnecessary. Daisy turns out to have been a flat character for a reason. She's served her purpose in the story, and she's never heard from again. Samir also does not grow but remains the loyal servant.

But Alex, the Nice Guy, certainly nothing much at the beginning of the story, a shoo-in to win the prize for Character Least Likely to Change, does grows through adversity. He first loses Julie to Ramses without much protest and then begins a flirtation with an American heiress only to lose her when Ramses casts everyone into disgrace by reanimating Cleopatra and causing a scandal at the museum. Once more resigned to his fate, trying to protect Julie in a brotherly manner, Alex moves through the story as everyone's strong right arm, a support to all, his personality only slightly darkened. Then he meets Cleopatra. Enslaved by her sexuality and her beauty, he gives himself up to her completely, and she in turn takes him as a consort. The effect of their coupling, both physical and emotional, gives new weight to his life. He tells Julie later that it was like discovering that what he had thought was hot water all his life was only lukewarm after all. When he loses Cleopatra, he loses his innocence completely, becoming cynical and bitter but also becoming a man, fully aware of life for the first time.

Finally, Cleopatra grows and matures from a wounded monster to a fully functioning human being, capable of loving Alex and developing a morality that prevents her from killing Julie for revenge. But just as she achieves full consciousness, Ramses comes to destroy her, and when she rises again at the end of the novel, she has full reason to be vindictive as she sets out to find the others once again.

Many of these characters are motivated by their own acceptance of their stereotypic identities. Ramses does the incredibly stupid act of raising Cleopatra from the dead because he sees himself as a Hero, and he must save her as he couldn't two thousand years before. It's an instinctive act based on his concept of who he is. Julie must remain true to Ramses no matter what because she sees herself as a Faithful Girl. If she questions him, she's not being loyal. Only when she finally turns from him can she discover what she wants instead of what she should want, and in the depths of her despair, she grows. Alex remains the true-blue nice guy because that's the only way he knows himself to be. Only great loss can make him cynical by destroying everything he believes in. And Cleopatra begins by acting on her most surface memories, those that identify her as a selfish all-powerful being. Only as time, the sun, and experience foster her physical and mental growth can she move past that to become a fully functional human being again.

Thus in playing with horror movie stereotypes, Rice sets up expectations about the characters, only to shift in midstream and surprise the reader with character growth and complications. In doing so, she uses character to move her plot, creating plot twists that are logical and right.

PLOT DEVELOPMENT AND STRUCTURE

The Mummy has a classic plot structure, in part because Rice originally intended the story as a screenplay, and the structure for a screenplay is much more rigid than structure for a novel. But classic does not have to mean predictable, and Rice adds twists and turns to her story by luring the reader into false expectation based on the way horror movie plots *usually* run. Since Rice never does the usual, the last half of the plot holds quite a few surprises.

The book begins with exposition when the archeologist Lawrence and his partner Samir open the tomb and read the inscriptions. Henry is introduced as the villain, and Ramses begins to stir. Then Henry kills Lawrence, and the rising action of the plot takes off. At this point, the reader knows that Ramses is the protagonist and Henry is the antagonist, and the central plot question is, "Will Ramses kill Henry before Henry kills everyone in the book?" In the rising action, then, the mummy is taken to London where Julie leaves the lid off the case and the sun hits Ramses' body. This reanimates him just in time for him to stop Henry from killing Julie. The action continues as Ramses learns to deal with the real world and Henry's villainy, Samir becomes aware that Ramses is the ancient pharaoh, Henry panics and kills his loan shark, Alex begins to worry, Elliott catches on, and Julie falls in love. Finally having learned enough, Ramses insists on going to Egypt, and the whole cast troops along with him for various reasons. Stuck together on the boat, they all grow tense and there are confrontations before they reach the midpoint of the story when they dock in Egypt.

At this point, all the characters are locked in their various struggles and cannot walk away from the action, but they are also mostly stereotypical horror movie characters, so the reader feels secure in assuming that Ramses will face Henry down in some final confrontation, thus winning Julie forever. Instead, at the point of no return, Rice has Ramses act entirely within his character as a hero and reanimate the mummy of his long dead lover, Cleopatra. One of the first things Cleopatra does is kill Henry, clearing the way for her to become Ramses' new antagonist.

Therefore, halfway through the book, it's a whole new ball game. The rest of the rising action after Ramses wakes Cleopatra shows the characters dealing with the assault on their assumptions that Ramses' action has created. By the time the reader reaches the climax where Ramses finally kills Cleopatra by accident, readers aren't sure who they're rooting for. In the falling action and resolution, all the characters pick up the pieces and begin new lives based on the recognitions the climax has brought them to, including the resurrected Cleopatra who now has modern reasons for vengeance in addition to her ancient ones.

Rice uses stereotypes brilliantly in this book. By introducing all the characters as types, she can move quickly through the intricate setup this multi-peopled plot requires. Then by galvanizing all her stereotypes into character growth at the midpoint, she can surprise readers without ever breaking character motivation. *The Mummy* is, at base, a classic action-adventure plot, but the intricacies of Rice's characterization both make the twists in the plot logical and raise it above the norm.

LITERARY DEVICE: MOTIF

A motif is a character, idea, action, or object that shows up over and over again in a story, the way the threatening music is played in *Jaws* whenever the shark is about to strike. The use of motif strengthens a story by giving it a common thread that runs through it from beginning to end, and also by giving it something concrete that can help the reader understand the theme or meaning of the story. One motif that occurs again and again throughout *The Mummy* is the motif of drinking. Although Rice uses the motif of drink mostly to move the plot, she also uses it to show characterization in both the choices of drink her characters make and in the way her characters discover meaning in their lives.

The plot of *The Mummy* begins in a tomb with Lawrence, an archeologist, studying vials of drink and a diary while he keeps a cup of coffee beside him to stimulate him as he works. The diary he is reading tells him that Ramses, the mummy behind him, has taken the elixir or drink of immortality and is now not dead but sleeping. It also warns him that the bottle with the elixir has been placed with similar bottles containing poison. Lawrence continues to read, ignoring the fact that he is surrounded by drinks that contain energy, death, and immortal life, concerned only with the mystery of the man in the coffin behind him.

At this point, Henry, the villain, arrives. Unlike Lawrence, Henry is a man who is sensitive to the power of drink because he is an alcoholic and knows that drink can transform life, if only for a few hours. When Lawrence refuses to give him what he wants and turns his back, Henry picks up a bottle at random and pours it into the coffee. At this point, drink represents the randomness of life. Has Henry picked up a poison or the elixir of immortality? He offers Lawrence the cup of coffee, cementing his character as a betrayer since the offer of drink is a universal sign of good will. Lawrence accepts the offer and dies of drink, both because he is poisoned and because alcoholism has destroyed Henry's character to the point that he has become a murderer.

Drink continues to move the plot as Henry tries to poison Lawrence's daughter Julie, thereby causing Ramses to rise from his coffin, and Ramses gives the drink of immortality to the plants in Julie's conservatory, thereby alerting another character to the fact that the drink exists and still works. The most important plot move in the book is also begun by drink when Ramses presses a bottle with the elixir to the lips of the mummy of Cleopatra and brings her back to life, sending her on a killing rampage. Henry's death also is attributable to drink since he is drunk when he sees Cleopatra the first time and shoots her, which makes her reach for him and break his neck. And the final plot move or resolution of the story occurs when Julie agrees to drink the elixir and join Ramses in immortality.

But drink does more than move the plot. It also characterizes people. Lawrence drinks coffee because he is so excited about his archeological find that he hasn't slept for twenty-four hours and can't bear to stop even then. He drinks to keep his consciousness because he's too happy and excited to sleep. Henry is the reverse of Lawrence. He drinks alcohol to dull his consciousness because he's too unhappy and frustrated to bear life fully awake. Ramses' craving for drink (and food) demonstrates the lust for life that the immortality elixir gives those who drink it. The English habit of drinking tea tells him about their repressed lives; he thinks when he drinks it that it tastes like half of it is missing. Elliott's desire for the elixir is so strong that he tries to blackmail Ramses to get it, loving life so much that he's willing to betray his ethics to keep his hold on it. And Julie's refusal of the elixir shows her conservatism and her reluctance to believe in a future with Ramses.

Finally, drink in *The Mummy* becomes a metaphor for life for many of the characters. Alex tells Julie that, having loved Cleopatra, he now has a new vibrant sense of life, as if he'd been drinking water that he thought was hot before, only to learn through experience that it was just luke-warm. And Julie's acceptance of the elixir the morning after she has tried to drown herself is more than just the acceptance of a life with Ramses. It's a rejection of her despair and desire for death the night before and an acceptance of life whatever the circumstances, even if she loses Ramses. In all these ways, Rice uses the motif of drink to bind *The Mummy* together in plot, characterization, and theme.

THEMATIC ISSUES

Theme in *The Mummy* is a problem, not because there aren't clues to what it might be, but because it was intended as action-adventure fiction, a kind of story that is usually called escapist fiction because it is more interested in providing an escape from real life for the reader than in making a philosophical statement. Still, there are plenty of hints as to possible theme in the different aspects of the story such as settings, the central plot question, the protagonist's internal conflict and character growth, the beginning and ending, the title, and motifs. A comparison to a similar work of literature also sheds some light on what the theme might be.

The settings, for example, provide two worlds, one of logic and reason in London and one of impulse and passion in Egypt. In London, Julie and Elliott turn from the immortality elixir because it isn't proper in the terms of their lives. In Egypt, they open up to the passion of life and accept it. In London, Alex is faithful and adoring to a woman he's known all his life who rejects him physically. In Egypt, Alex gives up rejection and turns to physical passion with a woman he's just met. Going to Egypt, then, seems to represent going back to these characters' emotional selves, the parts of them that have been repressed by living in a logical modern culture, indicating that the theme may have something to do with self-discovery. In the process of self-discovery, these characters leave behind their old inhibitions as something that was appropriate to the past, embracing their new emotional freedom as part of their futures. This seems to indicate that the theme might deal with leaving the past to accept the future.

The central plot question—Will Ramses succeed in protecting Julie from Henry and Cleopatra and find his place in the new world?—can be answered yes, maybe, and maybe. Since the Henry plot question is solved halfway through the novel, protecting Julie from Cleopatra and adapting to the new world seem to be the important questions. Both of these answers depend on Ramses leaving behind his old world to embrace the new. His old feelings for Cleopatra lead him to resurrect her, and his old assumption that he can do anything because he's king leads him to break laws. Both of these acts endanger his new life. Only if Ramses turns his back on the king he was and the queen he loved will he be able to make a new life for himself. Therefore, the theme may deal with choosing the future over the past.

This theme is reinforced in the protagonist's internal conflict, which involves choosing between the two worlds of Julie and Cleopatra. And it is also shown in Ramses' character growth, which leads him to accept the rules of others like Julie, to choose Julie over Cleopatra, and to share the elixir for the first time in three thousand years, making others equal to himself.

The beginning and the ending of the novel seem to go back to the two different worlds theme. In the beginning, Lawrence invades the ancient world by breaking open Ramses' tomb and dies. In the end, Cleopatra invades the modern world by breaking out of a hospital and lives once more. But both scenes also support the "choose the future" theme because Lawrence chooses the past and dies, while Cleopatra chooses the future and lives.

The title of the novel is another clue, since Rice could have simply titled it *Ramses the Damned*. By calling it *The Mummy or Ramses the Damned*, Rice emphasizes that Ramses begins wrapped in the past, and that only by removing the evidence of his past life can he truly live again. Once more, the theme seems to be dealing with casting off the past to live in the present. And the motif of drink, discussed earlier in this chapter, also reinforces this theme. Choosing to drink the elixir means choosing the future.

A comparison to a similar work of literature throws some final light on this question. An earlier book of Rice's, *The Vampire Lestat*, has many similarities to *The Mummy*, but also some important differences. The similarities show that Rice was concerned with similar ideas. For example, both titles are eponymous, which means that they're the same name as the hero in the story, showing that the book is going to center specifically on that character. Both characters are immortal, and both became that way through drinking, Lestat by drinking the blood of the old vampire who made him and Ramses by drinking the elixir that the old priestess gave him. Both tire of life as immortals, and both "bury" themselves twice in their lives, Lestat by going into the ground to sleep and Ramses by entombing himself away from sunlight so that he can sleep. Both are therefore "born" three times in their lives, and the third time is the charm for both since they both choose to remain alive after that "birth." Both are sexually free (Lestat loves many other vampires and experiences sexual ecstasy every time he drinks blood, and Ramses sleeps with twelve prostitutes, Julie, and Cleopatra in the course of his story), and both see themselves as above the law, not only because of their immortality but also because they see themselves as larger than life, kings among humans.

But there are important differences, too. Lestat can be killed by the sun, but Ramses needs the sun to live. For that reason, the events of the story can take place in the daylight which removes the dark mood of the night that must infuse Lestat's story. Both can make others immortal, but Lestat must kill them to give the Dark Gift, while Ramses can give the elixir without killing. This also means that those to whom Lestat gives the Dark Gift must kill to survive, while those to whom Ramses gives the elixir simply find themselves with increased appetites for food, drink, and sex. This makes Ramses' choices easier than Lestat's because he's not passing on a curse. All of these aspects make *The Mummy* a lighter book than *The Vampire Lestat* right up to the ending: whereas Lestat goes to his coffin to find the Queen of the Damned planning death, Ramses goes to bed with Julie, the good girl, planning sexual intercourse, a metaphor for life.

Therefore, the theme of *The Mummy* both inverts the theme of *The Vampire Lestat* and takes the same theme and makes it lighter. The theme that seems to come from the analysis of the different aspects of *The Mummy*—choose life and the future—seems to do both. Lestat cannot choose life since he's dead, so this theme is an inversion of his book. Yet the theme of his book also deals with self-knowledge and choosing the future, and in that way it reinforces Ramses' theme. Therefore, the theme of *The Mummy* is probably that choosing to live the life that's ahead rather than dwelling in the past leads to happiness. It's a simple theme, but *The Mummy* is simple fiction, meant to reinforce a reader's comfortable beliefs as part of the escape from reality it is meant to provide.

A FEMINIST READING OF *THE MUMMY*

A feminist reading of *The Mummy* shows that Rice has constructed a male-centered story in which women play traditional supporting roles with no real lives of their own. Some of this is because the story is set in the 1920s when few women had careers, which means that the occupations of the women in the story will most logically be those of wife, mother, daughter, and mistress. But even within these roles, women had dreams and desires, goals they pursued, lives outside of the men they loved or served. Unfortunately, the lives of the women in *The Mummy* revolve solely around the men they choose to love, and they have no real desires or identities of their own. A brief analysis of the story using basic feminist criticism questions shows these aspects in all four female characters.

Where are the women in this story?

Usually they're standing in some man's shadow. Julie, the female lead character, is first Lawrence's daughter and then Ramses' lover, reacting to what goes on around her in terms of how it will affect the men she loves. Daisy and Malenka, Henry's mistresses, are stupid and sensual and have no lives without him. Cleopatra, active and vicious as the antagonist in the second half of the book, is motivated in her rage and grief by the loss of her lover centuries before and by her determination to take revenge on the man who denied him immortality. Therefore her presence in the book is defined by two men. Without them, she has no goal and no reason for living.

What role does gender play in the story?

All the women are sexual objects to be wooed, won, and slept with. Then they can be discarded as Henry plans to do with both Malenka and Daisy, or married as both Ramses and Alex plan to do with Julie. If they become too powerful and their passions run too deep, they must be destroyed, as Ramses and the rest of the men plan to do to Cleopatra. All of these roles feature women being "done to." None feature women actively doing things themselves, achieving their own goals for their own motives since even Cleopatra is seeking revenge for a wrong done to another man, not revenge for herself. Therefore, gender in this story means that women are objects, things that are "done to" by men.

What image of women is conveyed?

Women are sexual and passive, which can be good or bad, or sexual and aggressive, which is bad. Good passive women restrain their sexuality until men make a commitment, as Julie does with Ramses. Bad passive women sleep with men who abuse them, as Daisy and Malenka do with Henry. Really bad aggressive women sleep with men and then break their necks, as Cleopatra does with just about everybody but Alex. Essentially, women in this story are bodies, and the way in which they give men access to those bodies determines their characters.

How is the relationship between women and men depicted?

Most of the relationships are distant, based more on sex than on emotional connection. Elliott loves his wife distantly, and she loves him in
return, not minding the distance. Henry uses women like sexual Kleenex,
and they either worship him for it like Malenka or use him in return
like Daisy. Lawrence longs for his daughter to be with him to share his
discoveries as an audience, and Julie, in turn, misses her father because
he was the center of her world. Ramses reacts to Julie at first as a sexual
being, trying to entice her into his bed. Julie resists until he changes his
approach and tells her he loves her, whereupon she gives herself up to
him, following him around for the rest of the story. When she is forced
to leave him, she tries to commit suicide, only accepting immortality
when he returns to give her life meaning. Alex seems to love Julie as a
person, but he replaces her quite easily with an American heiress, and
then finally finds the great love of his live in Cleopatra, a strong woman
who relates to men only through sex, although he begs her to tell him
her problems so that he can solve them for her. Part of the distance in
these relationships is an aspect of the times which said that women were
weaker than men and should therefore be protected and not bothered
with the problems of the world. Still, if the important love stories like
that of Julie and Ramses were truly love stories, the relationship would
be based on more than protection and sex. As long as the women have
no lives outside the men, however, they can't be expected to hold their
own in an equal partnership and are therefore left to serve and obey
(unless they're Cleopatra, in which case they kill).

How is the relationship between women and women depicted?

There are no relationships between women in this novel. The only time
two female characters meet, Cleopatra tries to kill Julie in revenge for
the death of Mark Antony.

This analysis points out the two problems with the portrayal of women
in this book. One is that they have no relationships outside the men in
their lives, and so they are totally isolated from one another and unable
to form the strong female friendships that most women count on in life
and that would allow them to speak freely as women. These relationships are particularly important in lives and stories that take place in
times where the genders are seen as unequal because in those times the
only free relationships will be those between people of the same gender.
This is beautifully shown in the close relationships between Lawrence
and Samir, Lawrence and Elliott, and Elliott and Alex, but there are no
female relationships to compare to these close male relationships.

The other problem with the female portrayals is that their motivations all stem from those relationships with men. Julie wants her father safe and happy, and when he dies, she turns to Ramses to make sure he's safe and happy. She has no goals, no desires, no motivations outside her relationships with her father and her lover. Daisy wants money more than she wants Henry, but she does whatever Henry wants in order to get his money. She is essentially a dumb blonde who lives a life that is completely physical, and her goals are to increase her physical comfort only. Since her physical comfort is tied to Henry, she's tied to Henry, and she never thinks of life without him. Malenka loves Henry and puts up with his beating her, taking her money, and insulting her. All that she cares about is that Henry stays with her. Cleopatra, who once ruled all Egypt and must have had some outside interests besides men, is now consumed with revenge for her long-dead lover, Mark Antony. Her secondary interests are sex and food, and she robs men in order to get them.

The point of this analysis is not to show that Rice is antifeminist or that Rice should have made all her female characters raving suffragettes. Daisy and Malenka are exactly the characters they should be, given Henry's character which dictates his choice of women. Julie and Cleopatra, however, deserve better, since Rice puts them center stage. They do not have to be strong, active, intelligent, or brave, but they should be as real as the male characters, as well-developed as Elliott or Henry or even Ramses the blue-eyed hero. That they aren't weakens the novel. Thus feminist criticism of *The Mummy* shows that, even though the book is clearly intended as escapist fiction, a more balanced portrayal of women with motives, goals, and lives outside of men would have made it much richer escapist fiction.

THE WITCHES

9

The Witching Hour
(1990)

When Dr. Rowan Mayfair pulls Michael Curry's body from San Francisco Bay, she brings him back to life with her extraordinary healing powers. Once back, Michael has extraordinary powers, too: he can now "read" any object placed into his hands, knowing details of the people who once handled it. But as *The Witching Hour*, the first book in Anne Rice's Witches Chronicles, opens, Michael also has a problem. While he was dead, he accepted a supernatural challenge to return to life to do something, and now he can't remember what it is. He meets Rowan again to see if she can help him discover his promise, and they fall in love. He leaves her to return to New Orleans, the place where they both were born, where he eventually learns what his promise was. When Rowan gets word that her mother has died there, she follows him. They meet Rowan's family and learn Rowan's destiny: as Aaron Lightner of the psychic detective group, the Talamasca, tells them, she is the thirteenth in the long line of the Mayfair witches. Aaron provides them with a complete history of the witches, a story of torture, murder, rape, incest, insanity, and possession, and Rowan is determined that she will not fall as her ancestors have. She is the witch who will free the family from the curse of the demon who has given the witches their power, the force the first witch called Lasher because he made the trees lash in the wind. At the Witching Hour on Christmas Eve, Rowan meets Lasher in the book's climax, playing out the last scene in Lasher's great centuries-old plan.

POINT OF VIEW

Anne Rice has once again told her own mythology in the multiple third-person limited point of view (using "he" and "she" instead of "I"), but this time she has made it tight by keeping it chronological; that is, she has told all the events in the order they happened. She begins with a modern plot about Rowan and her lover Michael, interrupts it with a long, chronological history of the Mayfair witches, and then returns to the modern plot smoothly. The modern plot is told from many third-person viewpoints, but each different scene has one narrator only, so each is seen only through that narrator's eyes. The long central section that makes up the history of the Mayfair witches is presented as a series of documents that range from first-person letters to third-person omniscient reports, but all of the documents are carefully titled so that the reader has the experience of encountering the file in the same way that Michael Curry does. It's a particularly effective use of point of view and, combined with the fascinating narration of the reports themselves, makes for very clear reading. Thus, even though Rice's novel is long and complicated, it is tightly controlled through her successful use of point of view.

CHARACTER DEVELOPMENT

In the hands of a less-skilled writer, the multiple characters of *The Witching Hour* might have been impossible to distinguish. Rice unfolds her story so carefully, however, that each character remains vivid on the page. Her protagonist or central character is Rowan Mayfair, the thirteenth Mayfair witch, and her goal is to save herself, her unborn baby, and her family from the menace of the antagonist, the demon spirit Lasher. Lasher is a worthy antagonist, or opponent, because he's crafty, seductive, and supernaturally powerful. The plot is their struggle, so the story question becomes, "Will Rowan defeat Lasher?" Rowan's identity is at stake here because she wants desperately to protect her newfound family. It's also at stake because she sees herself as different from the previous witches who fell under Lasher's spell, so she needs to be the one to defeat him in order to keep her identity as the strongest of the witches. The central question therefore determines not only the external struggle of the plot, which is Lasher's attempts to dominate Rowan and become flesh, but also Rowan's internal struggle to be worthy of her family and to fight her emotional tendency to be a victim.

Rowan is a particularly dynamic character, changing and growing as the events of the story impact on her. In the beginning, she is a loner, deliberately choosing men as partners that she can discard, saving all her affection for her foster mother. When her mother dies, she is left alone until she pulls Michael Curry's body out of the bay and brings him back to life. Meeting Michael later, she falls in love with him, and her character begins to open up, risking vulnerability for love. Shortly after that, she gets word that her real mother has died, and she flies to New Orleans and meets a huge family she had not known existed. This connection to a large and loving community breaks into Rowan's isolation even more, and this new development is followed by the news of her family history: she is the thirteenth in a long line of powerful witches, and the demon spirit that guides the family fortunes now belongs to her. By the end of the book, Rowan has moved from being an isolated, cold, and lonely surgeon to a loving wife and philanthropist, surrounded by family she welcomes with open arms. This character arc becomes even more important at the climax of the book because it raises the stakes for Rowan in the plot struggle. In the beginning of the book, she has only herself to fight for. Now the happiness of her husband, her unborn child, and the hundreds of Mayfair relatives who depend on her for leadership are all at stake. In spite of some inexplicable actions at the end, Rowan Mayfair remains a truly dynamic character.

Her husband, Michael, is also dynamic. Beginning as a loner who has had a near-death experience, Michael is tormented because he can now read objects with his hands, seeing the people who last handled the objects and picking up their emotions. He's also tormented by a memory he has of promising to do something while he was dead, but now he can't remember what. Thus the Michael of the beginning of the story is tortured, confused, and miserable, and the only thing that gives him hope is meeting and loving Rowan Mayfair. He begins to recover when he is with her, and the extended family they find when they reach New Orleans also helps to heal him. But it is the history of the witches that truly pulls Michael out of his misery because it shows him that Rowan may be in danger. As they work together to restore the great Mayfair house, Michael becomes stronger and surer until the end of the novel when despair faces him once more. This time, however, he has family and place to sustain him, and he ends his story on a note of blind faith, made possible by his character growth.

The remaining characters in *The Witching Hour* are static, but that doesn't mean they're not fascinating. Aaron Lightner, the wise man from the Talamasca, remains wise and understanding, sometimes not sure of the meaning of things, but always doing the right thing, tactfully and patiently. He is the moral core of the novel, the yardstick against which all other characters are measured. Although some of the family resist Aaron, those who accept him are the characters who have intelligence and tolerance.

Aaron shines particularly brightly against the other two important male characters in the book, Julien and Cortland, Mayfair ancestors who slept with sisters and daughters to ensure the line of witches. Julien and Cortland seduce and rape, making incubators of their relatives, selfishly doing whatever it takes to keep the Mayfair legacy going. Although Julien's character will be retrieved in the next book in the Chronicles, *Lasher,* here he is simply a creature of the flesh, wicked and powerful, although not nearly as wicked as Cortland, who simply takes what he wants, raping his own granddaughter and murdering innocent people to protect the wealth and power of the family. Both of these characters are static because neither changes during the course of their lives, but they are startling in their depravity without ever being cartoons of evil.

The women of the family are static characters, too, but they are drawn just as vividly. Each of the twelve witches of Mayfair history is an individual—no small feat for a writer whose book is crammed with dozens of Mayfairs spread throughout two centuries. Taken together, the Mayfair witches make a character arc of their own, rising in intelligence and power and then falling again as Lasher gains in strength; this group character arc helps increase the pressure on Rowan as the last inheritor. Stupid Suzanne is the first to call Lasher out of the ether and dies by fire because of it. Her daughter Deborah is brighter but more vulnerable, and her simplicity leads to her downfall when she fails to control Lasher and is sentenced to burn as a witch because of it. Her escape from the flames to her own choice of a swift merciful death shows how far she has come from her mother. Deborah's daughter, Charlotte, is much craftier than her mother and grandmother combined, running her own plantation and seducing her own father to make sure that she has a daughter to inherit the legacy. That daughter, Jeanne Louise, retains her power and extends it, producing another powerful witch by sleeping with her twin brother. Their daughter, Angelique, is essentially a name in a genealogy, not a character, but she does give birth to Marie Claudette, a powerful witch who moves the family from Haiti to safety in New Orleans. Her daughter Marguerite becomes even more powerful, but her obsession with voodoo and her attempts to bring Lasher into human flesh eventually drive her insane. With Marguerite the character arc of the line seems to falter because her witch daughter Katherine is weak, but Marguerite also produces the only male witch the line has ever known, the very powerful Julien. Julien saves the line when he rapes his sister Katherine, and she gives birth to the most powerful witch up to that time, Mary Beth, savvy businesswoman and voodoo sorceress.

At this point, the character arc of the witches' line peaks because the rest of the witches disintegrate. Mary Beth has two witch daughters, the first, cold, bitter Carlotta, rejects Lasher as she rejects everything in life. Then Mary Beth sleeps with Julien and gives birth to Stella, a powerful but uncontrolled witch who has all of her parents' lust for life without any of their common sense. When Mary Beth dies, Carlotta convinces Stella's brother to shoot Stella to death, but not before Stella has given birth to her cousin Cortland's baby, Antha. Pale, timid Antha tries to escape by running away, but Lasher kills her lover and Antha returns to have her baby, Deirdre, in Carlotta's house. Shortly after that, Carlotta attacks Antha, ripping out her eye and driving her off the roof of the house to her death. Carlotta then tries to bully Deirdre into giving up Lasher, and Deirdre runs away to find peace, only to be raped by Cortland instead and to give birth to the thirteenth witch, Rowan. Rowan is sent away to cousins in California, over Cortland's protests (Carlotta kills him to shut him up), and Deirdre is given shock treatments and tranquilizers until she becomes a vegetable. She has, in fact, sunk lower than Suzanne, the feeble-minded first witch. All of the witches are static characters, defined in the main by one characteristic: Suzanne the fool, Deborah the trusting, Charlotte the calculating, Marie Claudette the resourceful, Marguerite the voodoo priestess, Mary Beth the brilliant and strong, Stella the foolish, Antha the timid, and Deirdre the vegetable. But even though they are static, they are all vivid and fascinating and provide Rowan with a history that galvanizes her own character arc.

The most fascinating of all of them, however, is the one who refuses to be a witch. Carlotta should be a sympathetic character; she rejects evil and chooses God, and she fights Lasher with every particle of her soul. But as another character in the book points out, Carlotta has inherited the family capacity for evil. While she does fight Lasher, she does so by murdering and torturing her family, casting a spell of gloom and despair not only over the house which begins to fall apart but also over the entire Mayfair clan. She hangs onto life stubbornly, waiting until Deirdre dies and Rowan comes back, and then she malevolently dumps the entire family history on Rowan in the space of an hour, giving her a tour of the house that includes the severed human heads in jars that Marguerite used for voodoo experiments and the ancient corpse of a man wrapped in a rug in an upstairs room. She tells Rowan that she kept Deirdre under sedation until she lost her mind in order to rid her of the demon, and then taunts Rowan until Rowan uses her psychic powers to kill her. Even in death, Carlotta is in control, choosing her own time and way of dying, ensuring that her death will send the next Mayfair witch into her new inheritance with the guilt that Carlotta inflicted on everyone else in her life. The character of Carlotta never changes and never grows, but she remains fascinating as she sits in the center of the Mayfair history like a toad, glaring at everyone.

Lasher is also static because he's not a character; he's a demon, an unhappy soul who has plotted for centuries to breed a witch strong enough to give him a human body again. Lasher is childlike in his evil, controlling his witches through the gift of his power and providing them with sexual ecstasy. He cannot understand true, unselfish love, and his every act is based on his own needs. He loves and cares for the Mayfair witches because he needs them, but he deserts them to go to their daughters as soon as they give birth because his one goal in life is to regain a body. His plotting and patience for two centuries are broken now and then by murderous rages against those he sees as detrimental to his plan, but he is single-minded in his pursuit. Lasher is not intrinsically evil; he does not do the things he does in order to act against good. He simply moves selfishly through the world to attain his own ends, causing incalculable suffering that he never notices because he is fixated on his own goal. His taking of Rowan's baby at the end is not an act of evil to him; rather, it's the act toward which his entire existence has been aimed for two hundred years. His character is therefore unchanging no matter what occurs in the story, and he makes for a chilling antagonist, beating even Cortland and Carlotta in the Most Hateful Character Contest for this book.

Rice has constructed her characters brilliantly, making those who are central to the story, Rowan and Michael, complicated, dynamic characters, and those who are the supporting cast, the witches and Lasher, vivid, static characters. This use of both dynamic and static characters is the perfect choice for a book so crowded with necessary characters. Had Rice developed other characters in more detail, she would have confused the plot. Had she made her static characters any less vivid, they would have run together in a faceless lump. Instead, Rice gives us the Mayfair clan, incestuous, powerful, driven, and haunted, and makes sure we never forget any of them.

PLOT DEVELOPMENT AND STRUCTURE

The Witching Hour is beautifully constructed throughout and well-motivated almost to the end, as evidenced by the fact that despite the paperback edition's length (over one thousand pages), the reader never tires of the story. Rice needs a long book because she is once again constructing a double plot, this time a modern mystery story coupled with a saga, an historical account of a great family. Sagas began with the great oral stories of the ancient Norse but have been adapted by modern writers to tell the continuing story of noteworthy families. Rice's saga of the Mayfair witches is buried in the middle of her modern plot, but it's there for a reason. Besides acting as a plot on its own, it also provides motivation for Rowan and Michael and therefore becomes a natural part of the rising action of the novel. This means that the saga is not an unnatural intrusion but is instead a vital part of the modern plot, drawing readers into its own characters while increasing their concern about the modern characters.

Therefore, the exposition or setup for the plot is everything that leads up to Rowan pulling Michael out of the bay. When she brings him back to life and falls in love with him, she sets up the rising action, which consists of moving to New Orleans, meeting the family, fixing the house, reading the Mayfair saga, becoming pregnant—in short, everything in Lasher's plan. The climax is the "birth" and victory of Lasher. The falling action is the fight with Michael and Rowan's escape with the now human demon, and the resolution or return to stability is Michael's recognition of free will, which prompts his decision to believe in Rowan and to wait for her. It's an extremely tight plot, and it's well-motivated until the very end.

Unfortunately, the end has problems. As one critic put it, "Ultimately, what creaks loudest is not the haunted house, but the plot" (Ferraro, 77). Some of those creaks have been there earlier in the plot. For example, Carlotta tortures the Mayfair witches, and yet she lives to be ninety-something. Why doesn't Lasher kill Carlotta? Still, the plot moves so swiftly that Rice finesses the earlier plot cracks. Only at the end do characters begin to behave totally out of character, in ways they never would in real life.

For example, why does Michael, a man who is desperately in love and desperately anxious for a child and who has been a traditional male caretaker up until now, leave his pregnant wife alone for two weeks in a house haunted by a demon that he knows wants her? His action is absolutely inexplicable given his character, but given the demands of the plot, he must be gotten out of the way so that Lasher can seduce Rowan. So off he goes to San Francisco for two solid weeks.

And why doesn't Rowan, the most powerful witch ever, protect her unborn child from Lasher? And if he is too powerful to stop, why doesn't she kill him when he stands before her helpless in the body of her newborn child? And why does she leave Michael, the man she adores, floating face down in a swimming pool to leave with the demon, stopping only to turn on the alarm system so the fire department will arrive minutes later to resuscitate him?

Apparently, at this point Rice is overriding her characters, making them do things they normally wouldn't so that her book can reach the conclusion she wants it to. This changes a book that has been beautifully character-driven (that is, the events in the story happen because of the characters' needs and motivations) to one that is hopelessly plot-driven (that is, one in which events happen because the author needs them to, not because the actions are those the characters would normally perform). Rice does recover her character-driven plot once the climax is past, having Michael respond as he must because of the way his character has grown in the book, but the ending is still vaguely unsatisfying.

This ending is not unsatisfying because things are left open. Rice did not leave the ending open to ensure a sequel; she did so because she wanted the reader to deal with the ambiguous ending, and this is an excellent choice given all the foreshadowing and the character development that have gone before, particularly when capped by Michael's closing statement. Rather, the reason the ending is unsatisfying is that it is arrived at by sacrificing character, and the reader is left saying, "I don't care how good the last page is, those characters wouldn't have *done* that." Thus Rice's book unwittingly becomes the perfect example of both the tightness and rightness of the character-driven story and the ultimately unsatisfying nature of the plot-driven story.

LITERARY DEVICES: MOTIF

One of the most disturbing elements in *The Witching Hour* is the repeated motif of babies, particularly dead babies. If a baby is a symbol of anything, it should be a symbol of new life, but all the babies in *The Witching Hour* are produced as part of a great plan for an old life, a genetic inbreeding program to produce a great witch that can give the demon Lasher human form. In the same way, an aborted fetus should be the symbol of death, yet the aborted fetuses that Rowan sees in the research lab are giving life to others through their living cells. But the book does not imply that the babies should not have been born, or that the harvesting of the aborted fetuses is good and right. Instead, Rice uses the images of the babies to show that good and evil exist together in every situation, and that it is not easy to separate them.

She introduces the motif with Michael's child by his lover Judith. Judith is not ready to become a mother, and she tells Michael she wants an abortion. But Michael wants the baby desperately; he's even given it a name, Little Chris. Michael does believe in a woman's right to choose, but he also wants his child. He offers to take the baby on his own, telling Judith she'll never have to be the child's mother, but Judith points out that he's asking her to carry a child to term and then give it up. He is essentially asking her to be an emotionless incubator. She refuses and aborts the child, and Michael is devastated, from then on seeing aborted fetuses playing the monsters in every horror film he sees.

The reader's sympathy must be with Michael at this stage, but later in the book when it becomes clear that Lasher wants the same thing from Rowan, the readers' instinct is the same as Judith's: abort the unwanted fetus that is Lasher. When Rowan gives birth and leaves with the "baby" Lasher to care for it, her decision seems inexplicable. Yet it is the same thing that Michael wanted from Judith. Clearly, there are no absolutes in this situation.

In the same way, the fetuses in the research lab have their parallel in the Mayfair family. Rowan is horrified to see fetuses hooked to life support systems so that their cells can be harvested to save lives. Yet she's part of one of those experiments herself. The entire history of the Mayfair family is in essence one huge genetic research experiment in which the women act as incubators to produce a genetically superior fetus that will give life to Lasher. (Marguerite even steals babies for Lasher to practice on.) Rowan recognizes that the fetal research does save lives and therefore cannot be considered totally evil; she also recognizes that Lasher's grand genetic plan has produced a strong, successful family that supports her and loves her. Out of evil comes good, but can there be good if it springs from evil?

The good/evil problem continues in all the other abortions in the story. Carlotta wants to make Deirdre have an abortion, but she's stopped by Cortland. That's a good act on Cortland's part until it's revealed that the baby Deirdre is carrying was fathered by Cortland in a rape in order to produce another Mayfair witch. That's an evil act, and now Carlotta's abortion is looking better, but the baby turns out to be Rowan, the great surgeon and a good person. Now the abortion is a bad idea again until the end of the book when Lasher achieves his plan and is reborn into human flesh by taking Rowan's fetus. Now evil is unleashed on the world through Rowan, so Carlotta was right after all, was she not?

The worst of the questions comes at the end, however, when Lasher aborts the soul of Rowan's baby, driving it out of its fetal body so that Lasher can take possession. That is unmitigated evil, but that's Lasher. However when Lasher is born, Rowan faces a huge moral choice in a split second. This demon killed her baby, and she should "abort" it by killing it now, at the moment of its birth. But it is also her baby, she has given birth to it, and therefore killing it would be another abortion, which Rowan cannot bring herself to do.

Thus Rice has used a motif that is guaranteed to evoke strong feelings in the reader, but she then takes away all the easy answers and makes the reader first respond emotionally and then look at that response in a new light. Her repeated use of babies and abortion forces the reader to accept an underlying theme of this work, which may be that the difference between good and evil is not easy to discern because they are so often inextricably entwined.

THEMATIC ISSUES

The Witching Hour is so rich in motif and philosophy that the possible themes are endless. However, an examination of the usual clues to theme help narrow down the choices. That examination reinforces the ideas that the baby motif raises: it's difficult to separate good and evil, and therefore difficult to choose between them.

The Witching Hour has multiple settings: San Francisco, a cold, bloodless place; New Orleans, a place of magic and family and secrets; and Florida, the rational modern world that seems completely cut off from the passions raging in New Orleans. Of all these settings, New Orleans is the most important, and Rice's focus on this setting also emphasizes the importance of family and mystery in the story. In San Francisco and Florida, Rowan and Michael are cut off from family and therefore colder and more alone. Only in the danger and magic of New Orleans do they function fully. Therefore the importance of connection, always a theme in Rice's novels, is emphasized by setting. But New Orleans is not only the place of greatest love, it's also the place of greatest danger, and therefore the question of separating good and evil is reinforced in setting, too.

It's also reinforced in the main characters' internal struggles. Rowan's struggle is to love and open herself to others in the form of Michael and her family, to accept herself and her powers as positive, and to retain her free will and not fall victim to the demon. That she loses all of these struggles in the end, in part due to her choice of research and knowledge over love of family and Michael, in part due to Lasher's superior power, seems to indicate that the core of the book is about destiny and evil. But Michael's internal struggle refutes this idea. Michael struggles to accept his powers and find his place in the family and in Rowan's life throughout the novel, only to come face to face with horror and terrible loss at the end. If ever a character should succumb to a recognition of destiny and evil, it's Michael. And yet he rejects both, choosing instead to believe in free will and love as a means to goodness on earth. These characters' growth also reinforces the dual theme. Rowan's growth leads her to accept her family and Michael, making a commitment to both, but she breaks that commitment at the end, once more reinforcing the idea of human helplessness at the hands of destiny. Michael's character growth refutes this idea because he rejects the idea of destiny to write "I believe in Free Will" and to trust that Rowan loves him and will return to him. Once again, evil and good are entwined in the results of the same act.

The beginning and ending of the novel also present two sides. The beginning is about a doctor's helplessness to aid Deirdre, Michael's helplessness to deal with his new power and his broken memory, and Rowan's helplessness to deal with the memory of her dead foster mother. The end of the book both reinforces that helplessness as destiny as Rowan is victimized by Lasher, and refutes it as Michael sits bereft of his wife and child and chooses through free will to believe in the future. This is supported by another clue, the title *The Witching Hour*, which refers to the climax when Lasher becomes human. Although this would seem to indicate that the book is about Lasher, it actually moves the book back to Rowan and Michael and their differing conclusions because it is this event that brings them both to self-knowledge. Lasher's birth forces Rowan's terrible decision to choose science and the demon over love and family; it also forces Michael to confront his own beliefs about free will and evil.

Rice's literary inspiration also shows this interest in good and evil as a difficult choice. She drew on several Gothic novels, particularly *The Turn of the Screw* by Henry James, a story about a governess who encounters what may be a ghost or what may be the product of her twisted mind. She battles the spirit throughout the book, and her struggles leave one child insane and another dead in her arms as she watches the spirit depart defeated. Part of the spell that James's book casts is that the reader is never sure whether or not there are ghosts, or whether the governess is a heroine at the end or simply a maniac whose insanity has destroyed two children. Rice's novel also ends ambiguously (although there's no doubt that Lasher exists), and the question is really the same for both books: What is good and what is evil, and how can we ever know?

Another novel Rice has said influenced her is Mary Shelley's *Frankenstein*, about a scientist who "gives birth" to a monster and then deserts it, refusing to take responsibility for his child. The monster tracks Frankenstein down and makes him admit his error, and then both die. Rowan also creates a monster, but she is no denying Frankenstein; instead, she helps her child into the world. Both monsters kill and destroy, but neither monster is evil in the sense of deliberately choosing not to do the good thing. Both are children, selfish and demanding. When viewed in this light, Rowan's action is an act of love and responsibility, not science. Yet, she looses a demon on the world. Once again, the double question remains.

Rice has also suggested in interviews that *The Witching Hour* could be about sexuality or imagination, about "who's able to use it and who becomes a victim" (Gates, "Queen," 77). But her strongest flat-out statement of theme still seems to be Michael's credo at the end: "I believe in Free Will. . . . I believe that we can through reason know what good is. . . . I believe that through our finest efforts, we will succeed in creating heaven on earth, and we do it every time that we love" (1037). Michael says this in the face of all that he's seen, refuting all the evidence of history, and the fact that Rice chooses his statement of belief to close the book gives weight to the idea that, although *The Witching Hour* may be about the terrible difficulty of knowing the difference between good and evil and therefore the terrible difficulty of choosing between good and evil, Rice herself comes down on the side of free will and the ability to choose to do good in the world.

A FEMINIST READING OF *THE WITCHING HOUR*

A feminist reading of *The Witching Hour* reveals the surprising conclusion that this book about powerful women is really a story about victimized women. This in itself is not a bad thing, but since the witches are often presented as strong, independent women, and since Rowan Mayfair in particular is described over and over again as the most powerful of all the powerful women, their weakness and failures contribute to the idea that women are intrinsically victims. In the case of *The Witching Hour*, however, this is not true; although the women may have been described as powerful, their actions show them to be weak. A brief analysis of this novel using basic feminist critical questions shows this weakness.

Where are the women in this text?

The women are for the most part powerful witches, able to call down storms and end their enemies' lives. But in actuality, they are only calling on male power, and they get it only because the male, the demon Lasher, chooses to give it. Lasher can at any time refuse to give the Mayfair women anything, but he gives them what they want in order to keep them happy so they will complete his plan and have babies for him. As he moves them through history like chess pieces, he is always the one with knowledge and power while they play supernatural games and reproduce at his bidding.

The witches, however, do play other roles. As mothers, they are either cold and controlling, lavishing attention on the "legacy" child while often ignoring the other offspring, or they are weak victims, driven off roofs and into catatonia by the more powerful among them. As daughters, they are seduced, raped, and manipulated in order to ensure that the line continues. This goal seems to spring from family need but actually is driven by the great male power that drives the family, Lasher.

What role does gender play in the text?

Women seem to be powerful in the saga of the Mayfair witches (although the most powerful up to modern times is arguably the male witch, Julien). They can call on the power of nature in the form of Lasher, but they can't control it. While Lasher does do their bidding, he also kills their lovers and deserts them for their newborn daughters. Essentially, in this story, power is something that males have and females ask for.

In addition, this book has a strong sexuality and features many sexual women. Few of them prosper. The most overtly and freely sexual, Stella, has passionate affairs with her uncles and cousins, both male and female, and revels in her freedom, only to be shot in the head for it. Her counterpart, Julien, flourishes with the same sexual history. Most of these women are betrayed by their sexuality, falling victim to Lasher's invisible sexual advances because they can't deny their physical response. The one woman who can deny Lasher, Carlotta, is a cold, bitter, evil person, hardly a figure of admirable strength. The message seems to be that cold women aren't victims but they are evil, and that hot women aren't evil but they're doomed to be victims.

What image of women is conveyed?

Given the above analysis, the general image is that women are weak, dependent on men for power, and easily controlled through sex. The few women who are powerful on their own are cold, evil, and ultimately helpless in the face of male power, as Carlotta is helpless at the end to defeat Lasher.

How is the relationship between women and men depicted?

In general, men betray women. Rowan's Aunt Ellie is betrayed by her Uncle Graham. Graham betrays Rowan by forcing her to sleep with him by telling her he'll leave Ellie if she doesn't. The male government that is sworn to protect its citizens turns on Suzanne and burns her at the stake. A different government tries to do the same to Deborah, who is also betrayed by her dying husband and her two sons. Julien betrays his sister Katherine by raping her. Stella is betrayed by her brother who shoots her to death. Antha and Deirdre are betrayed by their male relatives who do not protect them from Carlotta's savagery. Deirdre is betrayed by her Uncle Cortland (who is also her grandfather) when he rapes her. In general, the successful relationships in this book are the unnatural ones, since the "nice" husbands in the stories end up dead of a wasting disease or of yellow fever or of alcoholism or are murdered by Lasher, but the consenting incestuous relationships go on forever. To the above list of incestuous rapes can be added the list of consenting incestuous pairings, including the monk Petyr who not only slept with his daughter Charlotte, but also indulged her taste for rapelike sex, something she seems to have passed down through the family tree. While there is nothing inherently wrong in rough sex or in the women who enjoy it, it becomes problematical here because this novel contains no scenes of tender lovemaking. Sex in this family is violent, which means sex in this book is violent.

How is the relationship between women and women depicted?

Aside from the mother-daughter relationships in this novel, the witches are alone. Although there are dozens of female family members, Rowan does not establish a close relationship with any of them. In fact, nowhere in the book is there even a sense of a coven, a kinship of witches. Each witch stands alone in her time, the head of the family but cut off from friendship, even when they try desperately to pursue it as Deirdre does with Rita Mae Dwyer. The most passionate relationship any woman has with another in *The Witching Hour is* the relationship that Carlotta has with Stella, Antha, and Dierdre, and her passion is to destroy them.

Rowan, in particular, is an example of this detachment. Although the names of three friends are dropped into the narrative when Rowan is about to be married, there has been no evidence of them in the text, so there are no real relationships there. This is reinforced when they all send their regrets and explanations as to why they can't support her on her wedding day. Rowan's use of other women in her career is cold and calculating; she makes friendly overtures to the nurses so that they will be on her side. She treats them as favored subordinates, never trying to establish real relationships with them because they are professionally beneath her. When she visits the law offices of Mayfair and Mayfair, she recognizes immediately that Lauren is the brains of the partnership and the one in control, and yet the relationship she cultivates is with Ryan, the male figurehead. Clearly, the most powerful of the witches has no interest in powerful relationships with other women.

This inability to form equal relationships is also demonstrated in her marriage to Michael. While she does form a relationship with Michael, for her part it is based on her appreciation of his ability to perform rape-like sex. She deliberately withholds what she's thinking from him, even though her actions often have an impact on his life. In short, she sees him as a sexual object, not a partner, an inversion of the usual patriarchal relationship. Thus Rowan denies the power of equal partnership and undercuts any close relationship she might possibly have with Michael.

Rowan's inability to form relationships also undercuts this novel's constant assertion that she is a great strong female character, the most powerful of the witches. But Rowan's greatest failing as the strong female character is that she is constantly weak and easily victimized throughout the story. If Rowan is the greatest of the Mayfair witches, it's little wonder that they've all come to such bad ends throughout history.

As the book opens, Rowan is a loner, not by choice because she loves being alone but because she fears connection. She has brief affairs with firefighters and policemen, subconsciously looking for someone to rescue her instead of trying to save herself. Her sexual preference is for rape fantasies, acting out her passion for being the victim, a person who cannot be responsible for her own life (sexual or otherwise) because she is helpless at the hands of others. A preference for rough sex does not automatically make a female character a victim, but when that is the character's *only* preference, readers may assume that this character is not confident in the power of her own sexuality. This portrayal of Rowan as a sexual victim is only strengthened by her decision to sleep with the uncle she hates so that he won't leave the aunt she loves. When he decides to leave anyway, she acts to protect her aunt and kills him, but she can only act to protect others, not herself. She even lets herself be victimized by Carlotta, falling into Carlotta's manipulations and killing her, only to feel guilty at her actions. Reading through her relationships, we come to the conclusion that anybody can victimize Rowan.

She is also professionally weak, working miracles in the operating room but ducking the jealousy of her fellow surgeons, manipulating the nurses so they'll like her instead of relying on her own personality (admittedly cold) and her own very great surgical skills to earn their approval. When she is appalled by the fetal research she is shown, she runs from the lab, but she does nothing to publicize and stop the research or to act on her horror. Finally, she gives up her career at the urging of her family, creating a plan for a medical complex that pleases them but cannot give her the personal satisfaction that surgery gave her. And she leaves the medical center behind when Lasher tells her she must come with him at the end. Even as a great surgeon, she's a weakling.

But it is in this last relationship with Lasher that her true role as a victim becomes clear. She loves Michael who in return gives her all his love, but she lies to him and sends him away in order to act out her rape fantasies with the demon, begging Lasher to "make it cruel" as she thrashes in ecstasy. This makes Rowan not only a cheating wife, but also a stupid cheating wife since she knows very well what Lasher is and what Lasher has done. Then at the witching hour, she stands helpless and horrified while Lasher enters her body and takes her baby, evicting its soul forever to take its fetal body. When Lasher is born, the incarnation of evil, she does nothing to save herself or to avenge her child, shutting off her emotions to examine him as a scientist, noting in particular his penis, the part of him that is most likely to victimize her again. And finally, she lets Lasher control her, leaving her beloved husband floating face down in a swimming pool to follow Lasher out into the night. If ever a woman was asking for it, it's Rowan Mayfair.

As a victim, Rowan makes a fascinating, fully developed, clearly motivated character, and were she portrayed as a victim, no feminist critic would dispute her legitimacy in the story. The problem is that Rowan is again and again referred to as a strong woman, an independent woman, the most powerful of the witches, the one who will defeat Lasher if anyone can. The damage that Rowan's character does, then, is not because she's a victim, but because she's a victim presented as an ideal twentieth-century woman: intelligent, capable, and strong. She isn't, and feminist criticism would only ask that readers take note of the fact.

10

Lasher
(1993)

The beginning of *Lasher* finds things in the same hopeless state that they were at the end of *The Witching Hour*. Rowan Mayfair is helpless in the hands of Lasher, the demon that has followed and enriched the Mayfair family for centuries and who has become flesh by taking over the body of Rowan's unborn baby. Grown to full height on the night of his birth, Lasher has taken Rowan with him across Europe to discover the secret of his past and to bear him another child like himself, abusing her terribly in the process. Meanwhile, Rowan's husband, Michael, sits shaken and silent until another strong Mayfair witch, thirteen-year-old Mona, comes to his house and seduces him. This, combined with the appearance of the ghost of the long dead Julien Mayfair, the only powerful male witch the family ever produced, brings Michael back to reality in time to deal with the search for his wife and the menace of the strange, abrupt men who claim to be from the Talamasca, the nonviolent organization that has studied the paranormal for centuries. At the end of the story, Michael must also deal with the return of his wife in a vegetative state due to the physical abuses she has suffered at the hands of Lasher, and with the return of Lasher himself, who has come to explain his actions and beg forgiveness as the last of a supernatural race called the Taltos.

POINT OF VIEW

As she has in several of her earlier novels, Rice pulls this multichar-
acter story together with multiple third-person limited point-of-view
narrators (using "he" or "she" instead of "I"), and once again, she in-
tersperses those scenes with first-person narratives told to the point-of-
view character by another character. It's a system that she's perfected,
and it only fails her when the first-person narratives seem misplaced, as
Lasher's narrative does at the climax of the story. Because Rice keeps all
the narratives together in chronological time, her story never becomes
confusing even though the point of view changes with each scene.

CHARACTER DEVELOPMENT

Once again Rowan Mayfair and Michael Curry are Rice's protagonists,
and their goal is the redemption of Rowan from the antagonist Lasher,
an immeasurably powerful demon and a worthy opponent. The story
question then becomes, "Will Rowan break free of Lasher and survive?"
and it affects the identities of both protagonists because Rowan wants to
see herself as a strong woman and not a victim and Michael wants to
rescue, protect, and avenge his wife. They are joined in their goal by an
old character who tells his history and a new character who explodes
like a firecracker on the page.

Rowan's identity as a strong woman was cast in doubt at the end of
The Witching Hour when she allowed herself to become Lasher's victim.
One of the Mayfair witches, Ancient Evelyn, has seen her as a victim
before that at her wedding, describing her as "a sacrificial creature for
the family, decked out in white with the emerald burning on her neck"
(151). Rowan is now being dragged through Europe by Lasher who continually tries to impregnate her through rape, and although she thinks
about killing Lasher, she cries at the thought and tells herself she's a fool
(226). Eventually, she even denies the responsibility of making him, telling him "I'm not Mary Shelley," even though in *The Witching Hour* she'd
seen the movie *Frankenstein* based on Shelley's book and longed to be
the mad scientist (231). By denying her own complicity in her predicament, forgetting that she has chosen to go with him in the name of
science and knowledge, Rowan reinforces her identity as a victim. When
she manages to crawl back home, she falls into a catatonic trance from

which she is rescued by her otherworldly daughter Emaleth, whom she promptly shoots, a reaction prompted by fear. Rowan can be considered a dynamic character because she does change, but her change is a disintegration into weakness and unconsciousness, and she fails to generate enough sympathy and understanding to be a truly strong protagonist.

Michael, on the other hand, moves beyond his usual passive state, and his growth is well-presented. When he hears that observers feel that Rowan is a captive, he is relieved because, although he agonizes over Rowan's plight, he feels glad that his "wily bride had not cuckolded him with the devil" (185). Male pride has been slow to awaken in Michael, but when it does, it wakens with a vengeance. That this awakening is due to his being seduced by a thirteen-year-old girl is even more evidence of his changing character since the incurably correct Michael of *The Witching Hour* would never have committed statutory rape. Michael's finest moment and the greatest evidence of his character arc come at the end of the story when he listens to Lasher's sad history of despair and torture. The sensitive Michael of the previous book would have understood Lasher, but the Michael of *Lasher* has been through the fire and he's mad as hell. Readers cheer when he tosses Lasher off the roof of the house, and the only regret is that the house wasn't higher.

Lasher the demon is once again a static character, and even his long drawn-out story of his lousy previous life cannot make him anything but a personification of evil. By the time readers get to Lasher's statement that "I dare you to hear me out and not forgive," forgiveness is out of the question (483). In fact, his self-serving story is mainly an irritant since the action stops completely while he whines. The only real question is why anybody listens to a character who so obviously has retribution coming to him in spades. But although Lasher is a static character, he's a great static character, made up of equal parts of selfishness, cruelty, and lust. There's a lot to be said for a character who is so evil that the reader itches to see his defeat, and Lasher is just that, one of the great villains of literature.

The male Mayfair witch, Julien, comes back in this book to warn Michael about Lasher and to tell his story, and in this case, evil is redeemed at least in part. Julien tells Michael that he had feared Lasher and served him, even to the point of raping his sister, Katherine, the person he saw as "his innocent self." Once convinced of Lasher's evil, Julien vows to fight him, telling God "I will go to hell if you save my family" (341). To that end he chooses to be earthbound when he dies so that he can hang around and advise the family from beyond the grave. He is the one who inspires Mona to seduce Michael, not the best possible move in the long run as it turns out in the following book, but definitely Michael's salvation in this one. His appearance to Michael strengthens Michael's resolve to kill Lasher at the first opportunity. Julien is not so much a dynamic or changing character as he is a revised one. Readers who experienced the Julien of *The Witching Hour* now get a look at another side of him, and he becomes a fully realized character full of flaws, anguish, and contradictory characteristics that make him seem completely human.

But the strongest of the characters in *Lasher* is a supporting character, thirteen-year-old Mona, who is refreshingly free of angst and who will never be a victim if she has anything to say about it. Just as Lestat was a welcome change from the depressing, despairing Louis in *Interview with the Vampire*, so is Mona a welcome change from the cold, weak Rowan. Unlike Rowan, Mona is not afraid of her powers or intimidated by the weight of her family. She's also not intimidated by social rules. She seduces her forty-eight-year-old relative by marriage, Michael, in part to bring him out of his depression, seeing herself as "wonder glue for broken hearts," but also because she wants his body (24). Mona will not be anybody's sexual victim, and she takes her pleasure with her good deeds. She also has an efficient way of evaluating people, dividing the world into kind and unkind; this plan seems too simplistic until one reflects that this kind of yardstick would have saved Rowan from Lasher (28). But Mona would have been merely a colorful static character if Rice had left her as she began. Instead, Mona changes through loss. In the beginning, she wears children's clothes, including a big bow in her hair, to hide the fact that she has a well-developed woman's body. This makes everyone around feel safe (even Michael tells her that as long as she has her bow, the world is all right) and hides her maturity. But when tragedy strikes again and again, resulting finally in the loss of her alcoholic child-mother to Lasher, Mona decides to grow up and handle the things that the adults around her have bungled. She signals this change by giving up her "ridiculous" clothes and dressing in her mother's clothing, like an adult. She then takes over the plans for Rowan's medical complex, as well as Rowan's place as the most powerful Mayfair witch. Her growth is motivated entirely by events, but Mona is never predictable or common. She is not only the greatest of the Mayfair witches, but she also ties with Lestat for Rice's most dynamic and fascinating character, one Rice herself has described as key to her work (Ramsland, *Witches Companion*, 291).

PLOT DEVELOPMENT AND STRUCTURE

Lasher is a relatively simple story for a Rice novel, turning on the central question of whether the protagonists, Rowan and Michael, can defeat Lasher. The exposition is Rice's previous novel, *The Witching Hour*, the rising action is Lasher growing stronger, abusing Rowan and murdering Mayfair women by impregnation while Michael and the rest of the Mayfairs try to protect themselves, and the climax is the death of Lasher at Michael's hands. This should make for a tight plot, but it's weakened by the addition of the first-person narratives that stop the story action in its tracks. Julien's story is fascinating, but Yuri's biography is a waste of the reader's time since he's hardly a major character. Worst of all, Lasher's apologetic biography goes beyond annoying, for the scene in which Michael sits down with Lasher at his dining room table to hear why Lasher has killed his child and brutalized his wife into a vegetative state comes at the end of a plot that has been designed to make the reader hate Lasher more than anything on the face of the earth. This annoyance is only increased when it turns out that Lasher is justifying his actions because his former life was a lousy one. At this point, the reader is not going to buy Lasher as an abused child. The final climax is extremely satisfactory, and the anticlimax with Rowan and her child is nicely ambiguous and chilling, but the breaks in the narrative for secondary character memories slow the forward movement of the plot.

It also doesn't help that the story doesn't seem to be in the control of any strong central characters whose actions move the plot. Rowan is obviously a central character, but she's a helpless victim for most of the story and a vegetable for most of the rest of it, so she can't do much to move the plot through her actions. Michael is in better shape, but he, too, waits and listens for most of the book. Lasher is active and moves the plot, but he's never a focal character, even when he finally tells his story. The character that the book belongs to both by default and by justice, is the beautifully strong, wonderfully developed character of Mona Mayfair, the thirteen-year-old witch whose intellectually and sexually precocious actions often move the plot, but Mona is too often offstage. Another problem is that Rice drops into the point of view of any number of fascinating but subordinate characters including Yuri, Ancient Evelyn, and Rowan's surgeon friend Lark. With all these narrators and no one strong central character, *Lasher* becomes the fifty-fifth chapter of

The Witching Hour instead of a full story in its own right, propelled more by the actions of Rowan and Michael in *The Witching Hour* than by the actions of anyone in *Lasher*.

LITERARY DEVICE: METAPHOR

As observed earlier, all of Rice's novels present deep themes about connection to others, and the metaphor that best symbolizes that connection is the metaphor of the Mayfair family. When Rowan discovers her family in *The Witching Hour*, she is awakened to the possibilities of connection, but she is seduced from them to bond with Lasher instead. As Rowan struggles to return, her family struggles to find her, not only those who are living but also the ghost of her ancestor, Julien, a man who once prayed to God that he was willing to go to hell as long as God kept his family safe. This sacrifice is echoed in the actions of the others in this novel who work to keep the family safe: in Mona who sleeps with Michael to reawaken him to life, in Julien who comes back to advise Michael, and in Michael himself who battles with Lasher for the soul of his wife. All of these struggles represent the willingness of individuals to sacrifice for other human beings, marking the connection of us all in one great human family. Rowan is welcomed back into the womb of the family to be reborn again in their love, and she sacrifices, too, killing her newborn alien daughter to ensure that not only her Mayfair family but also the family of humankind will be safe.

Thus for Rice family represents more than just the blood bond of the clan; it also represents love, loyalty, and connection with others, the act that makes us human. In the end it is really family that defeats Lasher because he cannot conceive of the bond that strengthens Rowan and the protectiveness that drives Michael. Isolated and selfish, he cannot understand love, and so he dies while the family continues free.

THEMATIC ISSUES

Theme in *Lasher* becomes clear if clues from the novel are combined with the metaphor of the family. The setting for most of *Lasher* is New Orleans, the home of the Mayfair family, a place of love and mysticism and power. When Rowan leaves New Orleans, she is powerless, but when she returns, she recovers the strength of the family. Her character growth is the realization of her own weakness and dark desires, and it is that weakness that causes her internal conflict because she cannot destroy Lasher, no matter how much he abuses her, because he is her "child," all the darkness of her personality made flesh. This is reinforced in the beginning scene of the book, which is told from the point of view of Rowan's inhuman fetus, the child of her intercourse with her dark side. The fetus is confused and frightened but dreams of her birth and the birth of a new world, just as Rowan desperately needs a rebirth out of the horror Lasher has plunged her into. The ending shows that Rowan has come through the horrors to her own rebirth: "She was Rowan. She was healed" (578). Thus the theme becomes the search for self-knowledge through acceptance of the darkness within, a psychological "homecoming" that is reinforced by Rowan's literal coming home to the Mayfair house in New Orleans. Even the title *Lasher* reinforces this theme when the novel is analyzed according to Jung's psychological theories. Jung said that the darkness inside all of us is represented in a Shadow figure, and Lasher is not just a demon: he is also Rowan's Shadow.

A JUNGIAN READING OF *LASHER*

Carl Jung, who first worked with the idea of the archetype in mythology, also extended his archetypes beyond the figures found in mythology. Instead of using Freud's idea of the conscious ego and the unconscious id (see chapter 3), he theorized that there was an ego and a "Shadow"—a dark side of the self that must be acknowledged before a person could be whole. Ursula K. LeGuin has described this dark side as "inferior, primitive, awkward, animallike, childlike, powerful, vital, spontaneous. . . . dark and hairy and unseemly" (64). Anne Rice has a shorter description of it; she calls it "Lasher."

Lasher acts as the Shadow for the entire Mayfair family. Because he exists, they lie and steal, rape and commit incest, murder and work magic, and so he is the ultimate bad influence on them. But he also is responsible for their health, wealth, and power. Without Lasher, the Mayfairs would not exist; therefore Lasher is not the evil outside but the evil within. LeGuin makes the same point about the evil in fairy tales, arguing that it is not opposed to good but is inextricably intertwined with it (66). The Shadow is not the Other, it's part of the whole being.

This is something that the representative of the Mayfairs, Rowan, must understand for the entire clan. As the most powerful witch, she is the one chosen to face the Shadow. But facing the Shadow means facing herself because the Shadow is all the qualities that the Ego suppresses because it can't bear to look at them. Rowan has repressed all her inner knowledge, but when she admits Lasher into her life at the end of *The Witching Hour*, she acknowledges the dark side of herself as she lies to her husband, cheats on him with the demon, and begs to be hurt and degraded through rape. LeGuin says that the person who denies her relationship with evil denies her reality, and Rowan finds her reality in her obsessive relationship with her Shadow at the end of *The Witching Hour* (65).

But Rowan cannot complete the end of the journey. As LeGuin also points out, in many fairy tales, the animal guide that has helped the hero throughout the journey then asks the hero to cut off its head. This represents the need for the hero to move beyond animal spirits to achieve a new whole life. When Lasher is born at the end of *The Witching Hour*, Rowan has the opportunity to kill him, to cut off the head of her animal spirits, and return to her real life reborn. But she hesitates because she is still fascinated with her dark side, the Shadow, and the Shadow overwhelms her and takes over her life.

Thus *Lasher*, in Jungian terms, is the story of Rowan's recovery of herself through her battle with her Shadow figure, Lasher. And her recovery is the archetypal struggle of the Ego and Shadow, the struggle between darkness and light. Lasher keeps her a sexual prisoner, using her darkest instincts against her, until she brings herself to strike out at him. Yet she cannot completely destroy him, and so she returns home only half-alive, part of herself still controlled by her Shadow demon. It is only when Michael kills Lasher, literally taking the head from his body as the hero does to the animal spirits in the fairy tale, that Rowan is truly free. Even then, she awakes only to the child of her union with Lasher. The child of union of the Ego and the Shadow is the new understanding of self that liberates the soul and causes it to be reborn. In the same way, Rowan drinks from her child and is reborn again into new life with new knowledge of her own dark secrets and the presence of evil in the world. That she fears this knowledge and represses it by killing it only shows that she has not completed her Jungian journey. This search for self-knowledge will continue in the third book of the Witches Chronicles, *Taltos*.

11

Taltos
(1994)

In *Taltos*, the third book of Anne Rice's Witches Chronicles, Rowan Mayfair recovers from her catatonic trance when she is told that her good
friend and relative Aaron Lightner has been murdered. Rowan goes to
Europe with her husband, Michael, to avenge Aaron's death, leaving
behind Rowan's young relative, Mona, another powerful witch who is
pregnant with Michael's baby. Once in Europe they join forces with Ashlar, the last of the Taltos, a supernatural race, and Yuri, a member of the
Talamasca, the centuries-old group that Aaron worked for. Together they
find the men who ordered Aaron's death and eliminate them. On the
plane trip back to New York, Ashlar tells Rowan and Michael the story
of the Taltos, beings of goodness and truth who can reproduce so rapidly, maturing to adulthood in a day, that they would overrun the world.
Since he is the last Taltos, however, he poses no threat. Meanwhile back
home, Mona has given birth to a Taltos daughter, Morrigan. When
Rowan and Michael come home, they aren't sure what to do, but Ashlar
solves the problem by following them, meeting Morrigan, and taking her
to Europe with him to begin the Taltos race again.

POINT OF VIEW

Anne Rice has once again chosen to use multiple third-person narrators (characters who use "he" or "she" instead of "I") to tell her story

and has once again made some of those narrators listen while another character relates his history in first-person flashback or memories. While the success of her third-person narratives depends entirely on the central character in the scene so that the narratives of Mona Mayfair are full of energy and sass while those of Rowan Mayfair are full of weariness and calm, her first-person narratives-within-a-narrative tend to clunk because of the way they are introduced. In one, a villain bargains for his life by telling a story; in another, a supernatural being recites his history for pages because the two main characters have asked him to do so. In both cases, the telling of the stories seems at odds with what is happening in the narrative. It seems to represent an artificial time-out while the author drops some information she thinks the reader should know, instead of a character desperate to tell this story because it is vital that his listeners understand. Still, the narrative hangs together and is never confusing, thanks to Rice's carefully controlled use of point of view. She keeps her multiple narrators in the now or present time of the story, leaving flashbacks for the storytellers. She also tells all her scenes in chronological order, that is, the order in which they occurred.

CHARACTER DEVELOPMENT

Taltos is plagued with static characters, people who walk through their paces without changing. There is nothing wrong with static characters if they are in supporting roles or if the plot is so strong that the events in it disguise the fact that the characters do not change and are not affected by it, but in *Taltos*, the three most important characters are static, and the events in the last half of the book are almost nonexistent. Only the introduction of two vividly dynamic characters keep the tension high in *Taltos*.

Rowan Mayfair and Michael Curry, the beautifully dynamic characters of Rice's earlier witch books, have now become static simply because they've been through so much before and their story has already been told. Once Rowan rouses herself from the catatonic trance she fell into after murdering her Taltos daughter, she takes off for Europe with Michael, and they both learn amazing things. But that's business as usual for them, particularly for Rowan who has given birth to two supernatural beings in the past year and shot one of them to death in her bedroom. When Rowan does act to kill for revenge, she does so with her mind, effortlessly. Both Rowan and Michael remain bloodless and be-mused throughout the book. Nothing they meet fazes them, and there-fore they cannot grow.

Ashlar the Taltos, the other major character, is the mirror image of the demon Lasher. Both beings are Taltos, but whereas Lasher is unmitigated evil, Ashlar is unmitigated good. Unmitigated evil is interesting because it poses a constant threat; unmitigated good is admirable but boring after a few pages because it doesn't do anything but stand there, being good. Since Ashlar always does the right thing while looking beautiful with his eyes full of love, he becomes not only a static character but almost a noncharacter, a symbol of the purity of a simpler time and place. Ashlar's lack of threat or personality becomes a serious drawback to this story because Rice's supernatural stories have always been driven by the sense of the unknown. All her vampires, mummies, and witches have the ca-pacity to do both good and evil, so the reader can never quite trust any of them, even the most admirable. But Ashlar the Taltos can only do good, which means there's really no story in the now that he can be an active part of, and he cannot change. In other words, he's a static char-acter. In only one scene does Ashlar show a flaw. When he meets Tessa, the only other being in the world like him, he kisses her gently and then tells the others to take her to the Talamasca. Even though she's the last of his kind, he has no interest in her because she's barren. Given Ashlar's gentleness and love for people, this is inexplicable unless Ashlar sees women, especially women of his own race, only as sexual objects and baby makers. Were this developed, it would have given more dimension to Ashlar as a character, but Rice returns immediately to her character-ization of static Ashlar as the Perfect Alien.

Stuart, Mark, and Tommy, the members of the rogue Talamasca trio that steal and murder so that they can witness the mating of the Taltos, are also static characters. Like all of Rice's people, they are wealthy be-yond belief, and so they turn to secret knowledge, something they can hoard besides money. Even so, their motivation seems strange. Kill three people so they can watch two supernatural beings make love and repro-duce? This may be possible for the unworldly, knowledge-mad Stuart who drinks the water at Glastonbury for luck, but Mark and Tommy are drawn as overeducated thugs, hardly the type to put themselves out for an otherworldly peep show. They are simply stick figures of evil, on stage so briefly and verbally (never in action) that the reader doesn't get much vicarious thrill when they're dispatched in a particularly horrible way.

This leaves the characters of Rice's subplot to hold the stage, and they do it beautifully. Both of Rice's teenage witches, Mona and Mary Jane Mayfair, are vibrant, interesting characters, but Mona, above all, claims this book as her own. Precocious beyond belief at thirteen, she has already mastered high finance and high seduction, luring Michael into her arms in *Lasher* so that at the start of *Taltos* she finds herself not only the heir to the Mayfair billions but also pregnant with the next heir, Michael's daughter, whom she has already named Morrigan. Mona's character growth in *Lasher* was also dynamic, moving her from a rebellious child to the brink of adulthood, but in *Taltos* she completes her growth, commanding first the attention and then the obedience of her family, connecting to Mary Jane in a free sisterhood, and finally accepting her monsterlike Taltos child with both maternal love and intelligent caution. At the end, when Mona vows to protect her child no matter what, it is not a childish vow but a very real tortured promise that takes into consideration the possibility that Morrigan will destroy the world and the Mayfair family with it. And through it all, Mona retains a joy for life that absolutely infuses every scene she narrates. When Mona says, "You know, you just know that it is magnificent to be alive," the reader does not think cynical thoughts but instead rejoices with her because it is indeed magnificent to be Mona (302).

Mary Jane, in contrast, is a been-there-done-that delinquent with the bluntness that is charming in a child and annoying in an adult. Since Mary Jane seems to be straddling the line between childhood and adulthood (a curious late bloomer standing next to the ferociously early bloomer Mona), she is alternately charming and annoying, and in the beginning she seems like a cartoon next to Mona. But as Mary Jane helps Mona with her increasingly terrifying predicament, she becomes a dynamic character, one who longs for education and family acceptance, but who is willing to stand by her newfound sister no matter what the cost. Rice has said that she loves these two characters in particular, and it shows in the way she has explored their fears and their dreams, and in the way she has developed their friendship, the first truly warm, close, unselfish friendship between women she has created in any of her supernatural books. Mona and Mary Jane are the best of all possible characters, the kind that are so interesting and so real that the reader must read on to see how they will handle the next crisis and how that crisis will change them.

PLOT DEVELOPMENT AND STRUCTURE

The plot of *Taltos* is hampered by two problems: the main characters are static, and the book itself is the sequel to a sequel instead of a new story using characters from a previous book. In the Vampire Chronicles, Rice first told Louis's story, then Lestat's story, then the mythology of the vampires, then a new story and a new problem for Lestat dealing with new characters, and finally the ultimate story and problem for Lestat dealing with the ultimate characters. But the Witches Chronicles are the story of the Mayfair witches, and then the rest of the story of the Mayfair witches, and then some more of the rest of the story of the Mayfair witches. This series therefore becomes as inbred as the Mayfairs, producing a book that is in flashes both brilliant and feeble.

The active plot of *Taltos* begins when news is brought to the catatonic Rowan Mayfair that Aaron Lightner, her good friend and relative by marriage, has been murdered by being run down by a car. This galvanizes her to regain full consciousness and to go to Europe to seek revenge on the organization that she assumes has killed Aaron, the Talamasca. It also sets up an exciting plot: Rowan is the protagonist (with her husband Michael Curry), her goal is to revenge Aaron and protect the rest of her family, and her antagonist is the Talamasca, a huge powerful organization and therefore an extremely worthy opponent for a powerful witch. This means that the central question of the plot is, "Will Rowan defeat the Talamasca?" It's an excellent plot question because it also has a direct impact on Rowan's identity, or her sense of who she is, because Rowan is devoted to the Mayfair family. If she does not avenge Aaron and protect her family, her identity will be threatened; therefore she will do everything in her power to achieve her goal. This goal is only strengthened by the subplot of the book, the struggle of Mona Mayfair to bear her child, the next inheritor or "legacy" of the Mayfair dynasty. Mona and her unborn baby are sure to become a target of the Talamasca if Rowan does not defeat them, so this increases the pressure on Rowan as the protagonist.

Therefore, the exposition of *Taltos* is the setup of Rowan's catatonia, the turning point into rising action is Aaron's death, the rising action is Rowan and Michael's pursuit of the antagonists, the climax is the defeat and deaths of the antagonists, and the falling action and resolution is Rowan and Michael's return and the safe delivery of Mona's baby. It's a lovely, tight plot, but there are a few problems with it: the battle is uneven, the struggle is too easy, and the outcome occurs much too early in the book.

When the leader of the rogue Talamasca, Stuart Gordon, is picked up on the street by Rowan and Michael and Ashlar, they force him to take them to the tower to meet Tessa, the female Taltos he has been hiding, and there he tells his story in order to bargain for his life. When his story is finished, he tries to escape, and Rowan kills him with her mind. This is cheating the reader in several ways. First, Stuart is outgunned. No matter how much he deserves to die (and the reader does want him to die), his death scene is a puny thing without struggle or suffering because there is no equality between protagonists and antagonist. All three protagonists are formidable because they have unlimited wealth and supernatural powers. Stuart, on the other hand, is old, stupid, and powerless. In other words, he never has a chance. He is therefore never a worthy opponent.

Second, the power of the Talamasca and the number of deaths this rogue group has caused (particularly the death of the much-loved Aaron) has led the reader to expect that the struggle between the two groups will be tougher and therefore more satisfying. Rice has foreshadowed or set up a great conflict that she then undercuts by having Rowan kill Stuart without breaking a sweat. She undercuts it even more by leaving Stuart's two henchmen to the hands of the Talamasca instead of to the protagonists, Rowan and Michael. The Talamasca dispatches them with suitable horror, but even this is not terribly satisfying since there are dozens of Talamasca and only two henchmen. Once more, it's not even a contest.

Third, Stuart dies on page 269 and his henchmen die on page 291 of a 467 page novel. That leaves 176 pages of falling action, more than one-third of the book. Most of this action becomes nonaction, a character telling the tale of his life, and it's a long life since the character is Ashlar, the Taltos, and he's been around since pre-history. Having removed the major natural (as opposed to supernatural) threat in the narrative, Rice has moved her plot from physical action in the real world to the life of the mind, and for the rest of the book, the story unfolds without tension. Therefore the ending of *Taltos* drags because the external conflict is solved too swiftly, and all that remains is endless storytelling, included because it is needed to set up the final scene in the book.

Taltos is, in fact, not so much a novel as a faerie mythology, the story of wondrous beings of peace and light who are almost wiped out by Christianity but who are recovered and reborn through the Mayfair witches. There is nothing wrong with book-length mythologies, but *Taltos* begins as a novel, promises the reader great conflict through the forces of good in the Mayfair witches and the forces of evil in the rogue Talamasca, adds the possibility of a supernatural child that will automatically be the target of the evil forces, and then disintegrates in mid-plot to become a bloodless recounting of a people whose greatest leader can only describe their life as "I don't remember rape. I don't remember execution. I don't remember grudges that lasted very long" (327). That this wisest of all Taltos can equate rape and execution with long grudges pretty well sums up the problem with this mythic tale: it has no depth, no passion, and no real beings—real in the sense of being any more than cardboard ideals of a prettified master race.

With this kind of confusion at the heart of it, *Taltos* can only fall apart at the end when the last of the Taltos, Ashlar and Morrigan, discover each other and go off to reproduce at their own personal Stonehenge. There are indications in the text that this is supposed to be ominous, but since Ashlar has just spent hours telling Rowan and Michael about how the Taltos mostly just want to sing, dance, and make love, it's hard to see how even thousands of Taltos let loose on the world could do more than send the globe back to the Summer of Love and make daisy-toting hippies of everyone again. Because Rice's mythology is bloodless, her climax is cold and reads more as an anticlimax, the last fizzle of the firecracker this book could have been.

LITERARY DEVICE: MOTIF

The major motif in *Taltos* is the tower. Towers have several meanings in literature. For example, they reach into the heavens and can be seen as symbols of human stupidity and arrogance in challenging God. The Tower of Babel in the Bible was seen as a challenge to God and destroyed because of it. The brochs, the earliest towers in *Taltos*, built by the Taltos as a refuge from their enemies, fit this aspect. Strongly constructed with huge double walls, they seem invincible, but they fall to the invaders anyway. In the same way, the Taltos erected tall stones to mark their territory only to see these fall, too. The towers erected to show the race's invincibility became symbols of their defeat instead because only God is invincible.

Towers can also be seen as a symbol of those who raise themselves above humanity, thinking higher thoughts and attaining a higher goodness. This is one of the reasons why cathedrals were built to soar into the sky, not as a challenge to God but as a symbol of humanity's soaring spirit. Ashlar's skyscraper in New York is this kind of tower, filled with dolls and wonderful plans for the children of the world. Ashlar also thinks about building public skyscrapers that will act as skyparks so that everyone can see the superior view he sees. His use of the tower shows not only the soaring goodness of his soul but also his generosity toward others.

Finally, towers are often used in literature as a symbol of male power, phallic symbols that assert male dominance while trapping women inside them. Alfred, Lord Tennyson's famous poem, "The Lady of Shalott" features this kind of tower, a stone building with a woman trapped inside who weaves night and day, forbidden even to look out the window on penalty of death. The ancient broch tower where Stuart keeps Tessa is like the Lady of Shalott's tower. Technically, Tessa is free to leave, but in reality, she has nowhere to go. In the outside world, she is raped and abused; only inside the tower is she safe at her loom, just like the Lady of Shalott. Thus, although Stuart doesn't literally keep her a prisoner, male power traps her inside, and Stuart knows this. He could have brought her into the Talamasca and made her safe in a world full of other people, but instead he keeps her alone in the tower, knowing she'll never leave him because she can't face the outside world alone. (An even more overt use of a tower as a male power symbol is the skyscraper in which Lasher imprisons Rowan in *Lasher*.) Rowan is literally a prisoner, tied hand and foot and repeatedly raped, a sickeningly real victim of male power. That the skyscraper she is trapped in is empty is a further symbol of Lasher's spiritual emptiness. Ashlar's tower is full of life and people and toys; Lasher's is full of emptiness and pain.

Rice's use of all of these towers seems to act as a metaphor for the uses and abuses of power by men, reflecting their owner's arrogance, spirituality, or cruelty. There is one other interpretation of the tower motif, however, and that can be found in a source close to a witch's heart, the Tarot. Tarot cards are used to understand the unconscious forces working on a question or situation. Tarot readers lay their cards out in a pattern, and then deduce significance from the card's meaning and where it falls in the pattern. The Tarot card of the Tower is a particularly powerful card, representing the rejection and destruction of outdated beliefs. One of the things Ashlar asks is that the humans of the world give up their outdated beliefs about the Other and accept all living beings, and the tower motif reinforces this, too. In this way, the tower motif helps illuminate the theme of *Taltos*.

THEMATIC ISSUES

Theme is difficult to analyze in *Taltos* because the book is really more interested in telling the myth history of the Taltos than in telling a story. The settings can't provide the usual clues because they're too numerous. In the same way the diffusion of the characters makes it difficult to focus on any one for character growth or internal conflict, especially since most of the characters are static. However, a look at Mona, the most dynamic character, shows that her growth is from child to mother, culminating in her total acceptance of her child, even though her child is not human, a move foreshadowed by the Tarot interpretation of the towers in the novel. In a parallel to Mona, Rowan comes to regret killing her daughter, realizing it was from fear of the unknown and not from certainty that the child posed a threat. This acceptance of the Other on faith is central to the survival of the Taltos, and that the book is concerned with the survival of these inhumans is indisputable. For one thing, the title tells the reader that this is their story, not the story of Michael and Rowan or even Mona. An analysis of the beginning and ending of the book shows that in the beginning, Ashlar is alone and despairing in his skyscraper. But at the end, he is with Morrigan and heading back to nature and the ancient monuments of their kind to begin the Taltos race again.

Therefore, the combination of acceptance of the Other with the revival of the Taltos race seems to indicate a theme encouraging the acceptance of the unknown on faith in the dawn of a new era, a plea for the acceptance of the Other no matter what the Other is. As Ashlar says, "Deep within us are the seeds of hate for what is different. We do not have to be taught these things. We have to be taught *not* to give in to them! They are in our blood; but in our minds is the charity and the love to overcome them" (422).

A MYTHOLOGICAL READING OF *TALTOS*

Since this book is in large part the mythology of the Taltos, a mythological comparison should shed some light on Rice's story. In fact, there is a clear mythological parallel to Rice's Taltos in the Celtic myths of the Tuatha de Danaan, the Children of Danu, also known as the Faerie and the People of the Otherworld. Like the Taltos, the Faerie were remarkable for their height and their pale beauty. Like the Taltos, the Faerie were not concerned with time; people who crossed over into the Otherworld might stay for a day and return to reality to find a hundred years had passed, or they might stay for a hundred years and return to find only a day had passed. And like the Taltos, the Faerie myths came from Ireland, Wales, and England, tying into the Authurian legend that Rice draws on in her Glastonbury setting. A comparison of their mythology and Rice's mythology points out both the strengths and weaknesses of the Taltos mythos.

In Rice's video biography, *Anne Rice: Birth of the Vampire*, Rice's sister says that they were taught that there were other worlds existing parallel to their own. This is the Celtic concept of the Otherworld, a world that it is possible to cross over into at life's "borders," places or times that are really neither one thing nor another. For example, crossroads are neither one road nor the other, bridges are neither water nor dry land, and dawn and twilight are neither day nor night. Particularly strong borders are the "Eves" such as All Hallows Eve, the break between autumn and winter that we celebrate as Halloween. And of course, there is the Witching Hour, midnight, which is neither the previous day nor the coming day. It is at the Witching Hour on Christmas Eve, a particularly strong border, that Lasher crosses over into the world of the flesh. And Ashlar promises Morrigan that they will conceive their child at dawn, another border, among the stones in England. Those stones are also part of Celtic myths that tell the story of the building of Stonehenge and the other monuments that Ashlar claims for the Taltos in Rice's mythology. And the Celtic name for Stonehenge, "The Dance of the Giants," echoes the name for the Taltos in antiquity.

Rice also echoes the Celtic myths in her use of women as sorceresses and battle leaders, particularly in the powerful character of Janet, the Taltos who refuses to follow Ashlar into Christianity, warns of the folly to come, and dies cursing everyone. Janet has a strong counterpart in the Celtic battle goddess, the Morrigan, the goddess of sex and death. She turns up later in Arthurian myth as Morgan Le Fay, the sorceress half-sister of Arthur who warns him that Christianity will lead to his downfall and opposes him throughout the legend, only to come for his body at the end and take it away to sleep in Avalon near Glastonbury until England needs him again and wakes him. Morrigan is a figure of both good and of evil, so when Rice gives her name to Mona's Taltos daughter, she's drawing on the myth to show that once again there are two sides to be considered, and that Mona's Morrigan will be a force to be reckoned with.

But while Rice's mythology draws on many powerful aspects of the Celtic myths, she fails to include the duality that Morrigan and the Faerie represent. As Rice describes the Taltos, they are simple, loving people who want to sing, dance, and make love, and who have no vices at all. This means there is no evil to balance the good, no dark to make the light seem brighter, no texture to give the myth depth and blood. In the end, then, it reads less like a myth than a fairy tale. Anyone who has read any of Rice's previous books knows that this is not because she is too squeamish to write darkness and blood, but evidently the Taltos were too squeamish to remember the dark parts of their history. As Ashlar tells it, "I do believe there were bad ones among us. . . . I think there were. There were those who killed perhaps and those who were killed. I'm sure it must have been that way. . . . But no one wanted to talk about it! They would leave things out of the tales! So we had no history of bloody incidents, rapes, conquests of one group of men by another. And a great horror of violence prevailed" (332–333).

Yet every major mythos in the world accepts both life and death, good and evil. The dual nature of the world is what makes myth interesting because it is in the conflict between good and evil that most myths demonstrate their meaning. The goddess Morrigan inspires sexual feelings, so through sex she brings life. Yet life alone would result in the nightmare that the Taltos present: unbridled reproduction that crowds the world with people. So Morrigan is also the battle goddess, bringing death with her crows flying around her. This duality is therefore also a circularity, a balance that the world needs. The Taltos myth lacks that balance because they refuse to accept the existence of evil in their lives.

Yet there was evil, as Ashlar's story makes clear. The Taltos world was one in which a woman could be attacked so that the men could suck milk from her breasts against her will, and Ashlar's insistence that "if she really didn't want us sucking her milk, well, within a reasonable amount of time, we stopped" does not mean that the Taltos did not have their own form of rape, "reasonable amount of time" notwithstanding (324). Coupled with Ashlar's later assertion that "simple women were cherished because they were gay all the time, and glad to be living and not afraid of giving birth," the Taltos paradise becomes a living hell for all but "simple" women who don't mind being barefoot and pregnant and therefore closer to death since childbearing for the Taltos meant earlier deaths for women. Ashlar obviously still sees women in the same light, for when he meets the last Taltos, Tessa, he does not welcome her into his home as the last of his clan as any Mayfair male would do for any Mayfair female. He instead turns her over to the Talamasca to die with strangers because she's barren and therefore of no use to him. Imagine thinking you were the only human left in a world of aliens, only to meet the only other living human in the world. Ours is a cold, violent, sexist world, yet it is unimaginable that we would walk away from each other as Ashlar walks away from Tessa because she is no longer sexually useful to him.

Therefore, at the same time Rice's mythology suffers from its refusal to acknowledge an evil that would balance its goodness, it also betrays the presence of an insidious kind of evil, a canker in the rose that spoils the myth without giving it depth. This failure to accept its own evil makes the myth seem false, and Ashlar's stress on remembering only the good parts makes it seem shallow. Rice's ability to construct a flesh-and-blood myth has been proven indisputably in *The Queen of the Damned*. *Taltos* would benefit greatly from a transfusion of the imagination that created that legend.

Bibliography

Note: Page numbers referred to in the text are to the paperback editions of Anne Rice's novels.

WORKS BY ANNE RICE

Cry to Heaven. New York: Ballantine, 1976.
The Feast of All Saints. New York: Ballantine, 1979.
Interview with the Vampire. New York: Ballantine, 1976.
Lasher. New York: Knopf, 1993.
Memnoch the Devil. New York: Knopf, 1995.
The Mummy or Ramses the Damned. New York: Ballantine, 1989.
The Queen of the Damned. New York: Ballantine, 1988.
The Tale of the Body Thief. New York: Ballantine, 1992.
Taltos. New York: Knopf, 1994.
The Vampire Lestat. New York: Ballantine, 1985.
The Witching Hour. New York: Ballantine, 1990.

Writing as Anne Rampling

Belinda. New York: Morrow, 1987.
Exit to Eden. New York: Morrow, 1985.

Writing as A. N. Roquelaure

Beauty's Punishment. New York: Dutton, 1984.
Beauty's Release. New York: Dutton, 1985.
The Claiming of Sleeping Beauty. New York: Dutton, 1983.

Reviews and Essays by Anne Rice

"A Cast of Killers." Book review. *New York Times Book Review*, 6 July 1986: 9.
"The Corpse Had a Familiar Face." Book review. *New York Times Book Review*,
    13 December 1987: 23.
"Daddy's Girl." Book review. *New York Times Book Review*, 5 June 1988: 24.
"David Bowie and the End of Gender." *Vogue*, November 1983: 434, 498.
"Eden in the Heart of the City." Review of *Southern Comfort* by Frederick Starr.
    New York Times Book Review, 31 December 1989: 7.
"A Lycanthropy Reader." Book review. *New York Times Book Review*, 5 April 1987:
    33.
"A Murder That Didn't Add Up." Review of *Blind Faith* by Joe McGinniss. *New
    York Times Book Review*, 29 January 1989: 9.
"Poetry and Poison." Review of *The Minus Man* by Lew McCreary. *New York
    Times Book Review*, 20 October 1991: 31.
"Presumed Innocent." Book review. *New York Times Book Review*, 28 June 1987:
    1.
"The Stranger." Book review. *New York Times Book Review*, 9 November 1986: 58.
"Welcome to the Lower Depths." Review of *Foreplay* by Catherine Roman. *New
    York Times Book Review*, 25 March 1990, sec. 7:13.

WORKS ABOUT ANNE RICE

General Information

Ansley, Leslie. "Queen of Halloween." *USA Today*, 25 October 1991: USW6.
Appelo, Tim. "The Haunted Life of Anne Rice." *Savvy Woman*, July 1989: 18.
Barton, Rick. "The Big Bite." *New Orleans Magazine*, November 1994: 54–57.
Bluestein, R. "Interview with the Pornographer." *Vogue*, April 1986: 212.

Boulard, Garry. "Anne Rice, Tourist Attraction." *Chicago Tribune*, 5 March 1995, sec. 12:1.

Brennan, Judy. "Rice's About-Face: Cruise Is Lestat." *Los Angeles Times*, 21 September 1994: F1.

Brumer, Andy. "Author Drawn to the Spirit of Vampires." *Atlanta Constitution*, 4 January 1989: C1.

Buchsbaum, Tony. "Not Such a Bloody Good Idea." *Times-Picayune*, 18 March 1990: E7.

Callum, Miles. "How the Vampire Lady Got That Way." *TV Guide*, 26 November 1994: 47.

Cheaklos, Christina. "Vampire Queen Buys New Lair." *Atlanta Journal Constitution*, 27 June 1993: A3.

Conant, Jennet. "Lestat, C'est Moi." *Esquire*, March 1994: 70–75.

Creekmore, Judy. "Invitation from the Vampire." *Times-Picayune*, 29 October 1992: OTR1.

Cuthburt, David. "GWTW 2: Margaret Mitchell Wouldn't Even Consider It . . . But Anne Rice Wishes She'd Been Asked." *Times-Picayune*, 3 September 1991: D1.

Dawson, Victoria. "Authors Writing New Chapter in New Orleans Literary Life." *Times-Picayune*, 25 February 1990: A1.

Doane, Janice, and Devon Hodges. "Undoing Feminism: from the Preoedipal to Postfeminism in Anne Rice's Vampire Chronicles." *American Literary History* 2 (1990): 422–442.

Donahue, Deirdre. "A Popularity As Undying As a Vampire." *USA Today*, 30 October 1992: D1.

———. "Rice's Ghosts Stalk *Witching Hour*." *USA Today*, 31 October 1990: D1.

Donovan. Sharon. "Contributing Factors: Haunting the Stacks with Anne Rice." *Library Journal*, 15 October 1990: 104.

Doyle, Jim. "Novelist Anne Rice Wins 'Mummy' Film Rights Suit." *San Francisco Chronicle*, 12 February 1994: A21.

"Experts Say King, Rice to Be Hot, Collectible Authors." *Your Money*, CNN, 18 February 1995.

Ezard, John. "Rice of Passage." *Guardian*, 12 January 1995, sec. 2:14.

Ferraro, Susan. "Novels You Can Sink Your Teeth Into." *New York Times Magazine*, 14 October 1990: 27–28, 67, 74–77.

Freedland, Jonathan. "Feeding Frenzy on Bitter Rice-Paper." *Guardian*, 6 July 1995, sec. 2:8.

Gates, David. "Queen of the Spellbinders." *Newsweek*, 5 November 1990: 76–77.

Gilmore, Mikal. "The Devil and Anne Rice." *Rolling Stone*, 13 July 1995: 92–103.

Ginsberg, Merle. "Interview with the 'Vampire' Author." *TV Guide*, 22–28 October 1994: 24–27.

Glentzer, Molly. "Sisters: Writing's in Their Blood." *Good Housekeeping*, September 1995: 221.

Grimes, William. "Grading the Gothic in Gotham." *New York Times*, 30 October 1992: C1.

Guillaud, Betty. "Southern Rep Fetes Quartet of Stars." *Times-Picayune*, 12 March 1989: F2.

Hirshey, Gerri. "Flesh for Fantasy." *Rolling Stone*, 20 November 1986: 91–94.

Hollinger, Veronica. "Anne Rice in the Academy: *Anne Rice* by Bette B. Roberts." *Science Fiction Studies*, March 1995: 129–130.

Hughlett, Mike. "Anne Rice Buys St. Elizabeth's Compound." *Times-Picayune*, 16 May 1993: F1.

Interview. "Charlie Rose." PBS. WNET, New York. 10 November 1994.

"Charlie Rose." PBS. WNET, New York. 25 July 1995.

"Good Morning America." ABC, New York. 24 September 1993.

"Larry King Live." CNN, New York. 11 November 1994.

"Larry King Live." CNN, New York. 27 July 1995.

"Showbiz Today." CNN, New York. 14 November 1994.

Jensen, Jeff. "Pair of Horrors Menace Marketeers." *Advertising Age*, 7 November 1994: 18.

Johnson, Brian. "Queen of the Night." *Maclean's*, 16 November 1992: 68.

Johnson, Judith. "Women and Vampires: Nightmare or Utopia?" *Kenyon Review*, Winter 1993: 72–80.

Kaplan, Michael. "Anne Rice Vamps Till Ready." *Rolling Stone*, 3 November 1988: 32.

King, Maureen. "Contemporary Women Writers and the 'New Evil': The Vampires of Anne Rice and Suzy McKee Charnas." *Journal-of-the-Fantastic-in-the-Arts*, 1993: 75–84.

King, Ronette. "Novel End for Landmark." *Times-Picayune*, 29 May 1993: RE1.

Lane, Anthony. "Sucking Up." *New Yorker*, 17 October 1994: 122.

Larson, Susan. "Books R Us." *Times-Picayune*, 24 November 1991: E6.

Lewis, Paul. "Interview with the Electorate." *Los Angeles Times*, 28 November 1994: B7.

"The Literary Life: How the Other Half Lives." *Esquire*, July 1989: 82–89.

Longino, Miriam. " 'Vampire' Captures Macabre Genius Behind Rice's Brooding Fictional World." *Atlanta Constitution*, 28 October 1994: P19.

Lorando, Mark. "Anne Rice Reflects on Lifetime." *Times-Picayune*, 11 July 1994: C1.

MacKendrick, L. K. "English & American: *Anne Rice* by Bette B. Roberts." *Choice*, February 1995: 938.

Mathews, Tom. "Fangs for Nothing." *Newsweek*, 30 November 1992: 74–75.

Matousek, Mark. "Witch Craft." *Harper's Bazaar*, November 1990: 112.

McCollum, Tom. "The Mayor's Choice." *Times-Picayune*, 6 May 1995: E1.

Miller, Laura. "Vampires in the Mainstream." *San Francisco Chronicle*, 22 November 1992: D1.

Murray, Steve. "Anne Rice Sticks Close to Her Book for 'Vampire' Script." *Atlanta Constitution*, 11 November 1994: P5.

Obejas, Achy. "Plugging 'Lasher' Anne Rice Sinks Her Teeth into Chicago." *Chicago Tribune*, 15 October 1993, sec. 1:22.

O'Briant, Don. "Rice's Reign." *Atlanta Constitution*, 31 July 1995: B1.

————. "Vampires, Monsters, Witches, and Anne Rice." *Atlanta Constitution*, 23 November 1990: C1.

Parks, Louis B. "Rice Warp." *Houston Chronicle*, 31 October 1993: Z8.

Perry, David. "Chronicler of the Damned." *Advocate: The National Gay and Lesbian Newsmagazine*, 17 January 1989: 52–53.

————. "Do the Rice Thing." *Omni*, October 1989: 26–28.

Peterson, Deborah. "The Vampire Chronicler." *St. Louis Post-Dispatch*, 25 August 1995: E1.

"Playboy Interview: Anne Rice." *Playboy*, March 1993: 53–64.

Plume, Janet. "Author Picks Uptown Home After It Calls Her to Buy It." *Times-Picayune*, 18 March 1989: RE3.

Podhoretz, John. "*Witching* Author Must Pick: Voyeur or Pro-Lifer." *Washington Times*, 30 October 1990: E1.

Preston, John. "Anne Rice: The Fire from the Heavens . . . That's What Makes Us Different from Other People." *Interview*, December 1990: 126–129.

Pugh, Clifford. "Queen of the Night." *Houston Chronicle*, 4 August 1995: D1.

Ramsland, Katherine. "Interview with the Vampire Writer." *Psychology Today*, November 1989: 34.

————. *The Vampire Companion*. New York: Ballantine, 1993.

————. *The Witches Companion*. New York: Ballantine, 1994.

Reed, Julia. "Haunted Houses." *Vogue*, November 1993: 280–283.

Rice, Anne. "Author Clarifies Remarks About Rights of Teens." *Times-Picayune*, 18 February 1994: B6.

Rinaldi, Mark. "Lestat's Last Stake." *St. Louis Post-Dispatch*, 17 August 1995: GO25.

Roberts, Raequel. "Vampire Dreams." *Houston Post*, 14 December 1992: B1.

Robins, Cynthia. "Queen of the Night." *San Francisco Chronicle*, 31 October 1993: IMA8.

Rose, Christopher. "South Central Belle." *Times-Picayune*, 19 January 1995: E1.

Summer, Bob. "PW Interviews Anne Rice." *Publisher's Weekly*, 28 October 1988: 59–60.

Thomas, Karen. " 'Vampire' Readers Say Film Has Book's Bite." *USA Today*, 16 November 1994: D1.

Tsagaris, Ellen M. " 'Men Must Be Manly and Women Womanly': Influences of Woolf's *Orlando* on Anne Rice's *The Witching Hour*." *Virginia Woolf: Emerging Perspectives*. Ed. Mark Hussey and Vara Neverow. New York: Pace University Press, 1994.

Van Matre, Lynn. "At the Newberry Library with Anne Rice." *Chicago Tribune*,
26 October 1993, sec. 5:1.

Virgits, Ronnie. "An Interview with Anne Rice: The New Orleans Experience."
New Orleans Magazine, June 1991: 48–50.

Wadler, Joyce. "Anne Rice's Imagination May Roam Among Vampires and Erotica, But Her Heart Is Right at Home." *People Weekly*, 5 December 1988:
131–134.

Warner, Coleman. "Rice Plans Museum For Dolls At Home." *Times-Picayune*, 26
April 1994: B1.

Waxman, Barbara. "Postexistentialism in the Neo-Gothic Mode: Anne Rice's *Interview with the Vampire*." *Mosaic*, Summer 1992: 79–97.

Whitall, Susan. "Interview with the Vampire Writer." *Detroit News*, 30 October
1992: C1.

Young, Tracy. "Endpaper: vampirecountry.com." *New York Times Magazine*, 15
October 1995: 100.

Ziv, Amalia. "The Pervert's Progress: An Analysis of *Story of O* and the Beauty
Trilogy." *Feminist Review*, Spring 1994: 46, 61–75.

Biographical Information

Anne Rice: Birth of the Vampire. Dir. and Prod. Anand Tucker. BBC, 1994.
"Anne Rice." *Current Biography*, July 1991: 54–58.
Ramsland, Katherine. *Prism of the Night*. New York: Plume, 1991.
Roberts, Bette. *Anne Rice*. New York: Twayne, 1994.

REVIEWS AND CRITICISM

Interview with the Vampire

Breen, Jon. L. Review of *Interview with the Vampire*. *Wilson Library Bulletin*, September 1976: 39.

Clemons, Walter. "In the Neck of Time." Review of *Interview with the Vampire*.
Newsweek, 10 May 1976: 108.

De Feo, Ronald. Review of *Interview with the Vampire*. *National Review*, 3 September 1976: 966.

Koger, Grove. "Genuine Gooseflesh." Review of *Interview with the Vampire*. *Library Journal*, 15 October 1989: 47.

Milton, Edith. Review of *Interview with the Vampire*. *New Republic*, 8 May 1976:
29.

Nelson, Alix. "Murder, Mayhem, Treachery, and Wretch-ery." Review of *Interview with the Vampire*. *Ms.*, May 1976: 27.

Parker, Julia. Review of *Interview with the Vampire*. *Library Journal*, 1 May 1976: 1144.

Reviews of *Interview with the Vampire*.

    Booklist 15 June 1976: 1453.

    Bookworld, 1 May 1977: E7.

    Entertainment Weekly, 27 August 1993: 23.

    Kirkus Reviews, 15 March 1976: 345.

    National Observer, 24 July 1976: 19.

    New Leader, 7 June 1976: 15.

    New York Times, 30 April 1976: C17.

    New York Times Book Review, 1 May 1977: 67.

    Publisher's Weekly, 8 March 1976: 57.

    Publisher's Weekly, 7 March 1977: 99.

    Publisher's Weekly, 9 May 1977: 157.

    School Library Journal, December 1986: 25.

    Village Voice, 29 March 1976: 44.

    Village Voice, 10 May 1976: 50.

    Village Voice Literary Supplement, June 1982: 18.

    Village Voice Literary Supplement, December 1986: 25.

    Wall Street Journal, 17 June 1976: 14.

Feast of All Saints

Goodfellow, Pat. Review of *Feast of All Saints*. *Library Journal*, 15 January 1980: 226.

Johnson, Alexandra. "Books in Brief." Review of *Feast of All Saints*. *Saturday Review*, 2 February 1980: 37.

Koenig, Rhoda. Review of *Feast of All Saints*. *New York Times Review of Books*, 17 February 1980: 17.

Reviews of *Feast of All Saints*.

    Booklist, 15 January 1980: 701.

    Bookworld, 27 January 1980: 6.

    Bookworld, 23 February 1992: 12.

    Kirkus Reviews, 1 November 1979: 1286.

    Locus, March 1992: 60.

    New York Times Review of Books, 15 March 1992: 28.

    Publisher's Weekly, 1 October 1979: 28.

    Publisher's Weekly, 9 May 1986: 157.

    Virginia Quarterly Review, Summer 1980: 107.

Cry to Heaven

Gates, David. "Queen of the Spellbinders." Reviews of *Cry to Heaven*. *Newsweek*, 5 November 1990: 27.

Hoffman, Alice. Review of *Cry to Heaven*. *New York Times Book Review*, 10 October 1982: 14.

Kakutani, Michiko. Review of *Cry to Heaven*. *New York Times*, 9 September 1982: 23.

Mills, Beth Ann. Review of *Cry to Heaven*. *Library Journal*, August 1982: 1483.

Reviews of *Cry to Heaven*.
> *Booklist*, 15 June 1982: 1337.
> *Bookworld*, 3 October 1982: 7.
> *Bookworld*, 10 July 1983: 16.
> *Kirkus Reviews*, 1 July 1982: 759.
> *Los Angeles Times Book Review*, 19 December 1982: 11.
> *New Statesman*, 30 October 1982: 37.
> *New York Times Book Review*, 24 July 1983: 23.
> *Publisher's Weekly*, 18 June 1982: 64.
> *Publisher's Weekly*, 13 May 1983: 55.
> *Publisher's Weekly*, 3 July 1987: 36.
> *Village Voice*, 5 October 1982: 42.
> *Village Voice Literary Supplement*, December 1986: 25.
> *West Coast Review of Books*, November 1982: 34.
> *West Coast Review of Books*, May 1983: 33.

The Vampire Lestat

Auerbach, Nina. Review of *The Vampire Lestat*. *New York Times Book Review*, 27 October 1985: 15.

Johnson, Eric W. Review of *The Vampire Lestat*. *Library Journal*, 1 October 1985: 114.

Kakutani, Michiko. Review of *The Vampire Lestat*. *New York Times*, 19 October 1985: 15.

Novak, Ralph. Review of *The Vampire Lestat*. *People Weekly*, 25 November 1985: 21.

Reviews of *The Vampire Lestat*.
> *Booklist*, 1 September 1985: 5.
> *Bookworld*, 1 December 1985: 28.
> *Fantasy Review*, June 1986: 25.
> *Kirkus Reviews*, 15 August 1985: 85.

New Statesman, 3 April 1987: 31.

People Weekly, 3 July 1987: 36.

Publisher's Weekly, 16 August 1985: 63.

Publisher's Weekly, 12 September 1986: 91.

The Vampire Lestat [audio]. *Publisher's Weekly*, 3 November 1989: 60.

Village Voice Literary Supplement, November 1985: 27.

Village Voice Literary Supplement, December 1986: 25.

Wall Street Journal, 26 November 1986: 28.

The Queen of the Damned

Diehl, Digby. Review of *The Queen of the Damned*. *Playboy*, December 1988: 37.

Estep, Steven. "Recommended Fiction of the 1980s: *The Queen of the Damned*." *English Journal*, October 1990: 82.

Kakutani, Michiko. Review of *The Queen of the Damned*. *New York Times*, 15 October 1988: 20.

Kendrick, Walter. "Brief Encounters: *The Queen of the Damned*." *Village Voice*, 11 October 1988: S5.

Kraft, Eric. "Do Not Speak Ill of the Damned." Review of *The Queen of the Damned*. *New York Times Book Review*, 27 November 1988: 12–13.

Novak, Ralph. Review of *The Queen of the Damned*. *People Weekly*, 7 November 1988: 41–43.

Reviews of *The Queen of the Damned*.

    Belles Letres, Spring 1989: 3.

    Booklist, 1 September 1988: 4.

    Bookworld, 6 November 1988: 8.

    Kirkus Reviews, 1 September 1988: 1270.

    Locus, November 1989: 57.

    Locus, January 1991: 58.

    Locus, November 1991: 58.

    Los Angeles Times Book Review, 6 November 1988: 13.

    Publisher's Weekly, 12 August 1988: 440.

    Publisher's Weekly, 18 August 1989: 56.

    [audio]. *Publisher's Weekly*, 7 October 1988: 87.

    Village Voice Literary Supplement, November 1988: 5.

    Wall Street Journal, 7 December 1988: A12.

    West Coast Review of Books 88 (1988): 20.

Rogers, Michael. Review of *The Queen of the Damned*. *Library Journal*, 1 October 1988: 101.

Sherman, Cordelia. Review of *The Queen of the Damned*. *Women's Review of Books*, April 1989: 17.

Van Gelder, Lindsy. "Biting Satire." Review of *The Queen of the Damned*. *Ms.*, November 1988: 76.

The Mummy or Ramses the Damned

Bodart, Joni Richards. "From the Editor." Review of *The Mummy*. *Wilson Library Bulletin*, March 1991: 4.

Carter, Angela. "The Curse of Ancient Egypt." *New Statesman & Society*, 1 September 1989: 31–32.

Corrigan, Patricia. "A Handsome Mesmerizing Monster." Review of *The Mummy*. *St. Louis Post-Dispatch*, 21 May 1989: C5.

Donahue, Deirdre. "Love Like an Egyptian." Review of *The Mummy*. *USA Today*, 28 June 1989: D6.

Gates, David. "Queen of the Spellbinders." Review of *The Mummy*. *Newsweek*, 5 November 1990: 77.

Hanna, Mark. "Ramses Alive and Well in London." Review of *The Mummy*. *Houston Post*, 28 May 1989: C6.

Kaganoff, Penny. Review of *The Mummy*. *Publisher's Weekly*, 5 May 1989: 70.

Larson, Susan. "Curse of *The Mummy*." Review of *The Mummy*. *Times-Picayune*, 11 June 1989: E7.

Libertore, Karen. "Anne Rice Unwraps Her New Immortal Hero." *San Francisco Chronicle*, 22 May 1989: F4.

Lovell, James Blair. "The Call of the Wild." Review of *The Mummy*. *Washington Post*, 18 June 1989: WBK4.

Novak, Ralph. Review of *The Mummy* [audio]. *People Weekly*, 24 July 1989: 21–23.

Prial, Frank J. "Undead and Unstoppable." Review of *The Mummy*. *New York Times Book Review*, 11 June 1989: 7.

Reviews of *The Mummy*.
> *Booklist*, 1 March 1989: 1051.
> *Bookworld*, 18 June 1989: 4.
> *Kirkus Reviews*, 1 March 1989: 328.
> *Locus*, August 1989: 11.
> *Pubisher's Weekly*, 2 June 1989: 57.
> [audio]. *Publisher's Weekly*, 2 June 1989: 57.

Rogers, Michael. Review of *The Mummy*. *Library Journal*, 1 April 1989: 114.

Stetson, Nancy. "Mummy's Girl." Review of *The Mummy*. *Chicago Tribune*, 28 May 1989, sec. 5:3.

Sussman, Vic. "Tapes of the Living Dead." Review of *The Mummy* [audio]. *Washington Post*, 11 February 1990: WBK11.

The Witching Hour

Altner, Patricia. Review of *The Witching Hour*. *Library Journal*, 15 October 1990: 106.

Bledsoe, Suzanne. "A Bewitching Tale of Demons, Sex, and Suspense." Review of *The Witching Hour*. *Detroit News*, January 1991: D3.

Bodart, Joni Richards. Review of *The Witching Hour*. *Wilson Library Bulletin*, 4 March 1991: 4.

Brown, Rita Mae. "The Queen of Darkness." Review of *The Witching Hour. Los Angeles Times*, 18 November 1990: BR1.

Corrigan, Patricia. "Scary Visions of Good and Evil." Review of *The Witching Hour*. *St Louis Post-Dispatch*, 28 October 1990: C5.

Gamerman, Amy. "Literary Bloodsucking in the Big Easy." Review of *The Witching Hour*. *Wall Street Journal*, 21 November 1990: A13.

Gates, David. Review of *The Witching Hour*. *Newsweek*, 5 November 1990: 76.

Harrington, Maureen. "The Witching Hour." Review of *The Witching Hour*. *Denver Post*, 20 November 1990: E1.

Isaacs, Susan. "Bewitched and Bewildered." Review of *The Witching Hour*. *Washington Post*, 28 October 1990: WBK1.

Lynn, Barbara A. Review of *The Witching Hour*. *School Library Journal*, May 1991: 126.

Madrigal, Alix. "A Tangle of Witches." Review of *The Witching Hour*. *San Francisco Chronicle*, 11 November 1990: REV1.

McCay, Mary. "Strange Brew." Review of *The Witching Hour*. *Times-Picayune*, 28 October 1990: E7.

McGrath, Patrick. "Ghastly and Unnatural Ambitions." Review of *The Witching Hour*. *New York Times Book Review*, 4 November 1990, sec. 7:11.

Mitchell, Kendall. "The Spell Is Cast." Review of *The Witching Hour*. *Chicago Tribune*, 11 November 1990, 14:4.

Parker, Suzanne. "The Good Witch." Review of *The Witching Hour*. *Detroit News and Free Press*, 25 November 1990: P7.

Passaro, Vince. "Choice Reads: *The Witching Hour*." *Self*, November 1990: 114.

Reviews of *The Witching Hour*.
  Booklist, 15 September 1990: 102.
  Bookworld, 28 October 1990: 1.
  Christian Science Monitor, 7 December 1990: 10.
  Kirkus Reviews, 15 August 1990: 1125.
  Publisher's Weekly, 4 October 1991: 85.
  West Coast Review of Books 6 (1990): 27.

Richmond, Dick. "One Way to Spend Intriguing Hours." Review of *The Witching Hour* [audio]. *St. Louis Post-Dispatch*, 7 February 1991: G3.

Shaheen, Richard. "Unseen Forces, Sinister Spirits Propel Anne Rice's Witch Story." Review of *The Witching Hour. Denver Post*, 26 October 1990: D10.

Siegel, Ed. "A Rewarding Tale After Toil and Trouble." Review of *The Witching Hour. Boston Globe*, 8 November 1990, 112: 1.

Steinberg, Sybil. Review of *The Witching Hour. Publisher's Weekly*, 21 September 1990: 62.

Walters, Colin. "Reader Beware: Seduction Awaits." Review of *The Witching Hour. Washington Times*, 12 November 1990: F2.

Ward, Janet. "Rice's *Witching Hour* Lacks Her Usual Bite." Review of *The Witching Hour. Atlanta Journal Constitution*, 18 November 1990: N10.

Zinsser, John. Review of *The Witching Hour* [audio]. *Publisher's Weekly*, 2 November 1990: 50.

The Tale of the Body Thief

Allan, Bruce. "Anne Rice's Bloodless 'Tale of the Body Thief.' " Reviews of *The Tale of the Body Thief. USA Today*, 30 October 1992: D5.

Bick, Suzann. Review of *The Tale of the Body Thief. The Antioch Review*, Winter 1993: 149.

Bregman, Sandra. "Rice Extends Vampire Bloodline." Review of *The Tale of the Body Thief. Washington Times*, 31 October 1992: B1.

Conway, Anne-Marie. Review of *The Tale of the Body Thief. The Times Literary Supplement*, 11 December 1992: 20.

Corrigan, Patricia. "A Tale of Two Bodies: Anne Rice Resumes Vampire Chronicles." Review of *The Tale of the Body Thief. St. Louis Post-Dispatch*, 27 September 1992: C5.

Gates, David. Review of *The Tale of the Body Thief. Newsweek*, 26 October 1992: 62.

Greenburg, Dan. "A Vampire Suckered." Review of *The Tale of the Body Thief. Chicago Tribune*, 18 October 1992, sec. 14:3.

Johnson, Robert. "Vampire Discovers Human Life Not All That Cozy." Review of *The Tale of the Body Thief. Denver Post*, 25 October 1992: F8.

Kaveney, Roz. Review of *The Tale of the Body Thief. New Statesman & Society*, 30 October 1992: 37.

Larson, Susan. "Undead Again." Review of *The Tale of the Body Thief. Times-Picayune*, 10 October 1992: E8.

Liberatore, Karen. "Cape Fear." Review of *The Tale of the Body Thief. San Francisco Chronicle*, 18 October 1992: REV1.

Loudermilk, Susan. "Lestat the Vampire Sees the Light of Day." Review of *The Tale of the Body Thief. Detroit News*, 18 November 1992: D3.

Parker, Suzanne. "Vampire Drained." Review of *The Tale of the Body Thief. Detroit News & Free Press*, 25 October 1992: G7.

Reviews of *The Tale of the Body Thief.*
   Booklist, 1 September 1992: 5.
   Kirkus Reviews, 1 August 1992: 943.
   New York Magazine, 14 September 1992: 110.
   Observer, 24 August 1992: 60.
   Observer, 10 October 1993: 19.
   Publisher's Weekly, 13 September 1993: 124.
   Times Literary Supplement, 11 September 1992: 20.
   The Tale of the Body Thief [audio]. *Library Journal*, December 1992: 210.
Roberts, Raequel. "A Vampire Lusts for Mortality in 'Body Thief.' " Review of
   The Tale of the Body Thief. Houston Post, 29 November 1992: C6.
Rogers, Michael. Review of *The Tale of the Body Thief. Library Journal*, 1 September
   1992: 216.
See, Carolyn. "Vampire Tans! News at 11." Review of *The Tale of the Body Thief.*
   Los Angeles Times, 25 October 1992: BR1.
Skow, John. Review of *The Tale of the Body Thief. Time*, 23 November 1992: 71.
Smith, Sarah. "The Vampire Strikes Back." Review of *The Tale of the Body Thief.*
   Washington Post, 30 October 1992: B1.
Summer, Bob. "Anne Rice Vamps Voluptuously." Review of *The Tale of the Body
   Thief. Atlanta Journal Constitution*, 4 October 1992: N8.
Vretos, Constantine. Review of *The Tale of the Body Thief. School Library Journal*,
   23 March 1993: 236.

Lasher

Adler, Dick. "Warlocks, Gore, and Purple Prose: Anne Rice Does It Again." Re-
   view of *Lasher. Chicago Tribune*, 17 October 1995, sec. 14:3.
Berry, Michael. "Ancient Evil." Review of *Lasher. San Francisco Chronicle*, 19 Sep-
   tember 1993: REV1.
Corrigan, Patricia. "Dashing Demons, Winsome Witches." Review of *Lasher. St.
   Louis Post-Dispatch*, 24 October 1994: F5.
Goodwin, Jo–Ann. Review of *Lasher. New Statesman & Society*, 26 November 1993:
   43.
Hand, Elizabeth. "The Demon Seed." Review of *Lasher. Washington Post*, 10 Oc-
   tober 1993: WBK4.
Larson, Susan. "Back to the Books." Review of *Lasher. Times-Picayune*, 12 Septem-
   ber 1993: D18.
———. "Toil and Trouble." Review of *Lasher. Times-Picayune*, 26 September 1993:
   E8.
Liss, Barbara. " 'Lasher' Loosens Anne Rice's Hold on Her Spirit World." Review
   of *Lasher. Houston Chronicle*, 3 October 1993: Z17.

Morrison, Patt. "All Souls." Review of *Lasher*. *Los Angeles Times*, 31 October 1993:
    BR3.
Parker, Suzanne. "Anne Rice Asks Fans to Ignore Logic and Taste." Review of
    Lasher. *Detroit News and Free Press*, 3 October 1993: J6.
Reviews of *Lasher*.
    Bookworld, 10 October 1993: 4.
    Entertainment Weekly, 27 August 1993: 23.
    Kirkus Reviews, 15 July 1993: 887.
    Locus, October 1993: 23.
    New York Magazine, 3 September 1993: 100.
    Observer, 31 October 1993: 20.
    Publisher's Weekly, 9 August 1993: 450.
Schleier, Curt. "Bewitched Sequel 'Lasher' Is Bothersome, Bewildering." Review
    of *Lasher*. *Atlanta Journal Constitution*, 3 October 1993: N10.
Sleeth, Peter. " 'Witching Hour' Sequel Demands the Midnight Oil." Review of
    Lasher. *Denver Post*, 19 September 1993: F6.
West, Paul. "Witchcraft Is Their Science." Review of *Lasher*. *New York Times Book
    Review*, 24 October 1993, sec. 7:38.
Whitwall, Stuart. Review of *Lasher*. *Booklist*, August 1993: 2012.
Young, Elizabeth. "Horror." Review of *Lasher*. *Guardian*, 13 September 1994,
    sec. 2:14.

Taltos

Boyer, Pat E. "Season of the Witch." *Times-Picayune*, 25 September 1994: E8.
Cole, Laura. Review of *Taltos*. *Library Journal*, 1 September 1994: 216.
Corrigan, Patricia. "A Different Kind of Ancient Spirit." Review of *Taltos*. *St.
    Louis Post-Dispatch*, 9 October 1994: C5.
Donahue, Deirdre. "Anne Rice Back at Her Old Haunt." Review of *Taltos*. *USA
    Today*, 29 September 1994: D6.
Johnson, Robert. "Talk Stifles Action in Rice's Land of Giants." Reviews of *Taltos*.
    Denver Post, 2 October 1994: E10.
Hodges, Michael H. "Witch Way." Review of *Taltos*. *Detroit News and Free Press*,
    1 October 1994: D34.
Keebler, Wendy. "You Review: Anne Rice's *Taltos*." *Detroit News and Free Press*,
    4 June 1995: MAG13.
Libertore, Karen. "Rice's Latest Tale a Monster Vision." *San Francisco Chronicle*,
    30 September 1994: E5.
Reviews of *Taltos*.
    Bookworld, 9 October 1994: 4.
    Spectator, 3 December 1994: 56.
Seaman, Donna. Review of *Taltos*. *Booklist*, 1–15 June 1994: 1725.

Simon, Clea. "Rice's New Sorcery Not So Spellbinding." Review of *Taltos*. *Boston Globe*, 30 September 1994, sec. 64:4.

Theroux, Alexander. "Witches a la Rice: Rich in Sorcery and Soap Opera, Serves at Least 600,000." Review of *Taltos*. *Chicago Tribune*, 9 October 1994, sec. 14:5.

Wilson, Gahan. "It's Witchcraft." Review of *Taltos*. *New York Times Book Review*, 4 December 1994, sec. 7:82.

Winter, Douglas E. "Son of a Witch." Review of *Taltos*. *Washington Post*, 9 October 1994: WBK4.

Memnoch the Devil

Allman, Kevin. "The Last of Lestat." Review of *Memnoch the Devil*. *Washington Post*, 6 August 1995: WBK2.

Corrigan, Patricia. "Just Don't Call Him 'Satan.' " Review of *Memnoch the Devil*. *St. Louis Post-Dispatch*, 23 July 1995: C5.

Hartman, Diane. "Expectations Fall in Memnoch." Review of *Memnoch the Devil*. *Denver Post*, 30 July 1995: E10.

Kelly, Susan. "Lestat Engages in a Devilish Seduction." Review of *Memnoch the Devil*. *USA Today*, 20 July 1995: D4.

Larson, Susan. "To Hell and Gone." Review of *Memnoch the Devil*. *Times-Picayune*, 9 July 1995: E7.

Libertore, Karen. "Sympathy for the Devil." Review of *Memnoch the Devil*. *San Francisco Chronicle*, 9 July 1995: REV1.

McLeod, Michael. "Anne Rice's Lestat Is Back for More." Review of *Memnoch the Devil*. *Chicago Tribune*, 31 August 1995, sec. 2:2.

Rabinovitz, Amy. "Rice Takes on Both God and the Devil." Review of *Memnoch the Devil*. *Houston Chronicle*, 30 July 1995: Z20.

Reviews of *Memnoch the Devil*.
  Booklist, 1 June 1995: 1684.
  Library Journal, 15 June 1995: 96.
  Publisher's Weekly, 5 June 1995: 51.

Smith, Wendy. Review of *Memnoch the Devil*. *New York Times Book Review*, 23 July 1995, sec. 7:14.

OTHER SECONDARY SOURCES

Auerbach, Nina. *Our Vampires, Ourselves*. Chicago: University of Chicago Press, 1995.

Blake, William. *Literature, the English Tradition*. Englewood Cliffs, N.J.: Prentice Hall, 1989.

———. "The Lamb." *Literature, the English Tradition*. Englewood Cliffs, N.J.: Prentice Hall, 1989: 620.

———. "The Tyger." *Literature, the English Tradition*. Englewood Cliffs, N.J.: Prentice Hall, 1989: 623.

Campbell, Joseph. *The Masks of God: Primitive Mythology*. New York: Penguin, 1969.

"Faust." *Benet's Reader's Encyclopedia*. New York: Harper, 1987.

Hartwell, David G. *The Dark Descent: The Evolution of Horror*. New York: Tor, 1987.

Holman, Hugh. *A Handbook to Literature*. 4th ed. Indianapolis, Ind.: Bobbs-Merrill, 1985.

Interview with the Vampire. Dir. Neil Jordan. Prod. Stephen Woolley and David Geffen. Screenplay by Anne Rice. With Tom Cruise, Brad Pitt, Antonio Banderas, and Kirsten Dunst. Warner Bros. 1994.

King, Stephen. *Danse Macabre*. New York: Berkley, 1981.

Le Guin, Ursula. "Introduction." In *The Book of Fantasy*, ed. by Jorge Luis Borges, Silvina Ocampo, and A. Bioy Casares. New York: Viking, 1988.

———. *The Language of the Night: Essays on Fantasy and Science Fiction*. New York: Perigee, 1980.

Lynn, Steven. *Texts and Contexts: Writing About Literature with Critical Theory*. New York: Harper, 1994.

Ramsland, Katherine. "Hunger for the Marvelous: The Vampire Craze in the Computer Age." *Psychology Today*, November 1989: 31–35.

Rosenburg, Betty. *Genreflecting: A Guide to Reading Interests in Genre Fiction*. Englewood, Colo.: Libraries, Unlimited, 1982.

Index

Aaron Lightner (*The Witching Hour, Lasher, Taltos*), 133, 136, 159, 163
Abandonment, 46–48
Abortion, 139
Akasha (*The Vampire Lestat, The Queen of the Damned*), 47, 58, 60–61, 66–68, 70, 74–79
Alcoholism, 2–4, 40, 80, 117, 123, 154
Alex (*The Mummy*), 118, 120
Allusion, 55–56, 89–92, 103–14, 125–26, 166
Amel (*The Queen of the Damned*), 68
Androgeny, 58
Anne Rice: Birth of the Vampire (video), 2, 168
Antagonist, 24–25, 27, 31, 50, 66, 74, 84, 101, 105, 121–22, 134, 138, 152, 163–64
Apocalypse Now, 55–56
Archetype, 17, 57, 110
Aristotle, 33–34
Armand (*The Vampire Lestat, The Queen of the Damned, The Tale of the Body Thief, Memnoch the Devil*), 47, 49–50, 73, 78–79
Arthurian legend, 168

Ash. *See* Ashlar
Ashlar (*Taltos*), 159, 161, 164–70

Babies, as motif, 139–40
Baby Jenks (*The Queen of the Damned*), 73, 77–79
Back story, 71
Beauty's Punishment, 5
Beauty's Release, 5
Belinda, 5
Blake, William, 90–92
Blood, as motif, 107–8
Body Thief (*The Tale of the Body Thief*), 83–87, 97
Brochs, 165
Brontë, Charlotte, 16
Brontë, Emily, 16

Campbell, Joseph, 57–58, 110
The Castle of Otranto, 15
Castrati, 2–3
Catharsis, 42
Character development, 3, 24–30, 45–50, 66–70, 84–88, 101–5, 116–21, 123, 134–39, 152–54, 160–63
Character: alter ego, 40–42; analog, 5,

11, 13, 23–24, 29–30, 43, 65, 80, 90, 111; arc or growth, 27–29, 46–49, 135, 137, 153; dynamic, 3, 29, 45, 47–49, 67, 84–88, 103, 119–21, 135, 153–57, 162–63; static, 29–30, 45, 49–50, 51, 86–87, 103, 116–18, 136–39, 154, 160–62. *See also* Antagonist; Character development; Observer; Protagonist; *individual characters*
Children of Danu, 168
Children of Darkness (*The Vampire Lestat*), 47, 58
"Christabel," 10
Christianity, 1–2, 168. *See also* Religion
The Claiming of Sleeping Beauty, 5
Claudia (*Interview with the Vampire, The Vampire Lestat, The Tale of the Body Thief*, 3, 11, 16, 21, 26–27, 28–29, 31–33, 39–41, 61, 80–81, 83, 91, 93–96
Cleopatra (*The Mummy*), 11, 118–20
Climax, 31–32, 50
Coleridge, Samuel Taylor, 9–10
Collective unconscious, 57. *See also* Jungian criticism
Community. *See* Connection
Conflict, 24–28, 30, 35, 38, 50, 74, 85, 125, 134–35, 143, 157, 164
Connection, 4–5, 11, 21, 28, 36, 40, 45–47, 52, 54–56, 74–75, 148, 156. *See also* Family; Relationships
Conrad, Joseph, 55
Cry to Heaven, 4–5

Daisy (*The Mummy*), 117, 119–20
Daniel, the interviewer (*Interview with the Vampire, The Queen of the Damned*), 21, 23–25, 30, 33–34, 36, 69, 79
Dark gift, 11, 14, 85, 87, 126
David Talbot (*The Tale of the Body Thief, Memnoch the Devil*), 83, 87, 91–93, 97, 102
Death Goddess. *See* Great Mother
Devil, 6, 103–5, 108–9
Dionysus, 61, 112
Displacement, 40–42

Dora Flynn (*Memnoch the Devil*), 99, 101–3, 112
Dracula, 13
Dracula's Daughter, 1
Drink, 122–24, 125
Duality, 14, 169
Dying God, 60–61, 110–12

Elliot (*The Mummy*), 118
Emaleth (*The Witching Hour*), 153
Enkil (*The Vampire Lestat, The Queen of the Damned*), 47, 60–61, 63
Evil, 5, 10, 12–16, 18, 21, 27, 33, 35, 43, 53, 85–88, 91–93, 98, 100–102, 108–9, 138, 142–44, 148, 153, 157, 161, 168–70; "inside evil," 13
Exit to Eden, 5
Exposition, 31–32

Faerie, 10, 168–69
Falling Action, 31–32
"The Fall of the House of Usher," 12
Family, 5–6, 13–14, 27, 30, 47, 50, 135, 153, 162, 163; as metaphor, 156. *See also* Connection; Motherhood
Fantasy fiction, 17–18
Faust, 94–95
The Feast of All Saints, 4
Feminist criticism, 75–80, 126–29, 145–49
Ficelle, 30
Flashback, 34, 43, 51, 160
Foil, 27, 49, 86
Foreshadowing, 73, 87, 140, 164
Frame, 33–34, 50, 54, 64
Frankenstein, 11, 144, 152
Free People of Color, 4
Free will, 6, 13, 85–86, 88, 92, 93, 96, 108–9, 143–45
Freitag's Pyramid, 30–31
Freud, Sigmund, 37–38, 57
Freudian criticism, 37–42, 53, 95–98; ego, 37–39, 97; id, 37–39, 42, 97–98; superego, 37–38, 97. *See also* Guilt; Repression; Unconscious

Gabrielle de Lioncourt (*The Vampire Lestat, The Queen of the Damned, The*

Tale of the Body Thief, Memnoch the Devil), 45, 48–49, 59–60, 69, 76–77, 78, 79
Genre, 9; escapist fiction, 6, 122; fantasy fiction, 17–18; Gothic fiction, 15–16; horror fiction, 12–15
Geraldine ("Christabel"), 10
Gilgamesh, 60
God, 6, 101, 103–5, 165–66
Goethe, 94
Gothic fiction, 15–16, 142; "paranoid gothic," 16
Great Mother, 57, 59–61, 68, 110
Gretchen (*The Tale of the Body Thief*), 87–88, 93, 94
Guilt, 14–15, 21, 25–26, 41–42, 85, 88, 91, 93–94, 95–96. *See also* Freudian criticism

Heart of Darkness, 55–56
Henry (*The Mummy*), 115, 117
Hero, 11, 57, 117, 119, 120, 158; dark hero, 16; picaro hero, 51–52
Homosexuality, 35. *See also* Relationships, between men
Horror fiction, 12–15
Houses, 5, 12, 15–16

Identity, 25, 27, 40, 47–48, 50, 67, 80, 84, 86–88, 93, 101–2, 120, 134, 152, 163. *See also individual characters*
Immortality, 15, 17–18, 21, 23, 33, 36, 53, 84, 87–89, 94–97, 118–20, 125
Interviewer. *See* Daniel
Interview with the Vampire, 3, 10, 15, 21–42; character development, 24–30; Freudian interpretation of, 37–42; literary devices, 33–34; plot development, 30–33; point of view, 22–24; thematic issues, 34–37
"Interview with the Vampire" (short story), 3, 21
Ishtar, 60
Isolation, 47–48, 50

James, Henry, 14, 142
Jane Eyre, 16

Janet (*Taltos*), 166
Jesse (*The Queen of the Damned*), 69, 77–80
Judith (*The Witching Hour*), 141
Julie (*The Mummy*), 117–19
Jung, Carl, 56–57, 58, 157–58
Jungian criticism, 157–58

Katherine and Jean, 3
Keats, John, 10
Khayman (*The Queen of the Damned, The Tale of the Body Thief, Memnoch the Devil*), 69, 79

"La Belle Dame sans Merci," 10
"The Lady of Shalott," 166
"The Lamb," 90–91
"Lamia," 10
Lasher (*The Witching Hour, Lasher*), 6, 10, 133–34, 138–46, 148, 151–53, 155–58, 161
Lasher, 6; character development, 152–54; Jungian reading of, 157–58; literary device, 156; plot development, 155–56; point of view, 152; thematic issues, 156–57
Lawrence Stratford (*The Mummy*), 117–18
Lestat de Lioncourt (*Interview with the Vampire, The Vampire Lestat, The Queen of the Damned, The Tale of the Body Thief, Memnoch the Devil*), 3, 5, 13, 15–16, 21, 23–33, 42–48, 51–53, 56–61, 64–67, 70, 78–79, 83–86, 88–103, 107–12, 125–26, 154, 163
Literary device, 33–34, 52–53, 73, 107–8, 122–24, 141–42, 156, 165–67
The Lord of the Rings, 17
Louis de Pointe du Lac (*Interview with the Vampire, The Vampire Lestat, The Queen of the Damned, The Tale of the Body Thief, Memnoch the Devil*), 3, 5, 10, 13, 15–16, 21, 23–26, 30–34, 41–42, 44, 69, 78–79, 102, 154, 163
Love, 10–11, 28, 67–69, 77–80, 106, 107, 128, 144, 156, 162. *See also* Connection; Relationships
Lovecraft, H. P., 12

Magnus (*The Vampire Lestat*), 16, 46

Maharet (*The Queen of the Damned, The Tale of the Body Thief, Memnoch the Devil*), 68, 70, 76, 77, 79–80

Marius (*The Vampire Lestat, The Queen of the Damned*) 47, 50, 69, 78, 79, 112

Mark (*Taltos*), 161

Mayfair, Ancient Evelyn (*The Witching Hour*), 152

Mayfair, Angelique (*The Witching Hour*), 136

Mayfair, Antha (*The Witching Hour*), 137, 146–47

Mayfair, Carlotta (*The Witching Hour*), 137–39, 142, 146–48

Mayfair, Charlotte (*The Witching Hour*), 136–38, 146

Mayfair, Cortland (*The Witching Hour*), 136, 137, 142, 146

Mayfair, Deborah (*The Witching Hour*), 136–37, 146–47

Mayfair, Dierdre (*The Witching Hour*), 137–38, 142, 143, 146–47

Mayfair, Emaleth (*Lasher*), 153

Mayfair, Jeanne Louise (*The Witching Hour*), 136

Mayfair, Julian (*The Witching Hour, Lasher*), 136–37, 146, 151–54, 156

Mayfair, Katherine (*The Witching Hour*), 137, 146, 153

Mayfair, Lauren (*The Witching Hour*), 147

Mayfair, Marguerite (*The Witching Hour*), 137–38, 141

Mayfair, Marie Claudette (*The Witching Hour*), 136–37

Mayfair, Mary Beth (*The Witching Hour*), 137

Mayfair, Mary Jane (*Taltos*), 162

Mayfair, Mona (*The Witching Hour, Lasher, Taltos*), 7, 151, 153–56, 159–60, 162–64, 167

Mayfair, Morrigan (*Taltos*), 159, 162, 165, 168–69

Mayfair, Rowan (*The Witching Hour,*

Lasher, Taltos), 6, 10, 19, 133–35, 137, 139–49, 151–61, 163–67

Mayfair, Stella (*The Witching Hour*), 137, 146–47

Mayfair, Suzanne (*The Witching Hour*), 136–37, 146

The Mayfair Witches, 1, 6, 10, 11, 15, 133, 136–38. *See also individual listings under Mayfair above*

Mekare (*The Queen of the Damned*), 68, 70, 76, 79–80

Memnoch (*Memnoch the Devil*), 99–102, 104–5, 108–12

Memnoch the Devil, 6; character development, 101–5; literary device, 107–8; mythological reading of, 110–12; plot development, 105–7; point of view, 100–101; thematic issues, 108–9

Metaphor, 5, 52–53, 92, 93, 107–8, 123–24, 126, 156, 166

Miami, 92

Michael Curry (*The Witching Hour, Lasher, Taltos*), 133, 135, 139–41, 143–44, 147, 151–56, 159–65, 167

Milton, John, 103–4, 108–9

Mona. *See* Mayfair, Mona

Monsters, 11–12, 16, 57, 86, 118, 144

Moral, 34

Morgan Le Fay, 168

Morrigan, the goddess, 68–69. *See also* Mayfair, Morrigan

Motif, 93–94, 122–25, 141–42, 165–67

Motivation, 26–28, 76, 84, 128–29, 139–40, 161. *See also* Character development

Motherhood, 69, 77, 80, 143

The Mummy or Ramses the Damned, 6, 11, 15, 23; character development, 161–21; feminist reading of, 126–29; literary device, 122–24; plot development, 121–22; point of view, 116; thematic issues, 124–26

The Mysteries of Udolpho, 15

Mythological criticism, 17, 56–61, 110–12, 157–58, 165, 167–70

Nature, 9–10, 48–49, 59
New Orleans, 1, 4, 6, 16, 47, 54, 133, 143, 156
Nicholas (*The Vampire Lestat*), 46, 49

Observer character, 22–25, 70
Other, 5, 13–14, 23–24, 35, 36, 47, 53–55, 90, 118, 167
Otherworld, 168
Outsider. *See* Other

Pandora (*The Queen of theDamned*), 69, 77–79
Paradise Lost, 103–5, 108–9
Petyr the monk (*The Witching Hour*), 146
Picaresque novel, 51–52
Picaro, 51–52
Plot development, 30–33, 50–52, 70–73, 88–89, 105–7, 121–22, 139–40, 155–56, 163–65; character-driven plots, 24–25, 29, 140; plot-driven plots, 140
Plot diagram: Freitag's, 31; modern, 32
Poe, Edgar Allan, 12
Point of no return, 31–32
Point of view, 22–24, 44–45, 64–66, 84, 100–101, 116, 134, 152, 160
Polidori, John, 13
Power, 36; in women, 10–11, 28–29, 59–60, 67–69, 80–81
Prest, Presket, 13
Proem, 65
Projection, 41–42
Protagonist, 24, 31, 33, 36, 43–45, 50, 66, 70–71, 84, 101, 121, 134, 152, 163–64

The Queen of the Damned, 5, 16, 23, 50–51, 61, 63, 170; character development, 66–70; feminist reading of, 75–82; literary device, 73; plot development, 70–73; point of view, 64–66; thematic issues, 74–75

Radcliffe, Anne, 15
Raglan James (*The Tale of the Body Thief*), 83–87, 97
Rampling, Anne, 5
Ramses the Damned. See The Mummy
Ramses (*The Mummy*), 11, 117, 119–22, 125–26, 128–29
Ramsland, Katherine, 40
Randolph Stratford (*The Mummy*), 118
Recognition, 11, 32
Redemption, 10, 152. *See also* Salvation
Relationships: between men, 79, 128; between women and men, 14, 78, 128, 146–49, 154; between women, 78–79, 128, 147–48, 162–63. *See also* Connection
Religion, 37, 41, 88, 90–92, 100, 105, 107, 112. *See also* Christianity
Repression, 38–41, 49, 96, 158. *See also* Freudian criticism
Resolution, 31–32, 50
Rice, Anne: childhood, 1–2; education, 1–3; family, 6; Freudian analysis, 40–43; marriage, 2–3; philosophy, 18; religion, 1–3, 41. *See also* Rampling, Anne; Roquelaure, A. R.; *specific titles*
Rice, Christopher, 4
Rice, Michelle, 3, 40–41, 80
Rice, Stan, 2–4, 40
"The Rime of the Ancient Mariner," 9–10
Rising Action, 31–32, 50
Rock Music, 55–56, 61
Roger Flynn (*Memnoch the Devil*), 99, 101, 103
Romanticism, 9–12, 18, 90
Roquelaure, A. R., 5
Rules of Darkness, 49–50

Sacrifice, 111–12, 156
Sagas, 139
Salvation, 10, 50, 85, 87, 95, 104–5, 109, 111
Samir (*The Mummy*), 118

San Francisco, 2–3, 21, 35, 54, 133, 142–43
Savage Garden, 109
Self-knowledge, 5, 25, 35, 83, 92–95, 124, 126, 144, 157
Sequels, problems with, 163
Servant of the Bones, 7
Setting, 12, 15–17, 33, 35, 54, 92, 124, 142–43, 156
Sexuality, 42, 52–53, 58, 78, 126, 144, 146, 148, 154
Shadow, 12–13, 157–58. *See also* Jungian criticism
Shelley, Mary, 11, 144, 152
Stereotypes, 117–18, 122
Stevenson, Robert Louis, 14
Stoker, Bram, 13
Stonehenge, 168
Stranger, 12–13, 157–58
The Strange Adventures of Dr. Jekyll and Mr. Hyde, 14
Stuart (*Taltos*), 161, 164, 166
Sublimation, 40–42
The Sufferings of Charlotte and Nicholas, 3
Supernatural, 5, 9, 15, 17–18, 25–26, 88, 90; in women, 10–11
Suspense, false, 72
Symbol, 7, 38, 52, 93, 107, 111, 141, 166

Talamasca, 133, 151, 159, 161, 163–64, 166, 170
The Tale of the Body Thief, 6; character development, 84–88; Freudian reading of, 95–98; literary device, 89–92; plot development, 88–89; point of view, 84; thematic issues, 92–95
Taltos, 6, 151, 159, 161, 167–70
Taltos, 6; character development, 160–63; literary device, 165–67; mythological reading of, 167–70; plot development, 163–65; point of view, 159–160; thematic issues, 167
Tarot cards, 166–67
Tennyson, Alfred Lord, 166
Tessa (*Taltos*), 161, 164, 166, 170

Theatre of Vampires, 15, 44, 49, 58
Theme, 18, 33–37, 53–56, 74–75, 92–95, 108–9, 124–26, 142–45, 156–57, 167
Titles, 36, 55, 94, 125, 143
Tolkien, J.R.R., 17
Tommy (*Taltos*), 161
Towers, as motif, 165–67
Trickster, 57–59
Tuatha de Danaan, 168
Turning Point, 31–32
The Turn of the Screw, 14–15; 144
"The Tyger," 90–92
Twins. *See* Maharet; Mekare

Unconscious, 37, 42, 94–98. *See also* Freudian criticism
Unholy Family, 27, 30, 47
Unities, 33

Vampires, 2, 5, 13–14, 16–17, 35, 69, 107
The Vampire Lestat, 5, 22, 125–26; character development, 45–50; literary device, 52–53; mythological reading of, 56–61; plot development, 50–52; point of view, 44–45; thematic issues, 53–56
The Vampyre, 13
Varney the Vampyre, 13
Vegetation God, 60–61, 110–12
Veil of Veronica, 99–100, 103, 112

Walpole, Horace, 15
Witches, 10, 14, 17, 23. *See also* The Mayfair Witches
The Witches Chronicles, 14, 16, 131–68
Witching hour, 168
The Witching Hour, 6, 10, 14; character development, 134–39; feminist reading of, 145–49; literary devicies, 141–42; plot development, 139–40; point of view, 134; thematic issues, 142–45
Women: motherhood, 69, 77, 80, 145; passivity in, 11, 76–78, 80–81, 127,

145, 148–49, 152; power and, 10–11, 15–17, 28–29, 59–60, 67–69, 78, 80–81, 145–46, 148–49, 154, 168; sexuality, 78, 127, 146, 148, 154, 161; as victims, 169. *See also* Relationships

Wuthering Heights, 16

About the Author

JENNIFER SMITH is a candidate for a Ph.D. in English and a Masters of Fine Arts degree in fiction at The Ohio State University. She is writing her dissertation on the strategic use of humor in 20th-century Western women's popular literature. She is the author of eight romance novels. Her first mainstream novel is to be published in 1997.